PUBLIC FORGETTING

BRADFORD VIVIAN

# *Public Forgetting*

## The Rhetoric and Politics of Beginning Again

The Pennsylvania State University Press
University Park, Pennsylvania

Library of Congress Cataloging-in-Publication Data

Vivian, Bradford.
Public forgetting : the rhetoric and politics
of beginning again / Bradford Vivian.
p.     cm.
Includes bibliographical references and index.
Summary: "Reconsiders the negative status attributed to forgetting in
both academic and popular discussions of public memory. Demonstrates
how a community may adopt idioms of forgetting in order to create new
and beneficial standards of public judgment concerning the lessons and
responsibilities of its shared past"—Provided by publisher.
ISBN 978-0-271-03665-6 (alk. paper)
1. Memory—Social aspects.
2. History—Philosophy.
3. Collective memory.
4. Rhetoric.
I. Title.

BF378.S65.V58 2010
153.1'25—dc22
2009034735

The Pennsylvania State University Press is a member of the Association
of American University Presses.

FOR ANNE — *unforgettable*

Great is the power of memory.
—AUGUSTINE, *Confessions*

For I am about to create new heavens and a new earth; the
former things shall not be remembered or come to mind. But
be glad and rejoice forever in what I am creating; for I am
about to create Jerusalem as a joy, and its people as a delight.
—ISAIAH 65:17–18

Outside Invale [Nebraska] not long ago, an old woman was
found burning a Dust Bowl diary written by her husband.
Her neighbor was astonished: why destroy such an intimate
family record? The horror, the woman explained, was not
worth sharing. She wanted it gone forever.
—TIMOTHY EGAN, *The Worst Hard Time*

# CONTENTS

# ACKNOWLEDGMENTS

I acknowledge, with gratitude, permission to use revised versions of earlier publications. Chapters 3, 4, and 5 have been adapted from, respectively, "Neoliberal Epideictic: Rhetorical Form and Commemorative Politics on September 11, 2002," *Quarterly Journal of Speech* 92 (2006): 1–26; "The Art of Forgetting: John W. Draper and the Rhetorical Dimensions of History," *Rhetoric and Public Affairs* 2 (1999): 551–72; and "'A Timeless Now': Repetition and Memory," in *Framing Public Memory,* ed. Kendall R. Phillips, 187–211 (Tuscaloosa: University of Alabama Press, 2004).

A number of individuals provided valuable assistance with early portions of this book, long before I myself knew that it would include such portions. Stephen Browne's mentorship concerning questions of rhetoric and public memory (and friendship, too) is omnipresent in these pages, even when not directly acknowledged. Chapter 4 began, in its earliest inceptions, as a paper in J. Michael Hogan's doctoral seminar on research and writing methods at Pennsylvania State University; my thanks to him for his assistance with it (and for helping me to mature as a researcher and writer in general) is long overdue. My former colleagues at Vanderbilt University, John Sloop and Charles Morris, also provided critical encouragement regarding early phases of this project. I am further indebted to the National Endowment for the Humanities; the generous NEH Summer Stipend I received in 2005 supported my work on the previously published version of Chapter 3. Last, but far from least, thanking one's daycare providers is unorthodox, but this book might have remained unfinished without the hard work and dutiful care of the staff at Brook Hollow Day Care in Nashville, Tennessee, and Elmcrest Small Wonders Day Care in Syracuse, New York.

Several others provided indispensable support in bringing this book to form. I am deeply grateful to Sanford Thatcher and Kathryn Yahner at Pennsylvania State University Press for steering my manuscript so expertly through the editorial process. I also wish to thank Andrew B. Lewis and Debbie Olson for their respective copyediting and indexing expertise. Syracuse University has provided me with an ideal intellectual environment in which to draft the balance of this project; I therefore owe great thanks to my Syracuse friends and colleagues Kendall Phillips, Amos Kiewe, and Arthur

Jensen for bringing me into their fold, and to the administration in the College of Visual and Performing Arts for making it possible. More generally, I wish to gratefully acknowledge the humbling goodwill and support I have received from the faculty, graduate students, and administrative staff at large in the Department of Communication and Rhetorical Studies.

Finally, I have been blessed in my efforts, as always, by the copious support of family. I am fortunate that I can thank my mother and father both for their parental encouragement and for their own scholarly influences on my work (as represented by significant portions of this manuscript). My son, Noah, taught me true, undiluted wisdom as I wrote this book, thereby enriching my research and writing immeasurably; I wish to thank him every day for the genuine gift that he is. Finally, this book is dedicated to my wife, Anne; she is the model and measure of incalculable goodness in my personal and professional life. Without her, nothing.

# INTRODUCTION

I met a traveller from an antique land
Who said: Two vast and trunkless legs of stone
Stand in the desert. Near them on the sand,
Half sunk, a shattered visage lies . . .
And on the pedestal these words appear:
"My name is Ozymandias, king of kings:
Look on my works, ye Mighty, and despair!"
Nothing beside remains. Round the decay
Of that colossal wreck, boundless and bare
The lone and level sands stretch far away.
—PERCY BYSSHE SHELLEY, "Ozymandias"

Memory is unavoidably, and sometimes maddeningly, inconstant. It sustains a sense of the past in bewilderingly protean ways. Shelley's "Ozymandias" commemorates the ruins of a once-grandiose edifice of memory—a colossus intended to so impressively amplify the fame of Ramses the Great that his renown would stand undiminished against the erosions of time. The massive idol promised to immortalize its subject in such grandeur that even those in future epochs who laughably considered themselves mighty would revere the monarch as "king of kings" and "despair" at the insignificance of their own trifling feats compared to his everlasting prestige.

The statue's memorial purpose was so great, however, that its obvious failure to achieve that purpose appears greater still. The inscription meant to permanently commemorate the king's reputation, to command the homage of travelers dwarfed by his monumental figure, now memorializes little more than rubble—heaps of crumbling stone sinking into the "boundless and bare," "lone and level" sands of "an antique land." The words etched into the statue's pedestal gesture, at best, to the inevitable withering of such a vainglorious effort at commemoration, to the vast absence that now envelops an originally towering effort to render the monarch's eminence enduringly present. The very monument dedicated to the king's undying memory has come to symbolize, and moreover *enact,* the epically prolonged death of memory as such.

Shelley's elegy to this bowed and decaying likeness reproduces poetic conventions used to dramatize the allegedly inherent vulnerability of memory to the rapaciousness of forgetting since antiquity. Numerous reflections on memory throughout the history of Western art, poetry, literature, philosophy, and religion emphasize the inescapable devastations of forgetting. "Men's Workes have an age like themselves," Thomas Browne wrote, "and though they out-live their Authors, yet they have a stint and period to their duration" (1963, pt. 1, sec. 23, 1:35). Grand works of memory reserved for elevated pursuits—allowing the voices of noble and heroic figures from former times to guide us perpetually—succumb time and again to a darker fate in which the forces of forgetting inexorably deplete their power to maintain a living past. The pattern is cruelly irreversible and ominously predictable. Shakespeare's plays and sonnets lavishly illustrate this pattern according to the "pervasive, all-embracing theme of 'Devouring Time'—a theme which inspired much of the greatest poetry and prose of the English Renaissance" (D. Bush 1969, 1451). *The Rape of Lucrece* catalogues the many corrosive effects of time, which relegate even the grandest mementos of a glorious past to "oblivion" (a standard literary term for forgetting):

> To ruinate proud buildings with thy hours,
> And smear with dust their glitt'ring golden tow'rs;
>
> 'To fill with wormholes stately monuments,
> To feed oblivion with the decay of things,
> To blot old books and alter their contents,
> . . . . . . . . . . . . . . . . . . . . . . . . . . . . . . . . .
> To spoil antiquities of hammered steel
> And turn the giddy round of Fortune's wheel.
>
> (1969, ll. 944–52)

Modern poets likewise lament the inevitable destruction of the past at the metaphorical hands of time. W. H. Auden muses,

> At any given instant
> All solids dissolve, no wheels revolve,
> And facts have no endurance—

And who knows if it is by design or pure inadvertence
That the Present destroys its inherited self-importance?

(1945, 430)

"Father Time," in David Lowenthal's description, traditionally was an agent of forgetting; this allegorical figure "came to symbolize decay and dissolution, his scythe, hour-glass, and crutches linking old age with poverty and decrepitude. . . . Time was a procurer of death who lurked among barren trees and ruinous buildings, waiting to devour his own children" (1985, 131). Forgetting, in this tradition, manifests the omnipresent corrosions of time, whereas memory offers precious recompense for its slow but pitiless ruination. If time is the dreaded agent of physical decay, then forgetting is its treacherous accomplice, which undermines all pretenses to perpetuity in human endeavor.

Such metaphorical threads persist in myriad depictions of the relationship between memory and forgetting—from mythology to philosophy, from theology to art, from literature to politics, and more. Memory is associated not merely with life but with individuals' and communities' assured transcendence of life, with their desires for lasting fame, even immortality. The goal that Herodotus sets for his *Histories*—ensuring "that human achievements may not become forgotten in time, and great and marvelous deeds . . . may not be without their glory" (2003, 3)—is a classic case in point. Forgetting is associated with the death of such remembrance and the "glory" it merits, with the slow but inevitable decay of all connection to a noble past, with the transposition of its familiar remainders into unidentifiable remains, even loss of such connection altogether. Milan Kundera's likening of "forgetting, which never stops enlarging its enormous cemetery," to a grave in which "lie buried values that have been underestimated, unrecognized, or forgotten" (2007, 17) intones an age-old association of forgetting with mortality and the tragic demise of human achievement. Forgetting, in these figurations, is not merely the opposite of memory; it parasitically haunts the act of recollection, thriving by virtue of a stealthy but lethal attachment to its host. Forgetting is memory's unshakable other, a ghostly counterpart shadowing luminous representations of former experiences.

Late twentieth-century investigations of social, collective, or public memory recast this historically irreconcilable relationship between memory and forgetting in characteristically modern fashion. Much of the diverse scholarship grouped under the heading of modern memory studies reflects preoccupations with archiving, documenting, or otherwise preserving traces

3

of an ostensibly organic past threatened by the allegedly increasing fragmentation of post–World War II culture. Beyond academic studies of public memory, moreover, individual and communal imperatives to remember— to recollect, recover, and preserve—offer hope of achieving some personal or collective continuity and stability in these times of social, economic, and political dislocation. The postwar epoch, whose effects continue to shape contemporary public life, has been typified by massive postindustrial economic transformations, the dramatically shifting valences of postcolonial and post–Cold War geopolitical arrangements, and the widespread dismantling of previous social, economic, and political orders. Such developments have understandably inspired diverse and passionate attempts to recover some sense of abiding communal history and heritage, as well as multifaceted scholarly efforts to document them, in the midst of local, national, and global upheavals.

Ours is an age in which archival documentation, revivals of communal heritage, and commitments to preserve memory at all costs consequently hold widespread cultural priority. A variety of scholars have documented the fact that many supposedly age-old traditions are in fact comparatively recent inventions; that the preservation of cultural heritage is a patently modern social, economic, and political preoccupation; and that, for better or worse, the increasingly large museum-going public (beyond academic or financial elites) embraces that preoccupation, sometimes as a somber activity and sometimes as escapist entertainment and consumerism.[1] Andreas Huyssen accordingly proposes that "we seem to suffer from a hypertrophy of memory," that "the obsession with memory itself [is] a significant symptom of our cultural present" (2003, 3), while Jacques Derrida might suggest that this obsession is symptomatic of the "archive fever" (1998, 12) to which we have succumbed.

Remembering as a collective means of preservation currently holds acute moral significance as well. Generational memories of heinous twentieth-century totalitarian regimes (from Nazi Germany to Stalinist Russia, from Mao Zedong's Cultural Revolution to Pinochet's reign of torture, from the Khmer Rouge to South African apartheid, and many more) have inspired awareness in Western liberal democracies of how illegitimate governments can violently impose historical revisionism on subjugated populations in order to concentrate their power and justify widespread suspensions of human rights or even genocide. Documentation of such events has impressed upon modern pluralist societies the need to preserve memory as a way of preserving the cultural lifeblood of oppressed peoples. Struggles for national sovereignty in former colonial states have likewise inspired myriad attempts to reinstate a once-repressed cultural past as the symbolic foundation of newly won sociopolitical identities. The result, Huyssen observes, "has been the emergence of memory as a key cultural and political concern in Western societies" (2003, 11), consistently yoked to universal ideals of democracy, human rights, and social justice. Civic discourse concerning popular folklore, communal tradition, and public history in the aftermath of such episodes often treats distorted recollections and outright forgetting as anathema to maintaining healthy collective memory and the forms of public identity it promotes. George Santayana's now-familiar adage, "Those who cannot remember the past are condemned to repeat it" (1906, 284), expresses the quintessential logic underlying imperatives for documentation, archiving, and preservation that shape the most ambitious memorial projects in modern times.

The laudable preservationist ethic that motivates contemporary efforts to cultivate rich cultural memory duplicates premodern trepidations over forgetting and the wreckage of memory it leaves in its wake. Forgetting, in academic as well as popular usage, continues to signify a loss, absence, or lack—not simply of memory but of live connections with a tangible past. Forgetting is acutely meaningful in both scholarly and public circles as the ontological opposite of memory, as a hindrance to mature understanding and full experience of a nourishing past. Paul Connerton speaks of a "commonly held if not universal" assumption "that remembering and commemoration is usually a virtue and that forgetting is necessarily a failing" (2008, 59). Ours is a culture that typically treats memory as a rich and vibrant means of preserving the past and forgetting as a form of commemorative passivity or neglect, a symptom of the undesirable dissolution of communal heritage or historical wisdom. In the late twentieth century, forgetting was most evidently associated with death, and memory with life, in the wake of unprecedented genocidal atrocities. The association was further buttressed by a growing awareness that the threatened traditions and memories of oppressed peoples contained precious relics of lives and histories otherwise eradicated by persecution in its many modern forms. Even today, in still other contexts, civic leaders routinely implore the public to "never forget" the example of those who perished in wartime or in national tragedy, as in World War II or on September 11, 2001.

The welter of late twentieth- and early twenty-first-century scholarship on memory understandably reflects the manifold priority that remembrance, conceived as an antidote to forgetting, has acquired in recent decades. Such scholarship has attained prominence by grappling with questions of historical discontinuity and communal fragmentation at a time when forgetting is viewed by every significant measure—cultural, political, moral, and technological—as a chief contributing factor of such ills. None of the preceding commentary, however, is meant to contend that modern memory scholars, as a result of these historical and cultural influences, shelter a naïve, unexamined faith in the organic fullness of all memory or an unflagging presumption that commemorative practices effectively preserve transparent connections with an unaltered past. Interdisciplinary literature comprising the field of modern memory studies demonstrates, to its credit, profound sensitivities to the instability, transience, and fragility of collective remembrance and communal tradition.

Regardless of such admirable sensitivities, however, studies in this vein collectively exhibit ambivalent attitudes toward the many ways in which instances of forgetting can play a positive, formative role in works of public memory. Despite a sophisticated awareness of the fact that public memories are selectively mediated, beyond a recognition of their inherent susceptibility to transmutation (the constant effects of forgetting, in part or full), contemporary treatments of such memory assign little, if any, positive value to the operations of forgetting as a significant factor in their formation and perdurance. Intentional or unintentional episodes of distortion, excision, or loss in regard to the past understandably signify not only commemorative but ethical failings when imperatives to archive, document, and preserve hold the moral high ground.

The scenes of public forgetting examined in this book suggest an understanding of, and analytic vocabulary for evaluating, the material nature and effects of forgetting that is fundamentally different from its most enduring representations in both classical and modern lore. Shelley's classically inspired rendering of Ozymandias's forgotten and piteously corroding monument symbolizes a qualitatively different kind of forgetting than, for instance, the publicly orchestrated toppling of a monument to Napoleon during the 1871 Paris Commune, an "act of anti-commemoration" intended, in Matt Matsuda's elegant treatment, "to proclaim a new euphoric order, shattering bronze and stone to rupture time and history" (1996, 21, 20–21). The idea that acts of organized state forgetting are synonymous with modern programs of atrocity or genocide, the Holocaust being the ultimate and omnipresent example thereof, is undermined by the iconoclastic procedures of state forgetting undertaken after the fall of the Soviet Union in 1989, when dozens of monuments to Lenin were removed from their places of pride in

Moscow, leaving only naked plinths: "Far from erasing the memory of the communist regime," Adrian Forty writes, the bare pedestals "became memorable in a way that they had never been when topped by statues" (1999, 10). Connerton economically pinpoints the crucial insight here: "Forgetting is not a unitary phenomenon" (2008, 59). The practices of forgetting that this book analyzes provide novel exposure to its manifestations and effects in public life by presupposing a definition of forgetting categorically distinct from far more familiar scenes of historical decay or genocidal destruction.

That said, a small cluster of recent studies have begun to revisit the topic of forgetting and explore the possibility that it can be a worthy alternative to memory in addressing either personal or collective dilemmas of the past. This book seeks to extend such emerging reassessments of forgetting on two fronts. First, sporadic affirmative treatments of forgetting remain essentially conceptual or theoretical in nature. It is one thing to accept the broad philosophical argument that forgetting can be a commendable response to the remembered past, including incidents of violence, injustice, or even atrocity that populate it; it is another to examine in detail how particular social agents argue for and enact such forgetting, and how one may evaluate its effects in concrete historical, cultural, or moral circumstances. For this reason, the majority of the book focuses narrowly on the rhetoric and politics of forgetting as a public practice—as a symbolic resource of public speech and action—instead of addressing it as a comparatively abstract ontological phenomenon or as an individual cognitive event. Second, a significant portion of late scholarly interest in forgetting seeks to revitalize premodern, though little-remembered, literary and philosophical terminologies according to which forgetting was once held in higher esteem. But the constitutive tropes and cultural symbolism of these antique, albeit approving, attitudes toward forgetting (such as willed amnesia or oblivion) endow forgetting with limited, potentially outmoded, value and utility in the context of modern public culture. Thus, the central purposes of this study are to provide: (1) an updated conceptual framework devoted to analyzing forgetting as an organized public practice; and (2) a series of case studies that reveal, by implementing that framework, how one may argue for and enact such forgetting in the political and moral languages of public life.

In structural terms, the book pursues these central purposes by demonstrating a deep terminological contrast. This study contends that examining traditional idioms of forgetting, with particular emphasis on the negative significance they assign to it, is a necessary first step in determining how one may adopt different idioms of forgetting that reveal (in counterintuitive ways) their vitality to particular cultures of memory and forms of public deliberation. The structure of the book mirrors this contention. Part 1 shows how our modern cultural resources for speaking of forgetting descend from consistently negative accounts of its legendary destructiveness in order to clear a conceptual space for identifying alternate heuristics with which to describe and assess its relative value in public culture. Part 2 offers close examinations of specific social, political, or ethical benefits that forgetting may contribute to communal affairs, thereby displaying in significant detail the sometimes great differences between the merits of forgetting as an organized public practice or mode of collective judgment and the bad reputation that both traditional and modern tropes of forgetting assign to it. Hence, the book's unfolding parts performatively mimic its basic thesis regarding the productive (rather than destructive) interplay of memory and forgetting: Part 1 recollects dominant tropes and figures of forgetting as a prelude to inaugurating, in Part 2, a constellation of new tropes and figures, new idioms of forgetting in public culture.

By virtue of this structure, the book proposes an alternate *public* conception of forgetting and, with it, an alternate apprehension of its value in shaping civic senses of time, history, and memory as resources of political and moral judgment.[2] Nonetheless, the following claim cannot be overstated: the interpretation of forgetting that this study advances in no way contradicts the irreproachable conviction to preserve memory as a way of preserving one's cultural heritage under threat of persecution and violence. Barbie Zelizer's splendid work on photojournalism and Holocaust memory, *Remembering to Forget,* is instructive in this respect. "Paradoxically," she argues, our socially acquired tendency to interpret "events as wide-ranging as contemporary barbarism, AIDS, urban poverty, and political suppression" with "Holocaust photos [has] helped us remember the Holocaust so as to forget contemporary atrocity" (1998, 13). Arguing against Zelizer's main contention—that we are obligated to remember past atrocities in reflective and constructive ways because the consequences of forgetting them are too appalling to tolerate—would be wholly foreign to the aims of this book.

The assumption, however, that an affirmative approach to forgetting is incompatible with such convictions and obligations rests on shaky logical premises. On close inspection, the apparent moral truth of Santayana's oft-cited maxim ("Those who cannot remember the past are condemned to repeat it") collapses in *reductio ad absurdum.* "Too often," Arthur Schlesinger Jr. quips, "it is those who *can* remember the past who are condemned to repeat it" (1966, 91). Elie Wiesel, Avishai Margalit, and Miroslav

Volf all acknowledge, contrary to conventional wisdom, that harboring recollections of torture and other injustices can incite desires for violent revenge among formerly victimized peoples.[3] Former Serbian president Slobodan Milošević's now-infamous speech on June 28, 1989, commemorating the six hundredth anniversary of the Battle of Kosovo exemplifies vividly the ways in which detailed collective remembrance can inflame rather than pacify ethnic hatreds. Even those who bear witness to such remembered hatreds, however, may represent uncertain bulwarks against their recurrence: "The thought that there is no consigning of deeds to a historical past," W. James Booth writes, "to the closure of 'what happened, happened,' but only a testifying to them, a making present of them, seems to make the witness into the 'gravedigger' of the present" (2006, 147). Forgetting, in logical terms, no more guarantees the repetition of past injustices than memory ensures their prevention.

Forgetting is admittedly a tragic force when it simply destroys symbolic affiliations with the past, whether by design or disregard, without imagining more conducive symbolic comportments between present and former times. This book nevertheless argues that in healthier forms forgetting can be used productively to maintain, replenish, or inaugurate vital cultures of memory writ large. In what circumstances, then, can one differentiate between productive and destructive manifestations of forgetting in public affairs? The book as a whole attempts to answer that question by examining rhetorical practices in which various agents somehow argue for and enact public forgetting.

The nature and effects of such practices contradict the notion that remembering and forgetting are categorical opposites. The analyses to come perceive memory and forgetting in a relationship of often reciprocal influence, or mutual creativity, in contrast to classical as well as modern renderings of their alleged incompatibility, which time and again emphasize the withering of living memory in the deathly embrace of forgetting. Contrary to these long-standing figurations, the case studies featured in this book identify ways in which forgetting is desirable to, even necessary for, maintaining cultures of memory that serve the needs of the present as much as they conform to the shape of the past, that nourish immediate social, political, and moral interests as much as they proclaim fidelity with former times, places, and events.

Strategically excising aspects of the collectively remembered past may prove essential to adapting collective remembrances in light of emerging social, political, and ethical dilemmas. Instances of ritualized forgetting may

prove salutary when one community seeks to symbolically interrupt historically accumulated antagonisms with another community (an official gesture
of forgiving and forgetting); when memories of violence and injustice breed
only desires for revenge and undermine efforts at political reconciliation;
when previously cherished traditions or institutions become outmoded and
stifle effective-decision making in response to new and unforeseen events;
or as a means of advancing a clear agenda for institutional reform when the
seemingly intractable dilemmas of the past inspire only confusion, apathy,
and resentment. Many have lamented, for example, that violence among
Israelis and Palestinians (or between warring religious traditions throughout
the Middle East, for that matter) might be quelled if memories on both
sides didn't run as deep as their hatreds. But this is only one, especially vivid
example of various ways in which public arguments to communally forget
could produce socially, politically, and ethically attractive outcomes.

The present study treats memory and forgetting, contrary to popular usage,
not as dialectical opposites but as densely interwoven dimensions of larger
symbolic or discursive processes. By virtue of such processes, we construct,
amend, and even revise altogether our public perceptions of the past, including our collective interpretations of its lessons, in response to the culture and
politics of the day. The claim that public bodies require healthy measures of
forgetting *and* remembering in order to nurture efficacious symbolic bonds
with their shared past is not paradoxical. Forgetting can be a necessary spur
to remembrance, provoking us to recognize the inherent selectivity of normative public memories and imagine anew, with each passing generation,
what our objects of memory should be, whereas collective remembrance
can become so inflexibly doctrinaire in form and content that it amounts
to a grossly simplified projection of former events, and thus an unintended
instance of forgetting the past in its truer heterogeneity. The activity of
remembering can unwittingly induce forms of forgetting, and forgetting
can be an instrument of remembering. These premises comport with a basic
sense of *remember,* defined as an act of mnemonic reconstruction—of recalling, yes, but differently with each act of recollection.

Rejecting the presumption that memory and forgetting are somehow antithetical, however, does not warrant the conclusion that memory and forgetting are therefore essentially one and the same. We depend on memory for our
individual and collective sense of identity, meaning, and purpose. The idea
that we know who we are now because we know who we have been is commonplace. We assign significance to past, present, and future (or anticipated)
events according to such subjective, temporally ordered experience.

But ordinary human experience attests that forgetting is also necessary for individual as well as communal well-being. Jorge Luis Borges's story "Funes, His Memory" tells the tale of a man afflicted with an insatiable, unedited memory that he himself likens to "a garbage heap" (1998, 135). Funes cannot take pleasure from present experiences because his memory is burdened with infinitesimal details of every past event. Borges's fable corresponds to some people's cognitive reality. Patients diagnosed with various cognitive disorders exhibit extraordinary powers of memory in their immediate and exacting recall of everything from musical scores to weather forecasts; but often they cannot function, mentally or physically, as self-sufficient individuals. Douwie Draaisma relates the representative case of Jacques Inaudi, a calculating prodigy who possessed "astonishing" powers of mental recall and was examined separately by Paul Broca and Jean-Martin Charcot as part of their pioneering nineteenth-century brain research. Draaisma reports that "the main striking feature" of these examinations was Inaudi's "general ignorance and exceptional forgetfulness in practical matters," leading to a "placid, rather indolent" personality (2000, 130).[4] In such cases, dramatically amplified faculties of memory suggest an imbalance in cognitive processes or personal abilities rather than a desirable enhancement of one's general capacities. One can possess too much memory and its content can be too vivid; one's capacity to preserve impressions of the past without exception can be a symptom of a disordered self, in both the temporal and psychological senses of the term. The fictional Funes and his real-life counterparts suggest analogous lessons concerning memory and forgetting in public life. In the parallel context of communal recollection, the ceremonial heralding of a new era or administration—the inauguration of new collective beginnings—is as crucial to a polity's sense of order and identity as its nurturance of ostensibly unbroken and comprehensive relations with the past.

Selves and publics alike require for their healthy functioning the ability to alternately enshrine or redact dimensions of their past—to call on memory and forgetting as distinct phenomena with apparently countervailing effects. Yet, in another sense, memory and forgetting are inescapably intimate. Personal as well as communal remembrance of the past a priori requires conscious or unconscious decisions concerning which of its surviving impressions should lie fallow, and why (regardless of individual or communal needs to treat memory and forgetting as epistemologically distinct phenomena). Such judgments suggest, by the same token, the operation of either conscious or unconscious reasons for remembering particular things in particular ways, for awarding some recollections privileged cognitive or communal attention to the diminishment of others.

We remember because we forget, and we forget in order to remember. Hence the paramount tension investigated across the following chapters: remembering and forgetting, in the context of public affairs, are not opposites; but neither, in postmodern fashion, should we presume them to be fictional versions of one another, or interchangeable social constructions differentiated only by arbitrary linguistic labels. Doing so would obfuscate our understanding of the critically distinctive function that each performs as a symbolic resource with which groups and individuals order and assign meaning to their existence. For this reason, the case studies that comprise the second part of this book examine the social, political, or ethical advantages of forgetting (or in one case, the dangers of a doctrinaire faith in memory) in places where we might least expect to find them: in grand civic commemoration, in modern historiography, in the formation of elaborate cultural folklore, and in some of the most cherished rhetorical artifacts of U.S. public memory and political statecraft.

The following inquiry into the rhetoric of public forgetting accordingly contributes to public memory studies in two ways. First, it explains how idioms of forgetting—something typically characterized as a hindrance (if not an outright harm) to the cultivation of fruitful remembrance—constitute occasionally necessary, even indispensable, aspects of those cultures of memory from which public institutions derive their purpose and authority. As such, this inquiry transmutes the dialectical opposition in which memory and forgetting are often cast in order to account for their dynamic interplay as formative ingredients of ongoing public speech, political action, and communal judgment. Second, such inquiry provides grounds for distinguishing between commendable and condemnable forms of public forgetting. (It also suggests, by the same token, secondary principles for distinguishing advantageous from disadvantageous modes of collective remembrance.)

This book makes such contributions by adopting a *rhetorical* methodology. The premise that social, collective, or public memory is communicative, discursive, or symbolic in nature is endemic to modern memory studies. Communal memory is the product of ongoing social or political debate over the contested meaning of the past. Maurice Halbwachs's landmark sociological approach to the connection between individual and collective memory remains normative in this respect, for he insisted that personal memory depends on socially engendered "frames of collective memory," language foremost among them (1992, 39).[5] Even individual memory, in other words, is collectively shaped and expressed. John Bodnar's definition of public memory provides an apposite summation of such orthodoxy in its reigning form: "Public memory is produced from a political discussion that involves not so much specific economic or moral problems but rather fundamental issues about the entire existence of a society: its organization, structure of power, and the very meaning of its past and present" (1992, 14). Public memory "takes the form of an ideological system," Bodnar observes, "with special language, beliefs, symbols, and stories," all of which serve "to mediate competing interpretations" of the past "and privilege some explanations over others" (14).[6] By this account, "public memory" is the result of a perpetual rhetorical process with which communities deliberate over how best to interpret the past as a resource for understanding and making decisions in the present. Deliberating parties thus craft in language as well as other symbolic or expressive forms a version of former persons and events appealing to public constituencies in light of present-day civic norms, interests, and controversies.

The logic of such definitional statements warrants the complementary assumption that public forgetting is an equally rhetorical phenomenon. Acts of public forgetting likewise culminate patterns of collective deliberation or contestation over the meaning and value of the past as it concerns immediate social or political interests. The crucial difference, however, is that such patterns of public dialogue, debate, and advocacy end in collective ratifications to discontinue or reject customary forms of remembrance instead of public proclamations to honor and sustain them. Speech, language, and symbolism devoted to this purpose stand apart from innumerable minor differences in popular or institutional recollection that comprise the quotidian substratum of public memory. Lowenthal makes this point in characteristically suggestive fashion: "Collective oblivion . . . is mainly deliberate, purposeful and regulated. Therein lies the art of forgetting—art as opposed to ailment, choice rather than compulsion or obligation. The art is a high and delicate enterprise, demanding astute judgment about what to keep and what to let go, to salvage or to shred and shelve, to memorialize or anathematize" (1999, xi). For this reason, the case studies featured in the second part of this book attend closely to the rhetorical techniques, the "art" of which Lowenthal speaks, embodied in particular forms and expressions of public forgetting. In order to distinguish constructive from destructive forms of such forgetting—in order to delineate their remarkably varied social, political, and ethical entailments—one must scrutinize in depth the artful language and strategic justifications that allow them to achieve public legitimacy.

Two final caveats, briefly stated, follow from this methodological orientation. The first is that this book avoids the temptation to apply the term *forgetting* in a solipsistic manner. Public forgetting operates in a categorically different way than vain and arbitrary alterations of the past, as Nietzsche describes them, which simply tidy up its uglier moments: "'I have done that,' says my memory. 'I cannot have done that,' says my pride—and remains adamant. At last—memory yields" (1990, 68). Chapter 2 establishes a relatively high conceptual standard that a rhetorical act of commemorative restructuring and transformation must meet in order to qualify as an example of public forgetting. Public forgetting arises from uncommonly pivotal moments in the evolution of communal time, history, and memory, during which either a single agent or a collective body initiates such forgetting according to a double movement: in this movement, advocates simultaneously articulate *a rationale* for interrupting, or even ending altogether, prevailing paradigms of memory and coin *a novel public idiom* with which the community's relation to its past, present, and future would be configured anew, or at least in profoundly altered ways. Forgetting, by this calculus, is set apart from ordinary and often unnoticed patterns of selective interpretation or partial recollection that weave the quieter, commonplace fabric of public memory.

Second, this methodology presupposes that public forgetting, like public memory, is irreducibly contingent in nature. Aristotle defines rhetoric as the art of understanding how to speak persuasively based on the contingencies of one public situation versus another; even if one sought to persuade different audiences about the same subject matter, those different bodies of listeners might expect to hear markedly different treatments of it. A similar logic holds true concerning the ethics and politics of public memory. Because publics remember only in a metaphorical sense—through competing narratives, speech acts, and symbols—communal memories of past events assume strikingly different forms based on the needs and interests of a given collective dilemma or controversy. By extension, the same must be said of public forgetting it gains currency within public speech, language, or symbolism as a situational response to contingent needs and interests, as a medium of judgment with respect to the perceived sense and value of the past. ("Forgetting," as Connerton says, "is not a unitary phenomenon" [2008, 59].) The chapters to come are not intended to yield categorical formulas for predicting what forms public forgetting can and should take in any and all circumstances (even the most meticulous comparative study of public memory in its conventional forms could not accomplish that task). The following chapters instead scrutinize *essential* rather than exhaustive instances of public forgetting that amply prove its strategic virtue to representative cultures of memory and the modes of public judgment they support.

To that end, the case studies in Part 2 of this book share the common purpose of analyzing rhetorical enactments of public forgetting in especially vivid idioms of collective life, ethics, and decision-making. The analyses scrutinize specific forms of forgetting not as stylistic practices unto themselves but as substantive resources of public judgment. The case studies in question thereby reveal the rhetorical work of forgetting not in arbitrary times and places but at the heart of collective practices commonly studied throughout public memory literature for the critical roles they play in allowing communities to derive important social, political, or ethical lessons from the past—namely, in national commemoration, in public history, in cultural folklore, and in the moral and political uses of memory in times of national crisis. The case studies are additionally balanced in their recognition that public forgetting, as a contingent rhetorical phenomenon, can originate in the voice of one or many, and can be a resource of the powerful and powerless alike.

But Part 1 of this book, as previously mentioned, accomplishes a necessary preliminary task. If we are to document various social, political, or ethical contributions of forgetting in public culture, then we will require conceptual resources for assessing its nature and effects that differ from those supplied by orthodox idioms of remembrance, which define memory as a public imperative and forgetting as a community's tragic failure to heed it. Huyssen and others posit that contemporary Western culture is relatively unique in the aim and extent of its characteristic "obsession" with memory; but the standard tropes and figures for memory and forgetting that express this obsession bear an ancient lineage. When individuals and communities today advocate for the virtues of memory as a safeguard against the vices of forgetting, they do so in terminologies distilled from a vintage store of theological, philosophical, and literary tropes or figures. Identifying the limitations of such conventional tropes and figures is a valuable first step toward adopting a set of heuristics with which to evaluate the comparatively positive nature and effects of forgetting in crucibles of public judgment. The chapters in Part 1 comprise, in this respect, an idiomatic history of the present as it concerns the conventional meaning and value assigned to forgetting in public life. What social, intellectual, and moral traditions have made it seem so imperative for us to think and speak of forgetting in such stridently negative ways—always as oblivion, liquidation, or amnesia, as the tragic loss, absence, or lack of memory? How might we learn to think and speak of it anew as a substantive resource of public judgment regarding communal lessons of the past?

# PART I

FORGETTING IN PUBLIC LIFE:
AN IDIOMATIC HISTORY OF THE PRESENT

## THE TWO RIVERS, PAST AND PRESENT

I contend that one cannot understand in full the nature of prevailing rhetorical resources for assigning significance to forgetting in public culture without studying their patent family resemblance to traditional tropes and figures of forgetting. The textual sources of these tropes and figures—all manner of intellectual, spiritual, and artistic reflections on memory and its fortunes in the Western tradition—are legion. The present chapter provides merely a synoptic overview of such tropes and figures in order to establish argumentative grounds for reconsidering equations of forgetting with oblivion that motivate seemingly unarguable present-day investments in public memory. Doing so will also establish a clear basis for comparison with succeeding chapters of this book, which seek to identify and apply alternate heuristics for evaluating the nature and effects of forgetting in particular cultures of memory.

Long-standing affinities among rhetoric, memory, and forgetfulness date to the classical origins of Western thought and culture. Foundational Latin treatises on rhetoric credit the poet Simonides of Ceos with inventing the so-called art of memory (*ars memoriae*)—a mnemonic method that enabled poets and orators to develop extraordinary powers of memory and remained an essential component of Western education for centuries.[1] Legend has it that Simonides, while dining at the house of a wealthy nobleman after a chariot race, was called outside by two young men seeking an audience with him; after he exited, the roof of the banquet hall caved in and killed the other celebrants still inside. Shortly thereafter, Simonides alone was able to name those who perished by remembering where he had seen them in the banquet hall, thereby identifying the dead so their families could commit their unrecognizable remains to a proper burial. "Prompted by this experience," Cicero recounts in *De oratore,* Simonides "made the discovery that order is what most brings light to our memory. And he concluded that those

who would like to employ this part of their abilities should choose localities, then form mental images of the things they wanted to store in their
memory, and place these in the localities" (2001, 2.354; see also 1.18, 1.157,
2.299–300, and 3.230). Thus began the formal tradition of mnemonics,
which Frances Yates (2001) has so masterfully documented, wherein orators assigned particular *topoi* (or lines of argument) to different places within
an imagined building. Orators exhibited astounding capacities for recall by
mentally walking through such imagined spaces as they spoke, discoursing
on topics according to the order in which they were there arranged. "And
it was as part of the art of rhetoric," Yates writes, "that the art of memory
traveled down through the European tradition in which it was never forgotten, or not forgotten until comparatively modern times" (2).

The dramatic episode that allegedly inspired the art of memory implicitly associates forgetting with death and memory with life (or at least a kind
of life). The Greeks' fear of being forgotten and deprived of lasting fame
after death operates subtly in the story of Simonides' mnemonic display.
The poet's feats of memory afforded those killed in the unforeseen tragedy a
measure of life after death, ensuring that their names and reputations would
survive in communal recollection. If Simonides had not remembered the
victims' names, then they would have been consigned to oblivion rather
than communal memory. To forget, in this instance, is to amplify the power
of death. Or better: forgetting as such betokens a kind of death.

The intellectual and performative tradition of mnemonics therefore originates in a manifestly negative depiction of forgetting as the opposite of, or
even a threat to, communal memory—and, to this extent, as a struggle of
life over death, of metaphysical redemption over physical oblivion. The cultural and intellectual movements that profoundly influenced dominant
Western perceptions of memory developed by appealing persistently to this
incipient symbolism, wherein memory connoted life, action, productivity, and presence and forgetting signified death, passivity, barrenness, and
absence. These tropes of life and death, or activity and passivity, survive in
modern ideals of memory and preserve the negative value of forgetting even
at this late date.

This antithesis between memory and forgetting, between life and death,
descends from the ancient mythological *topoi* of Lethe and Mnemosyne.[2]
*Lēthe* meant "forgetfulness" or "concealment" (conversely, the Greek word
for truth—*alēthia*—meant "*un*forgetfulness" or "*un*concealment").[3] Lethe
was also the name of a river in Hades; drinking from it causes forgetfulness, and in some tales souls imbibed its waters prior to reincarnation in

order to forget their past lives. Mnemosyne, in contrast, not only personified memory in Greek poetry but was mother of the nine Muses by Zeus.[4]
Memory, in this figuration, is impressively fertile—biologically, culturally,
and artistically. Souls in Hades could likewise drink from a river named
Mnemosyne, but its waters, unlike those of the river Lethe, enhanced their
recollections. Whereas the currents of memory ensure continuity between
body and soul, mortal and immortal life, those of forgetfulness erase abiding
connection between flesh and spirit, between earthly life and afterlife. From
antiquity to modernity, Western intellectual, literary, and religious authorities drew from the mythological symbolism of Lethe and Mnemosyne in
order to preserve forgetting as a synonym of absence, erosion, loss, or death.
The symbolism of life and death, of cultivation and destruction, operates at
the heart of major intellectual, religious, and artistic movements without
which both our historical and contemporary attitudes toward memory and
forgetting would not exist.

## Forgetting, from Antiquity to Modernity and Beyond

Plato's reflections on memory, wisdom, and morality are unsurpassed in
their influence on long-standing suspicions against forgetting. Plato adheres
strictly to the etymological meaning of the word "philosopher": philosophers are dignified by their love of wisdom (*philosophía*).[5] According to
Plato, one owes one's love of wisdom, and the preeminent title of philosopher, to the inborn providence of memory. Some individuals fortunately
possess souls that remember visions of ideal truth they acquired while traversing the heavenly sphere in disembodied form prior to their incarnation
in human flesh. In the *Meno*, Plato has Socrates instruct the title character
that his pedagogy consists in training oneself to activate intuitive wisdom
latent in one's soul. "Thus, the soul," Socrates expounds, "since it is immortal and has been born many times, and has seen all things both here and in
the other world, has learned everything that is. So we need not be surprised
if it can recall the knowledge of virtue or anything else which, as we see, it
once possessed" (81c–d). Learning, by the Socratic model, is recollection
(*anamnesis*). In the Myth of Er (at the end of Plato's *Republic*) a warrior dies
on the battlefield, then wanders in the afterlife among fellow souls as they
receive judgment and learn their impending human fates. These other souls
"journeyed to the Plain of Oblivion," where they were made to drink from
"the River of Forgetfulness" (X.621a), but the warrior is resurrected so he

may tell the living what he has witnessed. And in Plato's *Phaedrus,* Socrates relates a myth in which Theuth, a god, boasts to the Egyptian king Thamus of having invented the art of writing, proclaiming it "a branch of learning that will make the people of Egypt wiser and improve their memories," "a recipe for memory and wisdom" (274e). Thamus, however, objects that "if men learn this, it will implant forgetfulness in their souls" (275a). Writing, he retorts, is "a recipe not for memory, but for reminder"; it does not furnish wisdom from anamnesis "but only its semblance," the effect of which will be to fill pupils "with the conceit of wisdom" (275a–b). Plato riddles these and other dialogues with literary motifs all dramatizing this central theme: philosophers love wisdom the most, and become wisest above all others, because their souls remember the luster of its divine forms so well.

Foundational sources of Judeo-Christian teaching also identify forgetting as a neglectful, unrighteous condition. Old Testament prophets time and again adjure the Israelites to remember God's covenant with them, for the distractions of earthly pleasures repeatedly breed spiritual indolence among his chosen people.[6] Forgetting constitutes a breach of the divine covenant— the ultimate offense against God. Moses' exhortations to the Israelites not to forget this holy pact comprise a rhetorical leitmotif throughout the book of Exodus. "Remember that you were a slave in the land of Egypt," he proclaims in Deuteronomy, "and the Lord your God brought you out from there with a mighty hand and an outstretched arm; and therefore the Lord your God commanded you to keep the Sabbath day" (Deut. 5:15). God's faith in the chosen people is one with his steadfast oath to remember the original terms of the covenant: "He will neither abandon you nor destroy you; he will not forget the covenant with your ancestors that he swore to them" (Deut. 4:31). The Israelites honor God, and follow his divine example, in remembering the covenant; forgetting the covenant is tantamount to renouncing God. The biblical history of the Jewish people demonstrates the pragmatic urgency of such impassioned prophetic reminders: in exile, the survival of Jewish history depended upon its preservation in communal memory. The Jewish people are thus, as Jacques Le Goff would have it, "the people of remembrance par excellence" (1996, 132). In this sense, the Hebrew Bible and the ethos of the people it continually calls into being is a monumental work of memory.

Holy injunctions against forgetting are also central to Christian theology. Jesus' life, suffering, and sacrificial death introduce a new covenant between God and humankind: as Jesus' death redeems humanity of its sins, so humanity must honor that sacrifice by remaining faithful to the Holy Word, of which he was the singular human embodiment. The Eucharist establishes this new covenant—the definitive article of Christian theology—as one of remembrance, of demonstrating one's faith by not forgetting. Jesus breaks bread and distributes it among his disciples at the Last Supper, instructing them: "This is my body, which is given for you. Do this in remembrance of me" (Luke 22:19).

Augustine, greatest of the early church fathers, synthesizes Platonic and Judeo-Christian *doxa* concerning memory and the woeful prospect of forgetting in his enduringly influential testament of faith, the *Confessions*. "Great is the power of memory," he famously proclaims (X.xvii.26).[7] The seminal moment in Augustine's story of conversion is his realization that he had forgotten God's word in living a sinfully pagan life. He nonetheless rediscovers divine grace in the salvific fact that his creator has not forgotten him: "I call upon you, my God, my Mercy. You made me and, when I forgot you, you did not forget me" (XIII.i.1). For Augustine, Christian faith is defined by the belief that God does not forget us even when we forget God's call. This polarity between the steadfastness of God's memory and the heedlessness of human recollection is the sine qua non of Augustine's teaching.

Even in our forgetfulness of God's divine presence, according to Augustine, God sends signs that may help us reestablish our connection with divinity. Plato's influence looms large in this dimension of Augustine's thought, as articulated in the simultaneously theological and psychological treatment of memory in book 10 of the *Confessions*. Such signs—heavenly stimuli to remembrance—resemble Plato's ideal forms insofar as they incite us to rediscover our knowledge of God, our capacity for beholding God's radiance, dwelling within us since birth. Our souls, as in Plato, retain latent memories of the divine, before their incarnation in human form, if only we may train ourselves to remember God by reawakening those traces. Memory is the lodestar by which we recover our abiding relations with God: "Where shall I find you?" Augustine muses. "If I find you outside my memory, I am not mindful of you. And how shall I find you if I am not mindful of you?" (X.xvi.24). For Augustine, there is more at stake in such divine reminding than personal salvation. His charge to remember God as God remembers us provides a formula for gaining entrance to, and furthering the enlargement of, that kingdom of memory known as Christendom.

Even comparatively approving literary explorations of forgetfulness, evident throughout the history of Western letters, depict it as a hopelessly passive condition. Virgil, Dante, Milton, Goethe, Schiller, and many others employ the symbolism of Lethe in describing those liminal currents that run between life and death, remembering and forgetting, experience and oblivion. Dante's *Purgatory* infuses Lethe with patently Christian significance when Matilda informs the poet's narrative double that the river Lethe "removes as it flows down all memory of sin" (XXVIII.127–28).[8] Milton similarly recasts Lethe according to Christian motifs in *Paradise Lost,* but in his rendering the waters of forgetfulness stupefy rather than redeem:

> Far off from these a slow and silent stream,
> Lethè the river of oblivion rolls
> Her watery labyrinth, whereof who drinks,
> Forthwith his former state and being forgets,
> Forgets both joy and grief, pleasure and pain.
> (2007, II.582–86)

In Milton's epic, "Lethè the river of oblivion" leaves numbness, not regeneration, in its wake; it obliterates all experience, whether pleasant or painful— "both joy and grief, pleasure and pain." Goethe's *Faust,* moreover, includes an appreciation of such waters as thawing, replenishing currents. The wager Faust makes with Mephistopheles commences various scenes of forgetting in which the disavowal of one's past symbolizes spiritual liberation: "Let all past time for us be done and ended," he says. "For happiness Arcadian-free!" (1965, II.9563, 9573). These literary figurations *appear* to endow Lethe with estimable value—removing the memory of sin or pain, at however comprehensive a cost—yet forgetfulness in such depictions remains an ominously ambiguous proposition, signifying at best a form of amnesia. These canonical epics affirm the putative virtues of Lethe, of forgetting so defined, but only in the context of purgatory (Dante), amid humanity's fall from grace (Milton), and at the behest of Mephistopheles (Goethe). Forgetting, in this lineage, not only retains supernatural connotations but acquires a diabolical parentage as well, thus representing a doubtful salve to human woes.

This tendency, however, is not confined to the formulaic tropes of forgetting in Christian epics. Secular allusions to the waters of forgetting, of which there are many, similarly associate it with some form of oblivion, whether it be sleep, death, or both. "Tho will we little Love awake," Edmund Spenser wrote in *The Shephard's Calendar,* "That now sleepeth in Lethe lake" (1962, "AEgloga tertia," l. 23). Shakespeare's dramas include an array of such usages. In *Twelfth Night,* Sebastian prays, "Let fancy still my sense in Lethe steep; / If it be thus to dream, still let me sleep!" (1969, IV.i.58–59). Here, Lethe numbs one's "sense," possibly quieting dreams in "sleep." In *Julius*

*Caesar,* Lethe symbolizes the aftermath of violent death—the ultimate form
of passivity—when Antony, upon seeing the hands of Caesar's murderers
red with blood, laments: "Here didst thou fall; and here thy hunters stand, /
Signed in thy spoil, and crimsoned in thy lethe"(III.i.205–6). Shakespeare
makes the point explicit: "thy lethe" is synonymous with murder.

Similar references abound in myriad instances of early moden and modern literature. John Keats's "Ode on Melancholy" commences with the plea,
"No, no, go not to Lethe" (I.1), one of several methods by which to "drown
the wakeful anguish of the soul" (I.10), whereas his "Ode to a Nightingale"
makes the connection with death more explicit: "As though of hemlock I
had drunk" (I.2), the speaker swoons, "One minute past, and Lethe-wards
had sunk" (I.4) (1907, 247, 230). In either case, Lethe lulls the speaker into
some form of slumber, whether temporary or permanent. Samuel Beckett's
association of Lethe with passivity and death in his radio play *Embers* is even
blunter. Henry, the play's principal character, invokes the mythological river
when describing conversations with his dead wife: "That's what hell will be
like, small chat to the babbling of Lethe about the good old days when we
wished we were dead" (1970, 102). The figure of Lethe connotes an erasure of personality and self-possession in Sylvia Plath's "Getting There," the
characteristically biting conclusion of which, following a stream of deathly
imagery, renovates Lethe into a hearse-like automobile: "And I, stepping
from this skin / Of old bandages, boredoms, old faces // Step to you from
the black car of Lethe, / Pure as a baby" (1966, 38). Such long-standing
poetic or dramatic allusions to Lethe's soporific powers reappear even in
modern scientific nomenclature. William T. G. Morton, who first publicly
demonstrated the use of ether as an effective inhalation anesthetic (which
made modern surgery viable), exercised literary flair in calling his ether
"Letheon" (Fenster 2003, 210–11). By Morton's day, however, the symbolism was entrenched, thanks in large part to centuries' worth of canonical
literary works that depicted forgetting according to the mysterious imagery
of Lethe—as a figure of passivity, sleep, or even death.

Major facets of late Renaissance and Enlightenment thought, one could
argue, offered resolute alternatives to the classical and medieval tradition of
*ars memoriae* and, by implication, countered the foregoing negative depictions of forgetting.[9] Montaigne, for instance, railed against long-standing
European pedagogical methods, which in his view equated knowledge with
rote memorization: "To know by heart is not to know," he declared. "What
a poor kind of knowledge it is that comes solely from books!" (1957, I.26).
"Let him [the student]," Montaigne advised, "be asked for an account not

merely of the words of his lesson, but of its sense and substance, and let him judge the profit he has made by the testimony not of his memory, but of his life" (I.26). Harald Weinrich interprets Montaigne's polemics as a watershed development in which the formerly unquestioned authority of memory in intellectual pursuits gives way to the seemingly enhanced status of forgetting, primarily of medieval prejudices, as a requirement for enlightened knowledge (2004, 43 – 44). Cervantes' *Don Quixote*, published soon after, is generally regarded as the first modern novel precisely for its depiction of a man so bedazzled by romantic tales of chivalry that he no longer recognizes his own identity; indeed, his illusory recollections of a fabled past make him a pathetic object of ridicule (2005). By these measures, late Renaissance intellectual criticism and literature showed signs of a growing unease with the ancient art of memory and its influence on human knowledge.

Montaigne's polemics and Cervantes' novel presaged the more developed denunciation of scholasticism, dogma, and superstition that characterized Enlightenment philosophy and political theory. The ambitious Enlightenment project of "education" amounted to a pedagogical battle waged against memory in its musty scholastic garb (Gay 1969, 501 – 11). Descartes' methodological skepticism further legitimated such rejections of scholastic memory. One attains a secure foundation for rational thought, he maintained, by eliminating ideas subject to doubt in favor of maintaining clear and distinct chains of reasoning. Descartes' (2006) reflections on the proper techniques for forgetting as an instrument of sound and independent rational inquiry were ingredient to the very foundations of modern Western philosophy and mathematics.

But this putative early modern reversal in the respective value of memory and forgetting is deceiving. Forgetting remained a hindrance to intellectual refinement and the retention of knowledge in both the late Renaissance and the Enlightenment. The crucial development was not that forgetting attained a dramatically increased value but that leading thinkers of the day substituted the classical ideal of memory for modern, scientific ideals. Pioneering thinkers such as Descartes indeed contributed to the demise of the *ars memoriae* as well as the scholastic pedagogy to which it conformed; yet, as Weinrich admits, the Cartesian method produced "not only a new memory but also to some extent a new mnemonotechnics" (2004, 59), which severely circumscribed any validation of forgetting. The same may be said of numerous Enlightenment tracts that embraced similar methodologies: mature inquiry, as defined by leading philosophies of the day, depended upon trading one pedagogical ideal of memory for a competing ideal—one based on the clear retention of rationally discovered truths, which classical relics such *ars memoriae* and scholasticism occluded.

The characteristic tendency of late Renaissance and Enlightenment inquiry was to reinterpret the operations of memory according to emergent faculty psychology. Philosophical innovators of the period broadly agreed that sensations, ideas, and universal human experiences were best explained according to the mind's hierarchy of cognitive processes, including memory. John Locke's enormously influential account of human understanding provides an indispensable illustration of how such philosophies produced new and decisive models of memory. In Locke's analysis, the mind functioned best when ideas remained clearest, most reflective of the natural sensations or perceptions that inspired them. Language was a chief agent of forgetting because it naturally muddied one's comprehension of complex ideas. "When a word stands for a very complex idea that is compounded and decompounded, it is not easy for men to form and retain that idea so exactly, as to make the name in common use stand for the same precise idea, without the least variation" (1959, III.9.6). In Locke's interpretation, we use "moral words" (III.9.6) to refer to such complex ideas, a fact which indicates the gravity of this inevitable deviance from our originally clear understandings of particular concepts. The language of ordinary discussion incessantly obfuscates our apprehension of basic moral concepts upon which our judgments concerning such crucial subjects as law depend. "And hence we see," Locke writes, "that, in the interpretation of laws, whether divine or human, there is no end; comments beget comments, and explications make new matter for explications; and of limiting, distinguishing, varying the signification of these moral words there is no end" (III.9.9). The more we explicate the meaning of complex ideas, the further our original understanding of topics vital to human well-being passes into oblivion.

For these reasons, Locke argues vociferously against traditional "books of rhetoric," claiming they do little but "insinuate wrong ideas" and promote "error and deceit" (III.10.34). In doing so, he naturally argues against the classical mnemonic methods central to their pedagogy. But Locke intends his invective against the traditional conjunction of rhetoric and memorized wisdom to justify its subordination to competing ideals of language and memory. He does not argue categorically against memory in favor of forgetting; he advocates, to the contrary, a more scientifically accurate, psychologically grounded model of memory in order to counteract a linguistic form of forgetting. "*Any words*," he states, "*will serve for recording. . . . [F]or the recording our own thoughts for the help of our own memories*" (III.9.2; emphasis in original).[10]

Locke redefines memory as a system of recording, and thus prepares the way for the development of modern conceptions of memory. Chris Westbury and Daniel C. Dennett, for example, express a conception of memory indebted to Locke when they describe it as "the ability to store useful information and to retrieve it in precisely those circumstances and that form which allows it to be useful" (2000, 14). Good human understanding, by this definition, follows from ordered mental retention, from clear and rational recording and mental preservation of ideas. Endless "explications" in the style of "books of rhetoric" foment forgetting by obscuring originally clear and reasoned understanding, animating the passions and the "love to deceive and be deceived." For Locke, and the many Enlightenment figures who revered him as an intellectual giant, the proper functioning of faculty psychology held import beyond individual experience and understanding. The expanding, increasingly diversified marketplace of public discussion in their time allegedly fostered confused and counterproductive civic discourse. Those who participated in it did so with clouded ideas about moral and political issues. Civic bodies that disputed vital issues in misunderstanding, or forgetfulness, of their true nature would make accordingly deluded judgments—a notion that retains the status of conventional wisdom in liberal-democratic societies pledged to the institutional cultivation of memory.

Some have argued that the ascendance of modernist ideals in early twentieth-century science, politics, and art (which still exercise enormous influence over contemporary thought and culture) indicated not simply an increasing disillusion with the alleged goods of the past but a growing amenability to those of forgetting. The works of avant-garde movements such as Dadaism, Surrealism, and Futurism reflected, in especially provocative ways, a host of scientific, political, and artistic motivations for rejecting the authority of the traditional past. This interpretation, however, elides a crucial nuance: increasing recognition of the prevalence of forgetting, motivated by anxiety over the fragility of memory and history, does not amount to an affirmation of forgetting. Like the Enlightenment, mature twentieth-century modernism rejected classical ideals of memory and history, but precisely in order to erect new ones, not to embrace forgetting on its own terms. If anything, some of the most resounding intellectual and literary projects of the early twentieth century reveal that fuller assessments of forgetting only motivated the search for modern ideals of memory no less hostile to it than comparatively antique ones.

Freud's psychoanalytic theory, for instance, exerted vast influence in shaping modernist anxieties about forgetting and the mind's capacity for recollection. Psychoanalysis did not merely flourish as a therapeutic or intellectual project but, in Paul Ricoeur's description, "produced a sort of vulgate that has raised it to the level of a cultural phenomenon" (2004, 447). Indeed, the premise that unconscious drives covertly mold our conscious thoughts and behaviors is central to both modern and late modern notions of the self. One may cogently describe the *raison d'être* of psychoanalysis—to uncover and explain the secrets of the unconscious—as a project against forgetting. The presumption that we repress awareness of traumatic episodes from our past is elemental to Freudian methods. Freud distinguishes between repeating and remembering in this context: we repeat thoughts and behaviors that prevent us from remembering the original trauma in order to impede conscious awareness of it. "The patient," he writes, "does not *remember* anything of what he has forgotten and repressed, but *acts* it out. He reproduces it not as a memory but as an action; he *repeats* it, without, of course, knowing that he is repeating it" (1958, 150).[11] Forgetting is psychologically unhealthy: it leads to repression, which leads in turn to debilitating neuroses or psychoses.

Examining conscious thoughts and behaviors in order to discover their unconscious origins, to recover the repressed, is therefore a curative form of remembering. Freud summarizes the nature of this procedure according to a "division of labor" between patient and analyst: "The doctor uncovers the resistances which are unknown to the patient; when these have been got the better of, the patient often relates the forgotten situations and connections without any difficulty" (1958, 147). The unconscious, in Freud's theory, "is in no sense something that is merely unknown. The Unconscious is consequently an ex-known, something previously known that has been forgotten but has not thereby disappeared from the world" (Weinrich 2004, 134). Hence, psychoanalytic therapy consists in techniques designed to interrupt forgetting, to nullify the harmful effects of repressed trauma by achieving lucid, epiphanic recollection. (Freudian and Socratic methods thus resemble one another in the priority they assign to anamnesis.) In Ricoeur's estimation, "Psychoanalysis is therefore the most trustworthy ally in the thesis of the unforgettable. This was one of Freud's strongest convictions, that the past once experienced is indestructible" (2004, 445). Indeed, Freud posits that the existence of "screen memories" disproves the supposed impenetrability of "childhood amnesia": "Not only *some* but *all* of what is essential from childhood," he declares, "has been retained in these memories" (1958, 148). Psychoanalysis as Freud conceived it promised to address not only the memory blockages of individual patients but also the influence of the unconscious, and forms of forgetting intrinsic to it, on human society writ large.[12]

Marcel Proust's multivolume masterpiece *Remembrance of Things Past* (1934) likewise explored, in literary form, the possibility of using memory to recover one's past in its original texture. Implicit throughout his novel is the theory that conscious or voluntary memory, a category that necessarily includes the classical art of memory, provides one with scant hope of recovering past experience in its original richness. Such analytical recollection allows one to mentally catalogue mundane information but cannot enable one to recall sublime experiences that penetrated to the very core of one's being. Proust believed that involuntary memories were invaluable for achieving that purpose. The potency of involuntary memories in *Remembrance of Things Past* (the most famous example being the oft-quoted episode of the madeleine) lies in their wholly unexpected aspect: they wrench one out of the routine course of everyday experience with an ecstatic jolt, thereby triggering a flood of overwhelming spontaneous recollection. The *ek-stasis* of involuntary recollections, as Proust depicts them, returns one to seemingly lost, forgotten dimensions of one's past, the emotionally stirring recovery of which amounts to a reunion with previously abandoned facets of one's very self. The nature of the past that one encounters through involuntary remembrance is akin, in Proust's description, to "luminous moments" preserved in "sealed jars" waiting to be unsealed (2:994). Proust thus unequivocally rejects classical principles of memory; but he replaces them with passionately held beliefs in the power of spontaneous memory to enrich our lives. Memory, in his rendering, remains valuable for its capacity to relight pockets of personal oblivion.

Martin Heidegger's *Being and Time,* arguably the most important philosophical work of the twentieth century by its most important philosopher, also sets as its task a massive project of remembrance over forgetting. Heidegger laments that humanity at large (and not only philosophers) has forgotten to attend to the question of Being. His volume commences with this blunt assertion: "*The Necessity for Explicitly Restating the Question of Being. This question today has been forgotten*" (1996, 1). We have, in other words, forgotten how to reflect systematically on our unique existence as beings who can conduct such an investigation (as Da-sein). The disastrous consequences of this fact, in Heidegger's assessment, are not speculative in nature; one may observe them in the frightening embrace of destructive technologies deployed on an unprecedented scale as a wondrous remedy to the most formidable dilemmas of modern human existence. The quest to discover a mode of thinking and speaking by which one may remember Being in its unconcealed truth permeates Heidegger's entire philosophy.

His enormously influential corpus thus constitutes a sustained effort to re-collect the authenticity of being as *aléthia* (as unforgetting or unconcealment) over and against *lethe* (as forgetting or concealment). The elemental desire that Proust and Heidegger variously exemplify—to somehow recover, through remembrance, an elusive human essence eclipsed by the dislocations of modernity—lingers today in characteristically postmodern feelings of existential ennui.

Post–World War II history and public moral sentiment decisively stifled the avant-garde programs of forgetting that emerged during early and high modernism. Fervent postwar affirmations of remembrance over forgetting indicate the continuing appeal of life and death as respective figures of memory and forgetting. Collective memory is now widely accepted as a medium with which to preserve the fragile dignity of life amid state-sponsored mass murder and other modern forms of atrocity. Jewish survivors of the Holocaust naturally sought to comprehend its incomprehensible meaning with the biblical vocabulary of memory. On the one hand, the Nazis' attempt to annihilate all Jews represented an effort to exterminate every trace of their culture, and thus banish memory of their life and heritage from humankind. On the other hand, parallels between Old Testament Israelites exiled from their homeland and European Jews systematically exiled to a living twentieth-century hell were impossible to ignore. The various terms by which writers attached a concise name to the mass murder of European Jews, such as *Holocaust* and *Shoah,* all derive from the Hebrew Bible (Young 1988, 85–86). By either measure, memory remained the only viable medium through which their history and defining communal traditions might survive. Elie Wiesel gestures to the grave resonance between biblical and post–World War II history when he says, "To be a Jew is to remember" (Rittner 1990, 31).

Patterns of remembrance originally distinctive of Jewish Holocaust memory, however, now supply the dominant cultural vocabularies and rhetorical forms according to which liberal-democratic societies in general interpret the moral lessons of all historical atrocities. Wiesel's internationally renowned Holocaust memoir, *Night,* for instance, is widely celebrated as a preeminent model of moral testimony because of its sworn resistance to forgetting. Its opening passages formally recall biblical imperatives to uphold one's covenant with God through memory; yet the author's version of such imperatives endows memory with a spiritual potency even greater than biblical scribes might have intended. For Wiesel, the conviction to remember is all that remains after the Holocaust has obliterated not only his personal faith in God but, more profoundly, the apparent presence of God in the world:

> Never shall I forget that night, the first night in the camp, that turned my life into one long night seven times sealed.
>
> Never shall I forget that smoke.
>
> Never shall I forget the small faces of the children whose bodies I saw transformed into smoke under a silent blue sky.
>
> Never shall I forget those flames that consumed my faith forever.
>
> Never shall I forget the nocturnal silence that deprived me for all eternity of the desire to live.
>
> Never shall I forget those moments that murdered my God and my soul and turned my dreams to ashes.
>
> Never shall I forget these things, even if I were condemned to live as long as God himself. Never. (2006, 34)

Memory outlasts even the God who inexplicably vacated the now "silent blue sky," who was "murdered" in the fires of the crematoria, "which consumed my faith forever." Wiesel provides public witness to the atrocities from which he was somehow spared not in remembrance of a divine covenant but in spite of it. Remembering—or never forgetting—honors "those children" whose deaths he witnessed, who were deprived of the capacity to witness, who were not saved by any covenant. Forgetting is tantamount to a sin against humanity—a failure to accept the moral burden of testifying for those who cannot speak, of bearing witness to heinous crimes that must not go unanswered. Forgetting allows such monstrous crimes to exist in the absence of moral response and thereby compounds their destruction. It has become conventional wisdom in the aftermath of the Holocaust and other atrocities to assert, as Jean Baudrillard does, that "Forgetting extermination is part of extermination itself" (1995, 49) or to insist, with Theodor Adorno, that "the abundance of real suffering tolerates no forgetting" (1982, 312).

Logic of this sort permeates the canon of academic scholarship on social, collective, or public memory. Far from abandoning the ancient tropes of life and death, such scholarship has adapted those figures to explain the dilemmas of cultivating memory and history in late modernity. Pierre Nora's landmark studies in French national memory, for example, define the very idea of public memory as a nexus of state politics, civic heritage, and material culture. His account supplies one of the defining tropes of public memory scholarship writ large: *lieux de memoire,* or "realms of memory." To study public memory, using Nora as a model, is to study its public manifestations—its multimodal presence in the realm of public life.

Nora's oft-cited essay "Between Memory and History: *Les Lieux de Mémoire*" conveniently summarizes his core theoretical convictions. "A movement toward democratization and mass culture on a global scale," he argues, separates collective memory from state history (1989, 7). Historical perception is now "dilated, multiplied, decentralized, democratized" (14)—by all counts, memory is wider and therefore shallower. In Nora's reckoning, the multiplicity of memorial projects in postwar France reveals the decay of memory itself and, by implication, the imminence of collective forgetting. "There are *lieux de mémoire,* sites of memory," he says, "because there are no longer *milieux de mémoire,* real environments of memory" (7). Evidence testifying to the atrophy of civic memory exists everywhere, albeit in ironic form: modern culture is riddled with *lieux de memoire*—archives, historical sites, texts, symbols of the past, all proliferate seemingly without end—yet they remain mere fragments of the grand, unified memory that Nora seeks. Such dispersed, incoherently related *lieux de memoire* are not forms of memory at all, but portend its very destruction. "We speak so much of memory," Nora says, "because there is so little of it left" (7).

Nora describes the characteristically late modern abandonment of unified state history and cultural memory in terms that recall traditional antitheses between the vitality of memory and the depletions of forgetting. For him, memory signifies life, actuality, spontaneity—an organic force. Contemporary archival obsessions, in dramatic contrast, signify lost or lifeless memory; modern archives and recording technologies allow one simply to place remainders of the past in archival limbo, where they wither unattended. "Memory," he laments, "has been wholly absorbed by its meticulous reconstruction. Its new vocation is to record; delegating to the archive the responsibility of remembering, it sheds its signs upon depositing them there, as a snake sheds its skin" (13). The archive is, in his reckoning, "no longer living memory's more or less intended remainder" but "the deliberate and calculated secretion of lost memory" (14).[13] By this logic, a double anxiety over forgetting inspires Nora's ambitious effort to refurbish the bonds between national history and collective memory: not only the likelihood that contemporary archival fever disguises our neglect of a full, organic past but also that such fever evinces our forgetfulness concerning broader questions of how one might best commemorate the past at all. The result, in Nora's terms, is a kind of death.

Despite its deserved landmark status, Nora's conception of memory and forgetting is vulnerable to accusations of nostalgia: in lamenting the decay of a formerly cohesive state history and civic heritage, he posits a vibrancy of memory that might never have existed in the first place. James Young's commanding scholarship exhibits, in contrast, an unusually candid suspicion against conventional forms of public memory, such as monuments and museums. He approvingly quotes Robert Musil's remark that "There is nothing in this world as invisible as a monument" (Young 1993, 13) in order to argue that monuments to the past, despite their intended function as stirring incitements to communal memory, can engender memories as inflexible as the stone from which they're made, allowing the public at large to abdicate its communal responsibility for maintaining a fuller, more productive relationship to the past in daily civic affairs. Young is at his most eloquent when he critiques installations in Holocaust museums that display piles of personal tokens (shoes, clothing, suitcases, hair) seized from concentration camp victims because they fail so deplorably in the larger objective of fitting memorialization:

> That a murdered people remains known in Holocaust museums anywhere by their scattered belongings, and not by their spiritual works, that their lives should be recalled primarily through the images of their death, may be the ultimate travesty. These lives and the relationships between them are lost to the memory of ruins alone—and will be lost to subsequent generations who seek memory only in the rubble of the past. Indeed, by adopting such artifacts for their own memorial presentations, even the new museums in America and Europe risk perpetuating the very figures by which the killers themselves would have memorialized their Jewish victims. (1993, 133)

A badly conceived monument, however nobly intended, exacerbates the potentially irreparable loss of "spiritual works" or past "lives and relationships" by sanctioning a morally flawed mode of commemoration. The parallel that Young deftly draws between the vantage of "the killers themselves" and that offered by contemporary monuments to victims of the Holocaust dramatizes his primary moral insight: such conduits to the past perpetuate, even unwittingly, the forgetting of an entire people originally undertaken by means of unspeakable murder.

Across these various examples, however, Young preserves a commonplace opposition between memory and forgetting, understood as an opposition between life and death. To commemorate the past with a faulty monumental artifact is to compound the effects of mass murder by means of collective forgetting. To be unmindful of the lacunae inherent in any effort at historical narration or commemoration is to ignore, and thus forget, the ways in which one may preserve its fuller dimensions in the liveliness of cultural dialogue. One might argue that the overriding objective of Young's scholarship is to distinguish forms of public memorialization suited to achieving a kind of redemption—sowing the most fertile cultural seeds left behind by Holocaust victims so they may yield prolonged life—from commemorative practices that encourage relations with the past so formulaic and insipid that they amount to widespread forgetting.

Young underscores the fact that the past as we inherit it in narrative or memorial symbolism contains both "life-sustaining" and "life-threatening" myths by which we interpret the world," and calls on us to develop critical awareness of their differences (1988, 192). His work therefore features a remarkably astute moral and political attunement to the inherently selective, contested, and sometimes tragically ironic nature of public memory; but that attunement reaffirms standard incompatibilities between the liveliness of memory and the oblivion of forgetting. Taken together, Young and Nora's contributions to the field of public memory studies are qualitatively enormous (and rightly so). Their status as representatives of widely embraced critical approaches handily illustrates how the swell of academic reflection on social, collective, or public memory in recent decades preserves the traditional symbolism of recollection and oblivion, of life and death, as basic hermeneutic principles for understanding memory and forgetting in modern public culture.

Aside from understandable public and academic commitments to memory forged in the postwar era, one can find perhaps the most literal evidence that ours is an age in which memory and life are integrated as never before in a relatively banal phenomenon: widespread enthusiasm for the wonders of cutting-edge digital recording technologies.[14] The call to never forget is not only a moral and political slogan but, in the realm of digital innovation, a potential reality. Research divisions for Microsoft and Apple are developing technologies that fuse conceptions of individual life with digital memory storage. Microsoft's MyLifeBits project uses emergent technologies to digitally archive, on a personal basis, "a lifetime's worth of articles, books, cards, CDs, letters, memos, papers, photos, pictures, presentations, home movies, videotaped lectures, and voice recordings" (Microsoft Research 2008). Microsoft industry publications report that their lead researcher in this area, Gordon Bell, has donned such small-scale systems on a functionally permanent basis in order to record every waking moment of his life; he has gone "paperless" and is "beginning to capture phone calls, IM transcripts, television, and radio" instantly. Life, in this conception, is an exercise in immediate data storage and retrieval, of ceaselessly accumulated digital memory from which nothing is omitted. Advertisements for Apple's iLife software similarly invite consumers to compile a personal multimedia archive for the production of various digital memorabilia, including "beautiful books, colorful calendars, dazzling DVDs, perfect podcasts, and attractive online journals" (Apple 2008). Here, too, life is equivalent to a process of data storage and dissemination in which nothing is lost: Apple informs its consumers that "iLife" software is "the easiest way to make the most out of every bit of your digital life."

Emerging digital memory systems radically augment the scope and duration of personal memory far beyond the lifespan of the person in question. This increasing equation of memory with digital technology as an extension of personal experience contradicts the argument, advanced by some commentators, that the contemporary age evinces disillusionment with, or even ignorance of, the traditional fruits of memory.[15] The lavish tradition of *ars memoriae* has indeed waned but the recent proliferation of digital memory systems designed for flexible personal use indicates that contemporary culture remains as invested as ever in improving and enlarging the realms of memory. Instead of representing a break with long-standing techniques designed to enhance personal life through the enlargement of memory, such technologies demonstrate that the ancient equation of memory with life, and of forgetting with irretrievable loss (or erasure and deletion, to use modern computing terms), survives in ever more sophisticated digital formats. These technologies accordingly suggest that we remain as obsessed with perfecting memory as a system of accumulation and retrieval as our cultural forebears. Life, according to the digital calculus of MyLifeBits and iLife, is no longer the source of memory; memory now comprises the ever expanding horizon of life. To live is to be recorded and retrieved, effortlessly. In this sense, we have improved *ad infinitum* upon the classical *ars memoriae*.

One cannot deny that the art and culture of modernity, with its many fixations on present and future progress, brought the once-noble art of memory to an ignoble end. One cannot deny that the modernist penchant for rapid change and novelty, as well as postmodern enthusiasms for ahistorical pastiche and temporal discontinuity, led naturally to various flirtations with forgetting. In the main, however, our age remains notable not only for its anxieties over the degradation of tradition and glaring omissions from the archives of official history but also for its optimism in the power of increasingly sophisticated archival methods and increasingly ambitious memorial projects to counteract such losses. Massive public and private financing of archives and memorial centers, large and small; local and national political controversies over divisive historical episodes, from U.S. slavery to the Holocaust, involving advocates from across the social spectrum; numerous international efforts to promote awareness of human rights through the valuable medium of historical memory—all these developments typify powerful regional, national, and even global imperatives to remember in turn-of-the-century Western culture. Our age remains notable, in other words, for its passionate and democratically shared investments in cultivating memory as a medium of life and in viewing forgetfulness as a distressing symptom of absence, loss, and death.

Such worries are indisputably warranted in many cases. Yet the symbolism of life and oblivion, when taken as a universal framework for understanding our present-day relationship to former people and events, compels a reductive understanding of memory no less than forgetting, thereby overlooking their more complex interaction in public controversies over the meaning of the past. If one admits that even elaborate and sincere efforts at commemoration can produce politically or morally lamentable results (forgetfulness about the most valuable lessons of the past foremost among them), then one must concede the converse premise as well: not all forms of forgetting connote passivity, loss, ruination, or death in the context of public affairs. Some consciously considered public appeals to communal forgetting yield judicious responses to the dilemmas of the past in light of exigent cultural, political, or moral circumstances. Such responses potentially shape the boundaries and content of shared remembrance in desirable ways rather than merely diminishing its valuable store.

The conventional Western rhetoric of memory resists this more receptive approach to the subject of forgetting. To question the broadly accepted validity of that rhetoric, this chapter has shown, is to question the longstanding authority of tropes and figures intended to explain the virtues of memory and the vices of forgetting throughout Western history—a history well preserved in contemporary paeans to the fruits of institutional memory. Ancient and classical reverence for the power of memory, from biblical sources to Plato and Augustine, remains remarkably fresh in present-day beliefs that loss of memory amounts to both a severe moral failing and a lack of sustaining connection with divinity. Centuries' worth of celebrated poetry and literature bewailing the liquidation of human achievement and experience in the waters of forgetting continues to infuse modern fears over the potentially disastrous and irrevocable decay of historical works and wisdom from one generation to the next. And the notion that relighting our faculties of memory in times of mental or existential darkness demonstrates a kind of cognitive or ontological growth (variously present in Descartes, Locke, Freud, Proust, and Heidegger) today finds contemporary application in pervasive assumptions that memory serves humanity best as a clear, comprehensive, and securely archived fount of profound insight. The durable public persuasiveness of such time-honored commitments to the redeeming, enlightening, and improving powers of memory explains how particular social, intellectual, and moral traditions have made it seem imperative that we think and speak of forgetting in such stridently negative ways.

The key to demonstrating the merits of forgetting as a strategically useful mode of public judgment is to avoid merely replacing the established dialectic with an equally reductive one (instead of privileging memory over forgetting, privileging forgetting over memory). The primary motivation of the chapters to come is to conceive of memory and forgetting in reciprocal rather than dialectical terms. By delineating the telling differences between desirable and undesirable forms of communal forgetting, one also discerns why conventional forms of public commemoration sometimes fail to accomplish their intended social, political, or moral purposes. The central problem that preserves the dialectic of life and death as equivalents of memory and forgetting is rhetorical: beyond the traditional language and symbolism of oblivion, liquidation, or amnesia, one may employ alternative heuristics in order to identify the positive contributions of forgetting as a mode of public judgment with respect to both the wisdom and dilemmas of the past.

## FORGETTING WITHOUT OBLIVION

The symbolism of oblivion hasn't always been used to the detriment of forgetting (at least not intentionally). A host of past and present thinkers have employed the dark imagery of forgetting in order to assert its conventionally unacknowledged merits; however, such putatively affirmative treatments of forgetting as willed oblivion, symbolic erasure, or strategic amnesia assign merely inverted significance to the traditionally reductive understanding of memory and forgetting (as life and death). The operative question is why notable past and present appreciations of oblivion—which reverse the negative significance of tropes and figures traditionally used to disparage forgetting—offer dubious rhetorical resources with which to devise a critical vocabulary that discloses the reciprocal virtues of memory and forgetting in public culture. To address this question we cannot rely on conventionally negative tropes of oblivion, liquidation, amnesia, and the like; we will need to devise a heuristic framework better suited to reveal the positive contributions of forgetting within particular communities of memory.

The less renowned *ars oblivionis* emerges from the same cultural antecedents as the *ars memoriae*. The mythological dyad of Lethe and Mnemosyne, true to the Greek penchant for balancing dialectical alternatives, expresses simultaneously antithetical and intimate relations between memory and forgetting. The explicit symbolism of the mythological rivers is that Mnemosyne engenders a divinely tinged capacity for recollection whereas Lethe induces primordial amnesia. But the heavenly recollection associated with Mnemosyne in Greek myth, or the *philosophía* repeatedly affirmed in Plato's philosophy, is a rare and blessed kind of memory. By contrast, the forgetfulness that besets those who imbibe the waters of Lethe is a nearly universal human condition, an event necessary for the soul's embodiment in human form. Forgetting, in this generous interpretation, helps perpetuate the eternal cycle of birth, life, death, and rebirth that defines human existence.

From these ambiguous beginnings, Lethe retains profoundly indeterminate meaning, simultaneously evoking oblivion and renewal, death as well as rebirth, in the provenance of memory.

Classical practitioners of the *ars memoriae* recognized that one's trained memory might need occasional forgetting, just as Mnemosyne depended for its sense and value upon Lethe, its symbolic other.[1] Themistocles, who reputedly pined for an *ars oblivionis,* is the pedagogical counterpart of Simonides, legendary father of the *ars memoriae.* In *De oratore,* Cicero relates an anecdote in which Simonides offers to instruct Themistocles in his art of memory. Themistocles brusquely refuses, insisting that he would vastly prefer to acquire skill in forgetting. According to Cicero, Themistocles' memory was so absorptive that "nothing that had once been poured into his mind could ever again flow out of it; for him, an ability to forget what he did not want to remember was preferable to being able to remember whatever he had heard or seen just once" (2001, 2.300). The mythological pairing of Lethe and Mnemosyne finds its pragmatic double, as Cicero's anecdote suggests, in the classical insight that forgetting might be occasionally useful as a means to domesticate unusually plentiful accumulations of memory.[2]

From its earliest days, the art of memory raised questions concerning the self-sufficiency of sheer recollection. Unbounded memory inevitably became undesirable. Forgetting offered a countervailing faculty necessary for sustaining memory in its proper scale and order. This line of thought, although far less renowned than both classical and modern appreciations of memory, developed in a variety of theological, intellectual, artistic, and even political projects. A loosely collated *ars oblivionis* does exist; one may appeal to it when arguing for the relative value of forgetting, as a flurry of recent scholarship has done.[3] Considering the potential virtues of forgetting to present-day public life, ethics, and decision-making raises the crucial question of whether the traditional tropes and symbolism of that stepchild tradition represent a true departure from conventional idioms of memory and forgetting.

The following analysis shows that representative tropes of forgetting in the *ars oblivionis,* which has received renewed attention in memory studies of late, provide a highly circumscribed and possibly outmoded conceptual vocabulary with which to investigate how social agents advocate forgetting to persuasive and productive ends in modern public affairs. Time and again, such an approach seeks to assign merely enhanced value to forgetting under the existing rubric of oblivion, thereby failing to question the larger dialectic in which it symbolizes a kind of absolute void pitted against the plenty of memory. Displacing this dialectic, and thereby fashioning an alternate set of terms or symbols with which to study communal forgetting, would both validate the relative merits of forgetting on novel grounds and provide deeper insight into the subtler, nondialectical intimacies of memory and forgetting as mutually constitutive dimensions of public culture. The analysis supports this thesis in order to justify its subsequent proposal for adopting a conceptual vocabulary better suited to investigating the rhetoric and politics of public forgetting in terms other than those of oblivion.

## The Counter-tradition of Oblivion

A variety of rhetorical practices supply, as in the classical art of memory, the signature tropes of the so-called *ars oblivionis*. The spread of writing in classical Greek culture yielded a lasting set of metaphors with which to illustrate the notion that discrete instances of forgetting can assist one's intellectual growth. Plato's likening of the memory residing in one's soul to a wax tablet inspired a litany of similar metaphorical treatments: later writers commonly cited him in presuming that the souls of some individuals received firm and enduring impressions of truth, whereas others captured only its wispiest traces, easily dissolved in time.[4]

Plato's lofty imagery was inspired by a comparatively mundane feature of classical education: writing on wax tablets. The wax tablet was a handy, inexpensive device for acquiring and preserving knowledge, but it contained a finite amount of text. One smoothed the tablet's surface in order to create a fresh tabula rasa whenever space for writing ran short. Commentators throughout history have subsequently invoked the image of the wax tablet to illustrate the abstract premise that receptacles of knowledge (mental or otherwise) should be routinely cleared of detritus in order to ensure their proper functioning (Weinrich 2004, 20–21; Yates 2001, chap. 2).

Indeed, the habit of willfully forgetting in order to replenish the storehouse of memory forms a minor chapter in the history of the *ars memoriae*. At the highpoint of the Italian Renaissance, when intertwined rhetorical and mnemonic techniques attained arguably their greatest prominence, handbooks on rhetoric typically included a chapter detailing procedures for forgetting *(arte dell'oblio)*. Such chapters advised readers to forget by inverting standard mnemonic techniques: whereas one focused on vivid psychological images in order to remember certain *topoi,* one conjured mental images of decay, withering, erasure, and the like in order to dissolve psychological imprints that had outlived their utility (Bolzoni 1995, 143–48; Weinrich 2004, 200). Søren Kierkegaard later recommended this same strategy in more straightforward terms: "If there is something you want to forget," he wrote, "then try to find something else to remember; then you will certainly succeed" (1991, 152).

The ideal of forgiveness, variously interpreted in Judaism and Christianity, likewise comprises an essential resource of the *ars oblivionis*. The phrase "forgive and forget" is a modern cliché, but it distills, in banal form, centuries of theological reflection on redemption and social justice. Such reflections, as in the classical tradition, routinely used images of writing, erasure, and the clearing of space to endow forgetting with vital religious meaning and purpose.

Biblical origins of the sacred *ars oblivionis* are, like its profane counterparts, strikingly ironic. The notion that God keeps a Divine Book, which lists both the names of sinful souls he has doomed to oblivion and of those he will spare this fate, appears early in the Hebrew Bible. Moses pleads to God on behalf of the Israelites for worshipping the golden calf: "But now, if you will only forgive their sin—but if not, blot me out of the book that you have written." God's response confirms the existence of such a tally: "Whoever has sinned against me I will blot out of my book" (Exod. 32:32–33). As early as the book of Exodus, then, the question of forgiveness is fundamentally related to the question of forgetting—in this case, in a manifestly negative sense.

Subsequent books of the Hebrew Bible, however, dramatically invert the idea that forgetting—having one's name blotted from the Divine Book—is a sign of damnation. These books redefine the object of forgetting as one's sin rather than one's very name. One psalmist prays, to the contrary, for God to "blot out all my iniquities," to be forgiven as such, and by the time of Jeremiah the act of being forgiven means that one's sins will be forgotten: "I will forgive their iniquity, and remember their sin no more" (Ps. 51:9; Jer. 31:34). In their later forms, writing and erasure as metaphors for forgetting thus defined it not as an occasionally necessary intellectual faculty but as an integral component of spiritual forgiveness.[5]

Christian texts developed the ideal of forgiveness as a form of forgetting, and with it the standard tropes of writing and erasure, into the central article of Christian faith. Jesus subtly but surely invokes the imagery of writing, forgetting, and forgiveness in the Gospel of John when "scribes and Pharisees" beseech him to condemn an adulterous woman. Jesus rebukes them, proclaiming: "Let anyone among you who is without sin be the first to throw a stone at her" (John 8:7). The gospel reports that Jesus repeatedly "bent down and wrote with his finger on the ground" (John 8:6, 8:8) as he listened to the scribes and Pharisees rail against the woman's sin. Having dispatched her accusers, Jesus stands up from his writing and absolves her: "Neither do I condemn you. Go your way, and from now on do not sin again" (John 8:11). The significance of Jesus' writing in the sand graphically performs the moral lesson of this parable. He adopts the role of secretary as the scribes and Pharisees accuse the woman of iniquity, but the gospel fails to record the content of his writing. Inscribed in sand, it is lost to memory instantly. As in Jesus' parting words to the woman, her sin is lightly forgiven because it is already forgotten—no formal condemnation is needed, no record of it survives. The so-called Divine Book has become a repository of memory no more durable than a sheet of sand.

Europeans in early modernity fused this patently Christian imperative to forgive by forgetting with the classical symbolism of oblivion in diverse ways. During the sixteenth century, for instance, John Calvin wrote that forgiveness obligates one "willingly to cast from the mind wrath, hatred, desire for revenge" and "willingly to banish to oblivion the remembrance of injustice" (1977, 912). Theological injunctions to forgive by banishing memory of offense to oblivion found martial and political equivalents in standard clauses of European peace treaties during the seventeenth and eighteenth centuries. Agreements between warring Christian states in this period commonly formalized the end of bloodshed with a ritual of state forgiveness—a clause announcing an era of "amnesty and oblivion," which imposed a duty on former combatants to terminate all lingering hostilities, including attributions of blame for the original conflict (Weinrich 2004, 171–72; Fisch 1979; Joinet 1989). The Treaty of Westphalia (1648), for example, obligated its signatories to "perpetual oblivion and amnesty" regarding offenses committed during the Thirty Years' War. Following the French Revolution, Louis XVIII similarly declared a new era of "union and forgetting" (*union et oubli*) on ascending his throne (Ardant 1990, 57). "Remedial oblivion," Lowenthal adds, was similarly "a common tool of seventeenth-century English statecraft, with 'Acts of Oblivion' exempting from punishment men who had borne arms against Charles II or had opposed William III" (1999, xi). The trope of "amnesty and oblivion," as illustrated by these examples, codified in state policy the etymological kinship of *amnesty* to *amnesia;* "amnesty" descends from the Greek *amnestia* ("forgetfulness") and *amnestos* ("forgotten") (Ayto 1990, 236; Barnhart 1988, 400; Partridge 1966, 228, 253). Seventeenth- and eighteenth-century public declarations embodied, by virtue of this kinship, a transmutation of ancient theological figures of forgetting into secular and legal compacts: oblivion no longer signified the otherworldly realm to which knowledge of personal sin was banished but a ceremonial prerequisite for granting political amnesty in the world of statecraft.[6]

Routinely smoothing a wax tablet in order to continue writing, occasionally removing items from the mental storehouse of memory, blotting one's sin from the sacred book, or redacting traces of wartime animosity from the slate of political relations—such recurrent gestures illustrate the essential tropes of the *ars oblivionis*. These loosely affiliated traditions of forgetting have inspired an alternately implicit or explicit revival of interest in the subject.[7] The central difficulty here is whether the traditional language and symbolism of forgetting provides optimum heuristics for examining the rhetoric and politics of forgetting as a strategically valuable public practice.

A critical liability compromises the value of forgetting as defined by the representative tropes of the *ars oblivionis:* in each case, forgetting signifies negation. Forgetting holds productive value in these situations precisely because it lacks productivity. Forgetting produces a tabula rasa, deletes mental impressions, and mandates nothing less than "amnesty and oblivion" (or in more literal phrasing, amnesty *as* mnemonic oblivion—as amnesia). Forgetting so defined changes the nature of memory insubstantially, by subtraction (or in more dramatic terms, oblivion and amnesia). New memories, as well as those that remain, are essentially untouched by its discrete and unalterable truncations.

The metaphor of forgetting as a proverbial slate cleansed consequently rests on two questionable assumptions: (1) that the effects of forgetting are irreversible (erased text cannot be recovered, mental images can be displaced by new ones, and state amnesia can obliterate a recent wartime past); and (2) that forgetting and memory remain mutually exclusive in nature (however much the former tidies up a literal or metaphorical space in which the latter flourishes). Whether they concern personal recollections or international accords, such procedural templates amend the content of memory while leaving intact its traditional incompatibilities with, and dialectical superiority over, forgetting. By this calculus, memory remains a font of plenty (its only fault is its seemingly inexhaustible yield), whereas forgetting continues to signify destruction, lack, absence, and amnesia, however domesticated they appear. The timeworn antithesis between memory and forgetting holds, even in such seemingly mutual schemas.

Marc Augé's evocative treatise *Oblivion* (2004) fittingly illustrates such tendencies in contemporary thought. Augé purports to upend conventional wisdom concerning the purely destructive aspects of forgetting by arguing that "oblivion" is as indispensable to life as memory. But his version of this point implies a well-trod conception of memory, taken from the *ars oblivionis,* as a durable and uniform source of presence unaffected in its basic substance by forgetting: "It is quite clear that our memory would be 'saturated' rapidly if we had to preserve every image of our childhood, especially those of our earliest childhood. But what is interesting is that which remains. And what remains—remembrances or traces . . . is the product of an erosion caused by oblivion. Memories are crafted by oblivion as the outlines of the shore are created by the sea" (20). Erosion and oblivion carry romantic, nostalgic connotations here: the romance of decay, and nostalgia for a past we cannot recover. Augé's imagery recalls a series of familiar dialectical antitheses, despite his insistence on the primordial harmony between memory and forgetting. Memories are akin to the shore, "oblivion" to the sea that shapes it; forgetting helps to form memory, but only in its negative image—as an "erosion" that demarcates its borders; memory is defined by substance, solidity, whereas forgetting is defined by liquidity (as with Lethe), or lack of substance; memory is a product—that which oblivion helps to craft—whereas forgetting consists in ephemeral "traces." Hence the imagery of oblivion and liquidation shelters in Augé's vivid prose the very dialectic he intends to reject.

Forgetting, as defined by these persistent connotations, remains such a delicate topic of contemporary social analysis and ethical reflection that even those who wish to recognize its potential harmony with memory nevertheless assign it what one might call an integrated but unequal status. Harald Weinrich, for example, defends the *ars oblivionis* as a worthy tradition of art and criticism, but he ultimately espouses a conventionally adversarial stance toward forgetting insofar as he maintains that "Forgetting is always at our side, ready to spring out at us, whenever we want to remember. A memory that is to endure must therefore engage in a daily struggle against forgetting" (2004, 186–87). Paul Ricoeur, moreover, considers the degree to which forgetting shapes our sense of the past as a supplement to memory and history; yet he classifies forgetting as an effacement that memory would resolve—as a symptom of blocked or manipulated recollection—thereby reinforcing what the author himself calls "the asymmetry between forgetting and memory" (2004, 416–43, 448–52, 503). David Gross similarly appears to offer an account of memory and forgetting as equally necessary dimensions of individual and collective life but concludes his study by insisting, "It seems imperative that the value of memory be reaffirmed. For memory . . . allows us to recover and unfold again aspects of the past that, claims to the contrary notwithstanding, are perhaps not yet over and done with" (2000, 152). Such otherwise notable studies concede the limited value of forgetting only by default, as if resigned to tolerating its periodic necessity while nevertheless ardently reaffirming the putatively universal imperative to remember for the sake of individual and communal life.[8]

Scholars are thus willing to afford circumscribed value to forgetting in the context of social commentary or ethical reflection according to the conventional terms of the *ars oblivionis*. But these conventional tropes preserve the image of forgetting as an enigmatic and largely unmanageable basis of action; hence it is difficult to know what one affirms, exactly, in affirming absence or negation, oblivion or liquidation, as practical measures. The Spanish moralist Baltasar Gracián's commentary on the suspect nature of any so-called art of oblivion aptly summarizes the fundamental impasse here: "Know how to forget!" he exhorts, only to add: "This is more a stroke of luck than an art" (Weinrich 2004, 173).

Forgetting, long considered only a harbinger of oblivion—a negation, erosion, or absence—can be redefined as an organized public practice that may vitally shape both historical wisdom and the cultures of memory that perpetuate it. Memory can be a form of forgetting; and forgetting can offer a medium for reconfiguring memory, or *re*membering its content, in auspicious ways, to be investigated, not as a literary figure of negation or a merely evocative *topos* of social commentary and ethical reflection, but as a strategically productive component of public life, ethics, and decision-making.

## Public Forgetting: Essential Heuristics

*Memory* and *forgetting* are not necessary antonyms. *Forgetting* and *amnesia,* regardless of ordinary usage in public affairs and popular psychology, are not obvious synonyms; their most direct link is by way of a detour through the etymology of *amnesty. Forget* descends from the Old English *forgietan,* a composite of *for* and *gietan,* the latter akin to Old Norse *geta,* meaning "to get." To forget, at its root, means to miss or lose one's hold.[9] The word strongly connotes losing one's grasp of something, not the thing itself, or being errant in grasping something that one could still attain. Yet another classical metaphor for memory—that of an aviary, or birdcage—emphasizes this very connotation: "Possessing knowledge means having the bird in your aviary," whereas we "make mistakes," or forget, "because we grab hold of the wrong bird" (Draaisma 2000, 27). Kierkegaard also touched on this nuance when he posited, "One is not ignorant of what is forgotten, since one is ignorant only of what one does not and never has known; what one has forgotten, one has known" (1964, 295). *Neglect* seems a more direct synonym for forgetting than *amnesia,* which manifestly connotes the profound, potentially absolute loss of memory's object. By implication, to forget something (in personal or collective reminiscence) might mean that one has prepared, as a result of for-getting, to grasp it in a different or altogether new way. Wading in the river Lethe might herald the rebirth rather than death of memory.

One can justify this separation of forgetting from amnesia on grounds other than those of etymological nuance. Forgetting resists its equation with amnesia even in the context of infamous crimes against humanity. Margalit illustrates this point with a revealing insight: "When Hitler asked, 'Who today remembers the Armenians?' the resounding answer should have been, 'We all do.' Or, at least, 'The enlightened world does.'" "The irony in Hitler's question," Margalit continues, "is that in fact he counted on his listeners to remember the Armenians" (2002, 78). The operative claim here is not that appeals for the public to forget dimensions of its past are universally acceptable, especially when they justify indefensible crimes against humanity (in such cases, they should be condemned without question). The operative claim is, instead, that Hitler's justification for state forgetting represents an extreme limit case that proves a more general rule: asking others to forget something ironically draws attention to, and brings to mind or memory, that very thing. "It is pretty clear that just being told to 'forget it,'" Margalit insists, "does not quite secure forgetfulness: if anything, it increases the chance of remembering" (56). Memory contains dimensions of forgetting; and forgetting, it turns out, often reproduces (however indirectly) a degree of shared recollection.

Forgetting achieves persuasive effect as a rhetorical form—that is, as a speech or language act intended to influence thought, debate, or action in public affairs—not by asking audiences to become literally oblivious about segments of their shared past. On the contrary, the act of proposing that communities forget select aspects of their institutional memory directs public attention to the question of what those communities have remembered, according to which rhetorical forms and limitations, and in accord with whose interests. In their pragmatic outcomes, public appeals to forget neither solicit immediate and complete amnesia nor insert yet another selective interpretation of the past alongside myriad partial recollections that comprise the ordinary fabric of collective memory. Rather, such appeals function rhetorically by calling on the public to question whether communal affairs would be improved by radically altering the normative form and content of collective memories that have hitherto defined its past, and hence its current identity. In this context, the rhetoric of public forgetting need not be opposed to or contrasted with life—in this case, that of an entire community—but may constitute a formative and periodically advisable source of its well-being. The following heuristics offer unconventional and especially incisive resources with which to examine the ways in which public forgetting operates vitally in the formation and transformation of particular cultures of memory as well as the means of public judgment they promote.

## *Adaptation*

Ongoing studies in cognitive psychology that document surprising intricacies among memory and forgetting suggest instructive parallels between the role of forgetting in personal memory and in public culture. Cognitive psychologist Daniel Schacter alludes to the long-standing habit in our culture of judging the relative strengths and flaws of memory according to moral ideals in the title of his book *The Seven Sins of Memory* (2001). The title is ironic insofar as Schacter's work upends centuries' worth of conventional wisdom concerning the relative virtues and vices of human recollection. The so-called sins he examines (such as mental blockages, reconstructions, misattributions, or loss of recollections) have all been interpreted by the philosophical, theological, and psychological schools discussed in the previous chapter as errors in memory, as deviations from its normal functioning, and therefore as portents of its most dreaded end—forgetting. Schacter inverts such logic in contending that "it is a mistake to conceive of the seven sins as design flaws that expose memory as a fundamentally defective system. To the contrary, I suggest that the seven sins are by-products of otherwise adaptive features of memory, a price we pay for processes and functions that serve us well in many respects" (184). The proclivities for blockage, distortion, dissolution, and reconstruction that pervade human memory, which have vexed centuries' worth of commentaries on the subject, reveal the "adaptive strengths of memory" rather than "inherent weaknesses or flaws" (6).

The key to Schacter's rejection of long-standing conventional wisdom on this subject is his emphasis on *adaptation* in personal memory, which provides a profoundly different criterion by which to evaluate its functions than, say, preservation. By this measure, the distortions, deletions, and reconstructions that populate the family of forgetting, in its broadest designation, do not simply precede or follow memory (preparing a tabula rasa for its accumulation without fundamentally shaping its nature or scope). They instead comprise some of its most important internal dynamics. Schacter thus offers a nondialectical account of memory distortion, decay, and even loss by recognizing that patterns of mnemonic revision and adaptation are necessary, integral dimensions of memory itself.

One may draw an instructive analogy between Schacter's account of personal memory and corresponding issues of public memory. To view public memory as adaptive instead of preservative is to posit that acts of memorial revision, reconstruction, and even symbolic rejection are intrinsic rather than extrinsic factors in the evolution of public memory. These transmutations help to produce and reproduce visions of the past responsive to the dilemmas of contemporary public exigencies. In principle, such symptoms of forgetting in its many appearances are not dialectically opposed to the liveliness of public memory; they are often vital for its perdurance.

Of course, one must not overextend the analogy. Personal recollection flourishes by countless acts of amendment and reconstruction, but it can also suffer from an overabundance thereof. The premise that there can be too much memory, or burdensome mnemonic accumulation, parallels the notion that there can be too much forgetting, or mnemonic dispossession. Drawing an analogy between Schacter's account of personal memory and that of public commemoration does not allow one to conclude that collective memory and collective forgetting are one and the same. Memory and forgetting are intermingling forces that nevertheless retain nominally distinct identities, aligned neither in a dialectical antithesis nor as interchangeable (and therefore arbitrary) labels for the same phenomenon. Their intimacy in the context of public culture, as the present discussion conceptualizes it, implies rhetorical practices with which one invokes the prospect of forgetting not in order to negate collective memory per se but in order to transform its sense and value—to remember anew, in politically or morally transformative ways.

Hence, the episodes of public forgetting examined in the following case studies do not culminate literally in collective amnesia. Warring nations or adversarial publics that agree to an obligatory state of "amnesty and oblivion" do not effectively forget their mutual hostilities or prejudices by fiat, with no chance that they might resume. Such amnesty and oblivion is notional, not actual: it binds adherents to proceed *as if* they had actually acquired amnesia of mutual antagonisms and transgressions. In fact, the presumption that their mutual enmity is indeed forgotten and obliterated might make future conflict more likely rather than less; the trope of amnesty and oblivion resembles a forcible and potentially unhealthy repression of the past, not its erasure, and that which is repressed may return in forms more intense than before. Favorable instances of public forgetting consist in public speech acts or symbolic gestures designed to interrupt customary patterns of communal memory, strategically amending or even redacting its contents in order to denaturalize the normative authority of burdensome, seemingly unalterable historical obligations. Instances of forgetting in this spirit suggest how the prevailing appearance, sense, and value of the past could be radically adapted to better serve the political and moral needs of the present. Such is a very different outcome from presuming that the rhetorical work of forgetting entails proscriptions for communal obliviousness in which the past is mysteriously banished to a realm of no return.

## Counter-memory

The *telos* of public forgetting so conceived is not amnesia but counter-memory as Michel Foucault describes it. For Foucault, counter-memory involves not simply an opposition of one historical narrative against another but a complete transformation of the scope and substance of historical understanding in its existing forms. Foucault's classic essays "Nietzsche, Genealogy, History" (1977a) and "What Is an Author?" (1977b) illustrate this principle. His genealogical method defines the relation between past and present, between self and history, not according to continuity, inevitability, or identity, but according to ruptures, accidental outcomes, and irreconcilable differences between former and contemporary epochs. Foucault intends this manner of thought to undermine one's assured belief in the essential sameness of the past and present. Hence, Foucault's history of authorship in "What Is an Author?" is strikingly at odds with conventional wisdom: an author is not one who writes great literature according to inborn talent and vision; an author is a legal and political function used to identify and classify hierarchies of discourse, to establish copyright laws and means of punishment for their violation (1977b, 124). Foucault's text insinuates that re-remembering, as it were, the history of authorship produces a vastly different account of the same phenomenon—one in which the object in question is altered unrecognizably in relation to its previous form. In "Nietzsche, Genealogy, History," Foucault more expansively contends that history as we normally understand it encompasses not a unified narrative of truths and values seamlessly joining past and present but an arbitrary interpretation of events that conceals its investments in certain modalities of power. The history of history itself, as Foucault perceives it, betrays such investments. Until the nineteenth century, he observes, organized history celebrated those "great national ensembles" that "capitalism needed" for economic expansion; as such, "History was a discipline by means of which the bourgeoisie showed, first, that its reign was only the result, the product, the fruit, of a slow maturation, and that this reign was thus perfectly justified" (1998, 423). To tell the story of the great national past, in other words, was to ideologically justify bourgeois hegemonic power in the guise of seemingly undistorted, universally representative history.

Following these insights, public forgetting provides a language and rationale for abdicating traditional modes of historical narrative and communal remembrance in order to expose the arbitrariness of the past as we presently conceive it, thereby illuminating unacknowledged ways it could assume a radically different character. "We want historians to confirm our belief that the present rests upon profound intentions and immutable necessities," Foucault writes. "But the true historical sense confirms our existence among countless lost events, without a landmark or a point of reference" (1977a, 155). In this light, public forgetting neither negates the past *in toto,* as we currently remember it, nor prevents its translation into future recollections. It rather suspends, or even rejects altogether, the past's prevailing and seemingly natural truth, value, and destined course of development as they have yet been conceived in collective reminiscence. This suspension or rejection opens a rhetorical and political space in which one may voice an entirely new collective sentiment concerning the contingent meaning and utility of the past in relation to the present. Public forgetting culminates not in termination but in the type of transformation that Foucault ascribes to counter-memory: "a transformation of history into a totally different form of time" (160).

## Critical History

By implication, public forgetting embodies a conception of public time consistent with the Nietzschean vision of history that Foucault inherits. In Nietzsche's doctrine of the eternal return, history unfolds not by linear temporality but according to epochal cycles in which every end is also a beginning, in which every eschatological event paradoxically inaugurates a new era. Nietzsche rejects the dialectical philosophies of history that other nineteenth-century German thinkers promoted by formulating a philosophy of history in which difference holds unqualified positive value. Difference rather than primordial sameness, he insists, returns eternally in order to transform and produce historical time anew, without finality or entelechy. Public forgetting, in its most productive invocations, resides at the nexus of such a simultaneous end and beginning in the context of public time. Expressions of public forgetting do not call for mere termination of prevailing traditions of memory but reject their traditional forms as a warrant for calling into being a new, politically and morally transformative historical consciousness.

It is therefore consistent to say that public forgetting, as defined in this book, enacts Nietzsche's vision of critical history. His classic treatise "On the Uses and Disadvantages of History for Life" (1997) defines his iconoclastic attitude toward the role of history in public affairs. One might be tempted to interpret Nietzsche's comments on forgetting in this tract as an unqualified corrective to rampant human woes. Nietzsche imagines that human beings covet animals' carefree disregard for the past: "Man says 'I remember' and envies the animal, who at once forgets and for whom every moment really dies, sinks back into the night and is extinguished for ever. . . . Man, on the other hand, braces himself against the great and ever greater pressure of what is past: it pushes him down or bends him sideways, it encumbers his steps as a dark, invisible burden" (61). Humans are all too human in remembering too much. Constantly straining under the accumulated weight of the past stifles our ability to attend to present-day needs and interests. Of all modern thinkers, Nietzsche is most closely associated with the thesis that history can become burdensome to immediate personal and public endeavor.

One would nonetheless take liberties with this proposition if one interpreted Nietzsche to mean that forgetfulness should be the universal human condition, that we have license to invoke it haphazardly. "Forgetting is essential to action of any kind," Nietzsche maintains (62); but for him this statement does not support the conclusion that we should emulate beasts of burden by living a completely unhistorical existence. Nietzsche rather intends to prove the thesis that *"the unhistorical and the historical are necessary in equal measure for the health of an individual, of a people and of a culture"* (63; emphasis in original). Nietzsche is far from an indiscriminate relativist on the question of forgetting. Acts of concerted forgetting, in his estimation, require discriminating ethical judgment. One's decision to "from time to time employ the strength to break up and dissolve a part of the past" requires clarity "as to how unjust the existence of anything—a privilege, a caste, a dynasty, for example—is, and how greatly this thing deserves to perish. Then its past is regarded critically, then one takes the knife to its roots, then one cruelly tramples over every kind of piety" (75, 76). Modern readers might flinch at Nietzsche's vivid language in light of its later appropriation by Nazi party ideologues; one may measure the perversity of that appropriation, however, by the fact that the Nazis interpreted the meaning of Nietzsche's assertions here in a manner directly opposed to his intent. His conception of critical history presupposes that acts of willful forgetting can be acts of justice. They require one to identify with utmost clarity those "unjust," unbidden vestiges of the past (privileges, castes, dynasties) whose only value or authority lies in their agedness, whose very existence thus suppresses creative, spontaneous works and deeds in the present. Forgetting, in Nietzsche's formulation, does not reflect a casual relativism in which any and all elements of the past are equally valuable or valueless. It demands rigorous ethical scrutiny concerning which remainders of the past promote or obstruct the enhancement of contemporary life.

Nietzsche's definition of critical history does not, by the same token, entail willed collective amnesia, a declaration of amnesty and oblivion, whether it concerns the past *in toto* or acutely odious relics of it. Some contemporary commentators interpret Nietzsche's philosophy as frustratingly abstract and impractical, but his account of forgetting evinces a sober realism: however we may desire to break from the constraints or injustices of the past, we are ineluctably part of the lineage they form and would not exist as we do without them. Nietzsche's insistence that we cannot abrogate at will the heritage of which we are a culmination—that we cannot forget as such—tempers his conviction that, on occasion, we must judiciously abolish the most decadent remnants of our past:

> For since we are the outcome of earlier generations, we are also the outcome of their aberrations, passions and errors, and indeed of their crimes; it is not possible wholly to free oneself from this chain. If we condemn these aberrations and regard ourselves as free of them, this does not alter the fact that we originate in them. The best we can do is to confront our inherited and hereditary nature with our knowledge, and through a new, stern discipline combat our inborn heritage and implant in ourselves a new habit, a new instinct, a second nature, so that our first nature withers away. It is an attempt to give oneself, as it were *a posteriori,* a past in which one would like to originate in opposition to that in which one did originate. (76)

Amnesty and oblivion compound the decadence of the past precisely as we contest its authority over the present. To declare oblivious amnesia is to trade the outworn and burdensome illusions of our inherited past for an equally illusory historical consciousness of our own invention.

Critical history, as Nietzsche envisions it, accommodates strategic instances of unhistorical forgetting undertaken not in an effort at termination but in mindfulness of the eternal return. In forgetting, our judgments indeed dispel portions of the past; but by the same gesture, the past returns inescapably in a profoundly different configuration—one radically adapted to the needs of the present. Consistent with Nietzsche's philosophy writ large, forgetting is an exercise of self-discipline rather than delusion, a form of judgment in which we overcome our own invented or received perceptions of former times, people, and events as a mechanism for overcoming whatever self-defining flaws we have inherited from them. Forgetting propels the cycle of the eternal return in public time, ensuring that every consciously determined historical end is simultaneously an opening not simply to a new future but to a novel past with enhanced value and significance to present-day affairs.

But how can one assess more concretely the nature of that value and the future it heralds? What discernible end should a novel past serve beyond being novel? To this point, the claims that collective forgetting need not amount to amnesia and oblivion (Schacter), that its interruptive presence annuls the apparently apodictic nature of established histories (Foucault), and that one may forget in order to overcome the unjust or outmoded constraints of past traditions (Nietzsche) all stress the desirability of choosing to symbolically sever or recombine particular traditions of memory. The practical gains that accompany such actions, however, remain generally theoretical in Foucault's and Nietzsche's philosophies. Foucault emphasizes that the genealogical method renders normative expressions of historical truth and value available for potentially transformative political questioning, yet he characteristically declines to define the mode of politics such questioning would entail. Nietzsche declares the need to overcome the past, admirably recognizing the difficulties and dangers inherent in doing so, but says little about the type of future that such a gesture would inaugurate. Beyond the broad conviction that forgetting produces new forms of life and memory based on transformed conceptions of the past, how can one assess the civic goods that such forgetting engenders? Beyond being productive in general, what specific political goods should public forgetting ideally produce? And, most important, *when*—in what circumstances—does public forgetting help a community to realize those goods? Hannah Arendt's emphasis of natality in her political philosophy provides compelling answers to these questions.

## *Natality*

Arendt's description of public remembrance, as an indispensable medium for the constitution and reconstitution of political community, might seem incompatible with an affirmative model of public forgetting. Arendt stresses that the political deeds which call the *polis* into being would not endure, and thus the *polis* would not survive from one generation to the next, without the kind of organized remembrance that speech affords. She lauds Greek poets for practicing such reciprocity of speech and action: their epic tales bestowed "immortal fame . . . upon word and deed to make them outlast not only the futile moment of speech and action but even the mortal life of their agent" (1993, 46). Public memory allows human works, words, and deeds to attain "some permanence," she writes, "arresting their per-ishability" so that "these things would, to a degree at least, enter and be at home in the world of everlastingness, and the mortals themselves would find their place in the cosmos, where everything is immortal except men" (43). Ephemeral words and deeds establish the *polis* but the *polis* itself achieves "some permanence" as an everlasting space for their perpetual reduplication, for the attainment of immortality as such, in rituals of public remembrance. "The organization of the *polis*," according to Arendt, is quite simply "a kind of organized remembrance" (1998, 198). By this logic, forgetting appears to loom large throughout her philosophy as a force that would relegate works, words, and deeds to their customarily perishable status, that would disas-semble the everlasting legacies of speech and action upon which the *polis* is founded and so herald its collapse.

On closer inspection, however, Arendt recognizes that organized remem-brance must consist of a creative activity in the present rather than an unthink-ing *mimesis* of the past. Cultivating natality, or beginning again through col-lective speech and action, is a vital aim of communal recollection rather than mere repetition of the same. Arendt supports this claim with characteristi-cally lucid eloquence: "The end of a tradition does not necessarily mean that traditional concepts have lost their power over the minds of men. On the contrary, it sometimes seems that this power of well-worn notions and categories becomes more tyrannical as the tradition loses its living force and as the memory of its beginning recedes; it may even reveal its full coercive force only after its end has come and men no longer even rebel against it"

(1993, 26). In Arendt's dexterous thinking, the ongoing reconstitution of the *polis* conserves the value of its original constitution. Works, words, and deeds that attain "some permanence" in public lore should perdure because of their ability to inspire novel works, words, and deeds in the pursuit of contemporary political excellence. Stephen Browne, in commenting on Arendt's politics of remembrance, observes that "far from being merely nostalgic or retrospective, such work is always and at once new, discursive, and unpredictable" (2004, 48). Public remembrance is valuable in Arendt's account less as a medium of preservation and more as a continual device for the *re*production—or better, re*invention*—of the *res publica;* it signifies not so much proof of a polity's unbroken connection with its origins as a resource for the continual remaking and reaffirmation of its public identity. Any veneration for "everlastingness" in Arendt's writings conforms to the supremely vital project of cultivating natality in political speech and action, of beginning again, which envelops it.

Arendt's cardinal concern for preserving conditions of natality provides, by the spirit if not the letter of her philosophy, a warrant for pursuing the political goods of public forgetting as a procedure of radical commemorative reconstitution, as a necessary source of commemorative adaptation rather than simple termination or loss. The faculty of forgiving among fellow political agents is perhaps the most easily relatable (albeit somewhat controversial) source of natality in her writings. Forgiveness as Arendt speaks of it does not take place with the assistance of divine agency in a supernatural realm; it is a ritual of speech and action initiated and realized by members of the polis in the secular time and place of civic politics. The terms of forgiving as such, and the forgetting it implies, are distinct from religious idioms of forgiving and forgetting found in the *ars oblivionis,* where the sinner's past is literally blotted out, relegated to oblivion. The effect of forgiveness in Arendt's philosophy is not blotting out (or amnesia) but something like covering up, to use Margalit's phrase (2002, 126, 183–209), in which the bare presence of the past is preserved in a noticeably altered form that paradoxically draws attention to the very act of covering—that is, to one's public avowal to treat portions of the past in a self-consciously revised manner.

Forgiveness holds crucial political value in Arendt's philosophy for its capacity to release a polity from debilitating perceptions of its past—a past that limits a community's capacity for political action in the present. Forgiving allows political actors to counteract the effects of processes seemingly beyond their control. This potent source of communal agency appears to interrupt the ostensibly irreversible dominance of the past over the present:

"The possible redemption from the predicament of irreversibility—of being unable to undo what one has done though one did not, and could not, have known what he was doing—is the faculty of forgiving" (1998, 237). Arendt recognizes, as Nietzsche did, that lasting consequences of actions undertaken in the past condition our actions in the present—but they must not predetermine them. The *vita activa,* politics itself, is inconceivable in Arendt's system without the capacity to begin anew, to be released from commitments to a past not of one's choosing. Organized remembrance should indeed preserve former works, words, and deeds, even bestowing on them a kind of immortality, but in the form of institutional models for contemporary speech and action, not as predeterminations thereof. "Forgiving," Arendt proclaims, "serves to undo the deeds of the past. . . . Without being forgiven, released from the consequences of what we have done, our capacity to act would, as it were, be confined to one single deed from which we could never recover; we would remain the victims of its consequences forever" (237). Forgiving releases us not from the past as a whole but from its specific "consequences," from ostensibly irreversible chains of events initiated through prior actions (including our own), the course of which only appears unalterable.

Ingrained customs of institutional memory constitute prime expressions of such onerous irreversibility. Normative memories of past deeds and events need not, as a rule, depict present actions as necessary outcomes of predetermined historical processes; but twentieth-century history in particular has shown that they can, and often do. In such circumstances, public memory endows communal history—its future as well as its past and present—with the ethos of irreversibility as Arendt describes it. Unexamined reverence for that "one single deed" of which she speaks can constrict "our capacity to act" such that we "remain victims of its consequences forever" (or at least indefinitely). Forgiveness, as seen through this conceptual lens, transmutes public perceptions of temporal irreversibility into a source of immediate agency and thus replenishes the communal capacity for political action, for politics as such.

Forgiving, as a feature of the *vita activa,* requires a measure of forgetting. One remains free from irreversibility, from the apparent automatism that natural or historical processes engender, by willfully counteracting the influence of the past over current speech, judgment, and action—an influence commonly embodied in those works of public memory that preserve its authority as such. Describing Arendt's doctrine tritely as one of forgiving and forgetting, however, diminishes its gravity. Forgetting, to the extent that it is compatible with her thought, does not sanction self-deceiving proclamations of amnesty and oblivion. It avoids the sheer pragmatism that Paul Ricoeur, for example, finds so unacceptable in state pronouncements of amnesty, which seek to mitigate the effects of past injustices on "strictly utilitarian" grounds (by simply declaring they are forgotten) without forging deeper political or moral commitments (2004, 472). Rejecting apparently predetermined courses of action enjoined by previous deeds or withdrawing normative expressions of our obligations to the past—to forget as such—is a politically essential rather than merely utilitarian capacity in Arendt's philosophy. For her, nothing less than political freedom depends on it. It is consistent with the general ambition of Arendt's thought to say that the entire sphere of human existence known as the *vita activa*—in which decision-making by speech, judgment, and action holds at bay the politically destructive forces of violence and totalitarianism—withers when the present appears as merely an unalterable product of the past, when the past represents an incontestable blueprint for contemporary conduct.

Forgiving, as well as the forgetting that this study perceives at its heart, is only one of two crucial ways in which Arendt believes that political actors may mutually reset the proverbial clock of communal time. Forgiving allows individuals to release one another from the past they share, thereby neutralizing its putative irreversibility; but forgiving by itself does not dispel the uncertainty of the future, particularly one in which the normal course of events no longer appears predestined or assured. "The remedy for unpredictability," Arendt continues, "for the chaotic uncertainty of the future, is contained in the faculty to make and keep promises" (1998, 237). Suspending, or rejecting altogether, normative perceptions of the past in which its course of development appears intractable is a necessary prelude to inaugurating a new constellation of sociopolitical relations based on the promises of which Arendt speaks. Political agents must absolve one another from burdensome obligations to the past in order to preserve their collective ability to initiate the political deed *par excellence:* the act of beginning again, of establishing a new accord. "The two faculties belong together . . . binding oneself through promises," Arendt writes, "serves to set up in the ocean of uncertainty, which the future is by definition, islands of security without which not even continuity, let alone durability of any kind, would be possible in the relationships between men" (237). If forgiveness enables communities to derive a measure of collective agency over their past, then the forgetting that such forgiveness entails allows a community to do so by reinventing its constitutive norms and representative identity in light of "the oceans of uncertainty" that engulf its perceived future.

Lingering over the question of forgiveness as a political principle unto itself is not the aim of this discussion. Its purpose, rather, is to pursue the larger implications concerning natality, forgetting, and public time that political incarnations of forgiveness suggest. The foregoing interpretation of temporal and historical dynamics in Arendt's thought yields a critical analytic principle with which to distinguish desirable from undesirable instances of public forgetting. Public forgetting, as this book defines it, is an occasionally necessary procedure for transforming a public's perceived subservience to its past into an expression of its agency over the future. To this extent, the value of public forgetting consists not simply in eliminating prevailing modes of remembrance but in reconstituting existing sociopolitical relations so that new, politically and ethically transformative modes of remembrance can emerge. Judicious forgetting enables one, in Arendt's parlance, to make promises (to construct new sociopolitical relations) in light of the future as one now envisions it.

Public forgetting promotes or enacts a dramatically new communal perspective on the past in which former works, words, and deeds undergo radical alteration, losing their previous meaning and authority. The prime effect of this alteration is to simultaneously modify, in equally dramatic fashion, present-day sociopolitical relations originally founded in fidelity to that past. Public forgetting is a vital undertaking for public bodies not merely in order to terminate a past no longer serviceable to contemporary life or institutional politics but as a mode of speech and action that preserves the polity's ability to reinvent itself, to begin anew through collective action, in response to immediate or anticipated uncertainties that threaten its integrity.

The firmest grounds for an affirmative conception of public forgetting lie in this political good: its potential to generate novel public obligations by radically reinterpreting the perceived sense and value of a community's past, present, and future—in short, a tandem commemorative and political refashioning. By implication, public forgetting assumes the detestable appearance of forced amnesia when it suppresses the individual or collective capacity to begin anew, when it stifles one's ability to fashion novel sociopolitical relations (or to make and keep promises, the very hallmark of political freedom, as Arendt would have it). Public forgetting is laudable when it enhances the *res publica,* when it stimulates pluralist speech and action, and condemnable when it undermines communal practices in which such pluralism thrives. Public forgetting refers, in sum, to especially dramatic acts of counter-memory undertaken in order to identify novel grounds for public judgment about the meaning and value of the past, thereby inaugurating a new era of qualitatively transformed sociopolitical relations.

## Conclusion

Forgetting, as defined in this chapter, resides at the center of transformative junctures in the political formulation and expression of public time, memory, and tradition. In its most pernicious forms, forgetting resumes its timeworn place among the forces of violence and repression. In its most prudential forms, however, forgetting enacts a mode of public judgment regarding the political or ethical relevance of the past as well as the value of contemporary sociopolitical relations founded in compliance with its apparent lessons. Using the conceptual framework assembled in this chapter, the following chapters explore the rhetorical and political prudence of conventionally underappreciated forms of forgetting by attending to the speech, language, and symbolism in which leaders and ordinary individuals alike call on their fellows to forget.

# PART 2

PUBLIC FORGETTING:
ALTERNATE HISTORIES, NEW HEURISTICS

HALLOWED GROUND, HOLLOW MEMORY:
RHETORICAL FORM AND COMMEMORATIVE
POLITICS ON SEPTEMBER 11, 2002

Public commemorations influence collective thought and behavior by assigning normative meaning to signal dimensions of the communal past. Regardless of such authority, however, traditional state-sponsored commemorations fail as often as they succeed in their ostensible purpose: to enrich public understanding of the past and to stimulate robust civic participation in adherence to its lessons. "Being told to remember," Margalit observes, "and being properly induced to recall, is no guarantee that we can do so" (2002, 56). The mere command to remember according to "properly induced" rituals or guidelines often accomplishes contrary ends: it can breed ignorance about, or sponsor distortions of, the past—both of which resemble forgetting in its more undesirable, unconscious forms.

The destructive effects of grand state ceremonies are customarily exemplified by cases of totalitarian rule and violently enforced historical revision documented so extensively in post–World War II public and academic discourse alike. In the paradigmatic case of Nazi Germany, elaborate National Socialist spectacles helped to produce a quiescent citizenry largely content to ignore the genocide of the Holocaust. Twenty-first-century liberal-democratic societies rightly pride themselves for their informed aversion to such totalitarian rites of collective forgetting. To be clear, then, this chapter does not argue that its subject matter—state commemorations marking the first anniversary of September 11 in New York City—illustrates a form of public forgetting as extreme and inhumane as the spectacles of the twentieth century's most infamous genocidal regimes. The purpose of this chapter is to argue, nonetheless, that official commemorations on that occasion reveal a form of collective forgetting paradoxically at work in a representative and seemingly innocuous instance of contemporary public commemoration.

The ceremonies in question were steeped in conventional liberal-democratic idioms of remembrance intended to impress upon listeners their duty to never forget the events of September 11, 2001. However, the impassioned rhetoric of liberal-democratic remembrance so characteristic of contemporary state commemorations can entail a quietly pernicious mode of public forgetting and political judgment: a disavowal of institutional politics and difficult sociopolitical differences in favor of transcendent political symbolism and supposedly universal civic sentiment. State-induced forgetting in this case is not as blatantly propagandistic or politically abhorrent as in the vilest authoritarian spectacles of modern Western history, but the moral and political idioms of memory against forgetting which comprise the standard vernacular of liberal-democratic commemorations can nevertheless inadvertently encourage troublesome modes of forgetting.

## Words and Deeds

The complex and ambiguous affinities between words and deeds (*logos* and *ergon*) constituted a prevalent leitmotif of classical *epitaphios logos*. Consider Pericles' reluctance, in his famed eulogy for Athenian soldiers, to praise heroic deeds with simple words: "I could have wished that the reputations of many brave men were not to be imperiled in the mouth of a single individual, to stand or fall according as he spoke well or ill" ("Funeral Speech" 2.35; in Thucydides 1973). Demosthenes began his own funeral oration by professing a similar reluctance to entrust the memory of the dead and their heroism to the fallibility of mere words: "To speak as these dead deserve was one of those things that cannot be done. For, since they scorned the love of life that is inborn in all men and chose rather to die nobly than to live and look upon Greece in misfortune, how can they have failed to leave behind them a record of valor surpassing all power of words to express?" (2000, 1). Modern encomiasts, such as Abraham Lincoln in his celebrated Gettysburg Address, likewise invoke communal memory by measuring speech against action: the dead committed heroic acts in the past, but the living are bound by custom, however reluctantly, to speak of their actions in the present.

Despite their taciturnity, paeans to the memory of cultural idols contribute to the political viability of civic institutions. The eulogist displays for public audiences past deeds meant to inspire political action in the present, which will be imitated by future generations. Classical epideictic of the sort so famously illustrated in Pericles' and Demosthenes' funeral orations indirectly influenced deliberative affairs by promoting standards of civic excellence. In Gerard Hauser's terms, "Epideictic encouraged the constitutive activity propaedeutic to action: reflection on public norms for proper political conduct. . . . [E]pideictic constructs accounts of nobility worthy of *mimesis* [insofar as] its narrative character sets the conditions for a viable public sphere in which a people may engage in politics" (1999, 17–18). Ceremonial honors to the valor and sacrifice of state heroes do not simply provide consolation to the living but dramatize models of excellence worthy of imitation in the present. Chaïm Perelman and Lucie Olbrechts-Tyteca contend that epideictic speech is thus vital to political processes insofar as its rituals of praise and blame enshrine collective values by which future actions are justified (1971, 48). Whether in somber elegies or celebratory tributes, epideictic organizes the terms of public remembrance in order to shape perceptions of shared values and commitments serviceable to future deliberative agendas. The encomiast bemoans the dubious enlivening power of words precisely in order to enhance their capacity to inspire political action.[1] Such classical epideictic (or in modern parlance, ceremonial) ideals retain both normative influence and popular appeal, even at this late date, in shaping collective responses to national tragedies.

Public memorial services in New York City on September 11, 2002, marked the most important U.S. civic commemoration in recent times. They established official precedents concerning how future generations would memorialize and thereby derive models for judgment and action from the September 11 atrocities. On such pivotal epideictic occasions, citizens participate in officially sponsored symbolic rituals through which they derive order and purpose from seemingly senseless tragedy.

The role of place holds inestimable significance in the enactment of these commemorative rituals.[2] Memorials often are staged on the sites of historic events and thereby provide a sense of material connection with the past. After the terrorist attacks of September 11, 2001, the site of the former World Trade Center became a locus of national memory representative of the tragedies not only in New York City but also at the Pentagon in Washington, D.C., and in fields near Shanksville, Pennsylvania. By virtue of this connection, official memorial services held in Manhattan one year later offered the most symbolically representative national forum for the rites of public mourning and civic restoration.

The pregnant affinities between words and deeds understandably informed the character of this event. Fire, police, and military personnel committed heroic deeds on September 11; yet most of those who were murdered in the terrorist attacks were not soldiers or public servants willingly engaged in the defense of their country but innocent civilians preoccupied with ordinary affairs. Whereas celebrated encomiasts typically pay tribute to the tangible military or political achievements of willful agents, eulogists on the first anniversary of September 11 struggled to capture in words the prodigious loss of helpless, anonymous life. Instead of honoring the lasting attainments of celebrated individuals, speakers were charged with memorializing a massive and nameless absence.

Faced with this daunting prospect, New York City mayor Michael Bloomberg (who closely oversaw preparations for the ceremonies) balked at the prospect of marking the occasion with original speeches. "One of the things that I've tried very hard to do in the ceremonies for 9/11," he repeatedly explained, "is to keep politics out of it" (Archibold 2002).[3] Bloomberg personally chose a series of canonical texts rather than original speeches to be read by New York and New Jersey politicians throughout the day's ceremonies. On the morning of the first anniversary of the attack, after a city-wide moment of silence at 8:46 a.m., New York governor George Pataki recited the Gettysburg Address at the site of the World Trade Center. Following a subsequent reading of victims' names from the destruction of the twin towers, New Jersey governor Jim McGreevey recited the preamble and introduction to Thomas Jefferson's Declaration of Independence. During a sunset ceremony at Battery Park, Bloomberg read from the closing passages of Franklin D. Roosevelt's "Four Freedoms" speech. The day's only original address was a brief speech by President George W. Bush, delivered to conclude the memorial services, which nonetheless adhered to standard conventions of public eulogies.

This chapter analyzes the September 11 memorial readings by scrutinizing their function as illustrations of an epideictic *form* that promotes a widely representative ideal of public remembrance. Such unusual instances of public address—or public *declamation*—oblige one to reconsider conventional approaches to rhetorical criticism, which typically emphasizes the orator's technical or prudential skill in composing and delivering an original discourse in response to a given exigency. The indirect, symbolic communication of these declamations requires a different protocol of reading. In this case, orators were not responsible for the words they spoke as an author is responsible for the artistry or acumen of his or her composition; however, that fact begs the question of whether or not the epideictic provided efficacious terms for civic restoration. At issue is not the content of the speeches but their form, and above all the sociopolitical significance of the memorial planners' rhetorical choices.

One may describe the form of memorial declamations in question as *neoliberal* epideictic,[4] which is defined by its celebration of traditional political principles in an ostensibly nonpolitical idiom highly conducive to corporate media dissemination. Neoliberal epideictic reflects the constraints of democratic pluralism, political deregulation, and the free market economy on contemporary ceremonial speech. It seeks to nullify the profound inequities evident in a multicultural polity by acclaiming the historical transcendence of the nation's freedoms over historical crises, the citizenry's presumably essential socioeconomic solidarity to the exclusion of its constitutive political differences, and the virtues of private life over collective political activities. According to these terms, neoliberal epideictic employs an ostensibly nonpolitical idiom in order to celebrate the goods of free enterprise and consumer capitalism, rather than deliberative politics and partisan advocacy, as rightful byproducts of traditional U.S. liberties.

Nevertheless, this ostensible rejection of political speech is itself a form of social and political control. The public eulogies in Manhattan on September 11, 2002, dramatically broke with their classical antecedents by implying strongly that involvement in partisan affairs and acknowledgment of sociopolitical difference and inequity are incompatible with tradition and civic virtue. By urging them to remember and do little else, this exceptionally significant instance of neoliberal epideictic encouraged citizens to forget their collective capacity to engage in effective deliberation and decision-making. Celebrating remembrance for its own sake ironically can encourage the public to forget, in disturbingly unacknowledged ways, the very political obligations that both classical and modern commemorative rituals formally praise as essential attributes of civic excellence.

## Nostalgia for Invention

Mayor Bloomberg's attempt on the first anniversary of September 11 to honor the dead with self-effacing discourse, to achieve a solemn and nonpartisan tone, harked back to the formulaic obsequiousness of celebrated funeral orations. Yet a variety of commentators and ordinary citizens alike castigated Bloomberg and his staff for their rhetorical choices. Theodore Sorensen, speechwriter for John F. Kennedy's celebrated Inaugural Address, protested: "I keep hearing that words cannot express our feelings about what happened. . . . But it's not as though the American English vocabulary is limited. The imagination of our political leaders is limited, not the vocabulary" (Haberman 2002, B1). Roderick Hart concurred: "What we expect is that our leaders will make the effort to find some words appropriate, and we will identify with their effort. Not necessarily with the exact judiciousness of the words selected, but with the courage to try to find words" (J. Scott 2002, A29). The most vocal critics of the memorial readings, as exemplified by these reactions, decried the parochialism of the leaders who recited them.

In this view, artistic insipidness is not only a technical inadequacy but a moral deficiency. Pataki, McGreevey, and Bloomberg's spurious oratory revealed their moral failings as elected officials when measured against timeless standards of political leadership. Garry Wills asserted, "The culture loves it when people rise to the occasion. There are people who can rise to the occasion, and it's cowardice not to try. It's an insult to the dead at the towers . . . to slap on the label from somebody else's tragedy" (J. Scott 2002, A29). On this reading, the speakers' pedestrian intonation of canonical texts (their "cowardice") committed the very offense classical encomiasts painstakingly sought to avoid: insulting the memory of the dead.

By focusing so stringently on these affiliated moral and artistic failings, however, critics of the declamations understated their more substantive rhetorical and political significance. Detractors of the addresses declined to consider how and why these seemingly unimaginative eulogies might have conformed to or reflected widely accepted sociopolitical values. They underestimated the degree to which the bathetic *topoi* of the orations might have appealed to audiences as conducive to public commemoration and civic renewal. The commemorative readings likely carried a measure of institutional authority and popular appeal precisely because of their unoriginality and artlessness.

Influenced by modern notions of artistic originality, critics of the memorial address typically ignored the fact that epideictic forms, particularly the public funeral oration, are not principally artistic endeavors but civic institutions—*institutions of speech*. Pericles' expressed reluctance to speak of the dead exemplifies the classical belief that preserving the ritual form of funeral speech takes priority over the artistic innovations of particular speakers. In Nicole Loraux's terms, "the funeral oration was an *institution*" too politically vital to equate with the arbitrary skill of individual speakers: "an institution of speech in which the symbolic constantly encroached upon the functional, since in each oration the codified praise of the dead spilled over into generalized praise of Athens" (1986, 2). Even today, ritual performances of such epideictic forms are intended to symbolically preserve cultural tradition, collective memory, and political order—not to stand apart from or transcend them. The inimitable status accorded to Pericles' funeral oration, against which modern scholars habitually evaluate similar orations, belies the fact that the dictates of classical *epitaphioi* required orators to merely rearrange conventional *topoi* instead of inventing new figures of speech. The genre held institutional value for its tendency to conserve customary patterns of speech, and with them traditional figures of communal memory and political dicta, not to achieve artistic distinction (2, 3, 4, 5–10).

Epideictic is typically didactic in nature. Encomiasts sustain civic memory from one generation to the next by instructing audiences catechistically in putatively common accounts of collective origins, experiences, and ideals. Like many celebrated encomia, the ceremonial recital of Lincoln, Jefferson, and Roosevelt's texts on September 11, 2002, appeared to rehearse audiences, however implicitly, in foundational civic precepts as a means of rededicating the community to their pursuit in the wake of a national tragedy. For commemorative purposes, the very ritual or symbolic action of reciting traditional texts is often more essential to maintaining the continuity of collective memory than conjuring new turns of phrase.

The formulaic, didactic, and even redundant nature of common rhetorical rituals powerfully contributes to the appearance of continuity in public memories and political traditions. In his classic phenomenological study of memory, Edward Casey stresses the significance of *repetition* to commemoration: participants enact verbal and symbolic rituals that sustain collective memories from one generation to the next in familiar ways, at conventional times, in public forums (2000, 216–57). Ceremonial performances of established symbolic rituals offer vital incitements to collective participation in the preservation of communal memories. Indeed, *memory* and *mantra* are etymologically related; in a fundamental sense, to remember is to repeat a mantra—a sacred and commonplace text or litany of phrases (232).

The rich oral culture of early American history well illustrates the vital civic role of epideictic rituals used to inculcate audiences in basic communal traditions and values. Before and after the Revolutionary War, the annual Boston Massacre Orations contributed to the formation of a common patriot ideology (S. Browne 1999; Condit 1985). The Declaration of Independence, largely forgotten during the late eighteenth century, was revived, orated, and publicly praised during elaborate Fourth of July celebrations throughout the Era of Good Feelings. These select examples of the American epideictic tradition demonstrate that ritually enacting conventional commemorative forms perpetuates articles of civic memory and the political lessons they convey more pervasively than the transcendent artistry of singular oratorical masterworks. The rhetorical and political implications of these rhetorical rituals are far too critical to address solely according to post-Romantic models of eloquence.

In light of these observations, the very form of public address—indeed, of public memory—featured on the first anniversary of September 11 deserves as much, if not more, attention than its content, however unoriginal it may be. For this reason, the following analysis focuses primarily on the symbolism of that form instead of pursuing a traditional speech criticism or close textual interpretation. State eulogies on September 11, 2002, collectively eschewed literal or direct modes of communication. Commencing memorial services on that date by reciting the words that Lincoln spoke at Gettysburg in 1863 to refer to the nation's founding eighty-seven years prior ("Four score and seven years ago"), or eulogizing victims of twenty-first-century terrorism with the words that American colonists used to justify revolt against the eighteenth century's greatest military power, makes no literal sense, particularly as devices with which to foster a lucid public understanding of historical events. Hence, a conventional rhetorical criticism devoted to explicating the intended strategies behind original compositions would fail to capture the full symbolic ramifications of the ceremonial discourse.

At best, the speakers' words conveyed an indirect, implicit, or allegorical meaning. Local and national audiences were presumably unfamiliar with the nexus of historical and political referents in Lincoln, Jefferson, and Roosevelt's words but nonetheless recognized in them a familiar and reassuring form of speech. In Hayden White's terms, "the form of the poetic text," as well as "oratorical declamation" (among other discursive modes), "produces a meaning quite other than whatever might be represented in any prose paraphrase of its literal verbal content" (1987, 43). Thus *what* was said on the first anniversary of September 11 mattered less than *how* it was said.

This emphasis on rhetorical form rejects artificial literary distinctions between form and content, or textual and material reality. Janet Lyon's conception of form in her analysis of modern political manifestoes provides an apt alternative to such rigid classifications: "Far from being no more than scaffolding for expressions of angry dissent, the manifesto's formal contours actually produce and intensify the urgency of its particular imperatives. They do so in part by activating the symbolic force of the form's role in earlier political confrontations: to write a manifesto is to announce one's participation, however discursive, in a history of struggle against oppressive forces" (1999, 10). Epideictic speech, like political manifestoes, commonly adheres to familiar rhetorical forms. Its "contours" do not provide mere ornamentation but acquire a semiotic dimension, signifying its customary meaning and value in the perpetuation of civic norms and traditions. Through ritualized performances, the form itself acquires an institutional character, or ethos, that conditions the legitimacy and appeal of its "imperatives." Kenneth Burke describes how rhetorical form, rather than logical proof alone, solicits assent to particular motives: "We know that many purely formal patterns can readily awaken an attitude of collaborative expectancy in us. Once you grasp the trend of the form, it invites participation regardless of the subject matter. . . . [A] yielding to the form prepares for assent to the matter identified with it" (1969, 58). The symbolic meaning attributed to commonplace forms of address helps to explain audiences' perceived identification with the legitimacy of routine statements of public values, ideals, and judgments.

This methodology accordingly pursues James Jasinski's recommendation that "the interpretive burden faced by rhetorical critics" requires analysis of "the performative conditions or performative traditions that enable and constrain discursive action" (1997, 197). In his estimation, "Invention is a social process in that the words employed by any author [or orator] are always already part of a performative tradition in which the author is situated and from which the author draws" (214). The central issue of this investigation is how the rhetorical form, or customary patterns of public speech, represented by the September 11 declamations demonstrates the ways in which our traditions of epideictic performance are evolving to shape interrelated commemorative and civic ideals in the present era, as well as the larger political disadvantages — or inadvisable forgetting of significant sociopolitical duties and differences — that such developments imply.

### Epideictic in the Neoliberal Era

Conventional rhetorical forms, despite the appearance of continuous memory and political stability they invoke, are subject to inevitable mutation over time as orators employ them in response to unforeseen exigencies. State eulogies featured during public memorial services on September 11, 2002, illustrate a seminal moment in the emergence of *neoliberal* epideictic. The funeral orations in question allow one to delineate the manifestation of a contemporary form of speech that renders the signature *topoi* of U.S. democratic traditions compatible with prevailing neoliberal priorities. These declamations do not illustrate every manifestation of neoliberal epideictic. Nonetheless, the official encomia offered to local, national, and even global audiences on the first anniversary of September 11 provide valuable insight into the models of public speech according to which we increasingly praise our civic traditions and sanctify the memory of those who embody them.

Neoliberalism is a political orientation hospitable to global free market capitalism and international media conglomeration. Predicated on the priorities of free trade (including privatization, social-spending cutbacks, deregulation, deficit reduction, and economic globalization), neoliberal policies promote the profit-making capacities of markets while minimizing the goods of nonmarket institutions. According to Robert McChesney, neoliberalism "posits that society works best when business runs things and there is as little possibility of government 'interference' with business as possible. In short, neoliberal democracy is one where the political sector controls little and debates even less" (1999, 6).[5] To date, studies of neoliberalism have focused on the conjunction of governmental policies, corporate practices, and media cultures responsible for the emergent political, economic, and social hegemony of neoliberal values. Scholars have investigated in far less detail how the diminishment of substantive civic debate to which McChesney refers enhances the cultural currency of neoliberal vocabularies of excellence. We have yet to assess sufficiently the rhetorical means by which common forms of speech have coalesced into the public idioms of neoliberalism and endowed its precepts with the legitimacy and appeal of *doxa*. Although state eulogies admittedly represent only one of many epideictic forms, the anniversary declamations nonetheless demonstrate provocatively how ritualized public praise of neoliberal ideals (including the sordidness of politics and public institutions, the ingenuity of free enterprise, the democratic potentialities of information technology, and the enrichments of global consumer capitalism) increasingly promotes public imperatives to simply remember.

## Patriotic Liturgies

The widespread impact of the terrorist attacks on Americans from diverse cultural, ethnic, and religious backgrounds called for a commemorative idiom suited to both national and international media coverage. Cable news television and other corporate media during the previous year powerfully shaped the national sense of collective loss and mourning after the events of September 11 ("Finding a Way" 2002, 10; Purnick 2002, A22). Contemporary eulogists marking the anniversary were constrained by editorial conventions of corporate media, which compel today's speechwriters to employ a language of "value-free conversation" suited to mass communication. The recitation of cherished words may be rhetorically banal according to Romantic conceptions of the art, but it provides an oratorical performance well suited to the defining verbal and visual elements of corporate news media—namely, "sound bites and photo ops" (Haberman 2002, B1). In one editorialist's apt assessment, "Speechlessness may also suit the times. [Contemporary politicians] are not trained in oratory, and their audiences are skeptical and impatient. In a society fragmented by race, ethnicity and class, it is harder to find language and allusions that resonate widely and to find meanings that can be broadly embraced" (J. Scott 2002, A29).

During the neoliberal era, corporate media conventions effectively influence the nature of contemporary public address by emphasizing terse, memorable slogans more reminiscent of advertising catchphrases than refined eloquence. Denise Bostdorff and Steven Vibbert show how corporate public relations campaigns increasingly engage in the epideictic strategy of "values advocacy," through which they appeal to presumably noncontroversial cultural values in order to improve their image and deflect criticism of policies and practices (1994). The examples of neoliberal epideictic addressed in this essay indicate how such forms of corporate communication are being adopted as the idiom of contemporary civic spectacles. The result is a vocabulary of public commemoration that encourages the polity to forget, in dangerously unacknowledged ways, relevant details of its own national past, including the historical sources and significance of the very commemorative idiom in question. By implication, the normative authority and popular appeal of such a vocabulary solicits the community merely to rehearse customary tropes of memory while disregarding, or forgetting, the practical political commitments that ideally attend them as per the classical model.

Bloomberg and his staff adhered to corporate media conventions by providing concise, thematically broad orations, and imitated classical encomiasts by offering novel arrangements of familiar *topoi*. Along with the Preamble to the U.S. Constitution, Jefferson's Declaration of Independence and Lincoln's Gettysburg Address comprise the so-called American Testament (Adler and Gorman 1975, 9–13). Generations of exegetical commentary inform contemporary audiences' reception of these texts. Popular and political discourse designates them as central articles of U.S. civil religion. So conceived, their most venerated passages are said to communicate nonpartisan truths available to all Americans, irrespective of historical or cultural circumstance. Their nominally sacred character recommends them as integral epideictic resources in the neoliberal era: such ubiquitous, allegedly self-evident, and "value-free" expressions of U.S. political ideology offer a seemingly nonpartisan form of speech bearing presumably universal (or democratic) significance for heterogeneous audiences.

Neoliberal epideictic embellishes the exegetical tradition according to which documents such as the Declaration of Independence and the Gettysburg Address have attained their quasi-sacred status. It paradoxically identifies such texts as the transcendent ground of U.S. political principles and institutions: they authorize and govern our secular and political affairs while retaining the status of quasi-sacred, transcendent symbols of democratic wisdom and virtue. Neoliberal epideictic renders the content of their signature maxims immune from partisan appropriation or definitive interpretation, suggesting instead that one may apprehend the simultaneously recondite and transcendent truths of these documents through dutiful personal meditation rather than public debate. As such, it assigns allegorical meaning to benchmarks of U.S. political speech. In our fiercely democratic and presumptively postmodern age, when politicians and citizens alike disparage markers of sociopolitical status and cultural hierarchy, the allegorical symbolism frequently invoked in neoliberal epideictic appears to lend audiences the interpretive freedom to derive deeply personal meanings from the most ubiquitous articles of U.S. civil religion. The ceremonial readings on September 11, 2002, evoked precisely this indirect, allegorical meaning rather than adopting Lincoln, Jefferson, and Roosevelt's words as literal statements.[6]

By presenting sacred templates of American political speech as allegorical symbols, as a profusion of patriotic signs, neoliberal epideictic yields presumably a more democratic yet nonpartisan social and political text invested with the ethos of sacred tradition.[7] In such semantic plentitude, heterogeneous audience members allegedly find personal grounds for rededication to essential, if unspoken, principles of U.S. democracy. Neoliberal epideictic thereby illustrates Roland Barthes's (and, in rhetorical studies, Michael McGee's) premise that in contemporary culture readers (or auditors) have assumed the position of authors (or speakers), fabricating coherent texts out of continually recycled discursive fragments (Barthes 1977a, 1977b; McGee

1990). Only by this logic could one conclude, as the September 11 memorial planners did, that revered expressions of American political values would provide appropriately *non*political *epitaphioi* on that occasion.

By this logic, the public recitation of Jefferson and Lincoln's words on September 11, 2002, was intended to symbolize the transcendence of U.S. freedoms over sociopolitical crises and instability, their essentially unbroken continuity through periods of historical rupture and discontinuity. Event planners invited such an interpretation by arranging Jefferson and Lincoln's texts in a nonchronological manner. True to the associative structure of allegory, Lincoln's nineteenth-century address preceded Jefferson's eighteenth-century document in the morning services. For contemporary audiences, the chronological inversion (*hysteron proteron*) of Lincoln and Jefferson's texts invoked familiar sociopolitical axioms more readily than a historically accurate arrangement would have.

Conventional wisdom regards Lincoln's Gettysburg Address as a definitive interpretation of Jefferson's Declaration. Its renowned first line identifies the achievement of the revolutionary "fathers," specifically their dedication to equality professed in Jefferson's document, as the event that unifies the nation's past, present, and future while giving meaning and purpose to the sacrifices of its soldiers: "Four score and seven years ago our fathers brought forth on this continent, a new nation, conceived in Liberty, and dedicated to the proposition that all men are created equal" (1989b, 536). In his comprehensive account of the speech, Wills asserts: "The Gettysburg Address has become an authoritative expression of the American spirit—as authoritative as the Declaration itself, and perhaps more influential, since it determines how we read the Declaration" (1992, 146–47).[8] The address reflects Lincoln's belief that the Declaration comprised a transcendent expression of indispensable freedoms, "a standard maxim for free society, which would be familiar to all, and revered by all; constantly looked to, constantly labored for . . . augmenting the happiness and value of life to all people and of all colors everywhere" (1989h, 398). His elegy at Gettysburg accordingly transformed forensic principles authored specifically to justify colonial separation from Great Britain into universally applicable, and typically unquestioned, assumptions concerning the origins and extension of American freedoms. Lincoln famously expressed the country's enduring bond with its revolutionary origins in his closing prediction that "government of the people, by the people, for the people, shall not perish from the earth" (1989b, 536).[9]

Unlike the deceptive simplicity of Lincoln's prophecy, Jefferson's declaratory language holds legal and political connotations specific to July 1776, and consequently addresses contemporary audiences in comparatively pro-lix and antiquated eighteenth-century phrasing. Bloomberg and his plan-ners therefore selected only the Declaration's Preamble and Introduction, its least political passages, as the second declamation on September 11, 2002. Divorced from Jefferson's indictment of King George's crimes against the American colonies, as well as his closing appeal to "our British brethren," the Declaration's Preamble and Introduction speak in apparently transcen-dent terms about the nature of government and its universal aims, based on "self-evident" truths, to preserve the "unalienable Rights of Life, Liberty, and the pursuit of Happiness" (1994, 24). By themselves, the Declaration's Preamble and Introduction conform to *any* historical period and politi-cal body: its abstract and conditional language addresses purely theoretical scenarios: "When, in the course of human events, it becomes necessary for one people to dissolve the political bands which have connected them with another" (24). Drained of specific historical, legal, or political content, McGreevy's reading of the Declaration on September 11, 2002, consisted of seemingly apolitical civic platitudes.

The combined ethos of Lincoln and Jefferson's texts, so ordered, sym-bolized the nation's abiding connection with the original enunciation of American liberties, suggesting that the past, present, and future of U.S. free-doms were both destined and continuous, irrespective of historical or politi-cal circumstances. Modern Americans may be able to recite much of the Declaration's Preamble and Introduction by rote, but popular and political wisdom accepts the Gettysburg Address as a pithy and morally true (if not historically precise) distillation of its essential meaning. By this logic, the authoritative status of Lincoln's speech renders sociopolitical truths embod-ied in Jefferson's document perpetually available to present and future audi-ences alike, regardless of immediate cultural or political differences. David Zarefsky noted that none of the selected texts "have anything to do specifi-cally with terrorism or the attacks. . . . They are much more transcendent in their appeal. . . . [W]hat he [Bloomberg] is trying to express is that this is an event that transcends politics, by using texts that evoke a kind of resonance between then and now, and recommits us to the ideals that are contained in those texts" (Steinhauer 2002, A1). In this manner, the declamations adhered to a defining formal requirement of celebrated public eulogies: the didactic rehearsal of civic axioms intended to restore the public's perceived connections with its communal origins, rededicate it to its original civic mission, and thereby reaffirm its traditional bonds of sociopolitical solidarity in times of crisis, tragedy, or uncertainty.

The morning declamations of Lincoln and Jefferson's words symbolized the nation's unbroken affiliation with its origins and destiny; Bloomberg's evening recitation of Roosevelt's "Four Freedoms" speech, accompanied by President Bush's statements, displayed essential civic virtues necessary to galvanize the citizenry in the face of impending threats to its freedom and stability. In his 1941 address to Congress, Roosevelt employed universal terminology at a time of geopolitical turmoil, propounding recognizably American conceptions of freedom that everyone should enjoy. On September 11, 2002, Bloomberg recited Roosevelt's vision of "a world founded upon four essential human freedoms"—namely, "freedom of speech and expression," "freedom of every person to worship God in his own way," "freedom from want," and "freedom from fear" (Roosevelt 1999 [1941], 123). Preceded by Jefferson and Lincoln's politically sacred expressions of the American experience, Roosevelt's modern phrasing similarly assumed the ethos of revealed truth concerning the origins, nature, and scope of U.S. liberties. Thus, even the somewhat idiosyncratic choice of Roosevelt's speech evoked the formal, exegetical qualities of the so-called American Testament.

Although it was the most unconventional reading featured in the day's ceremonies, Roosevelt's speech nevertheless fulfilled a conventional twofold purpose. On the one hand, Roosevelt's address (like Lincoln's) proclaims fidelity to the origins of fundamental U.S. liberties while also portending their unceasing enlargement—or in the logic of the ceremonies, transcendence. The portion of his speech that Bloomberg recited is marked by a rhythmic pattern in which Roosevelt asserts that each freedom must be secured "everywhere" or "anywhere in the world" (123). Echoing the symbolism of the Gettysburg Address, such recognizably U.S. liberties form a transcendent model of universal freedom.

Roosevelt's speech is a prime example of numerous statements in which he reinterpreted the meaning of the Declaration of Independence in light of the economic ravages of the Great Depression and the international conflicts of World War II. Prior to and throughout his presidency, Roosevelt asserted that economic inequities hindered citizens' abilities to realize the pursuit of happiness, which the Declaration stipulated as an unalienable right, and called for an "economic Bill of Rights" applicable at home and abroad (Roosevelt 2005 [1932]). In the "Four Freedoms" address, he maintained that the country was still animated by the "perpetual, peaceful revolution" initiated in Jefferson's document and that "freedom from want" when "translated into world terms, means economic understandings which will secure to every nation a healthy peacetime life" (1999 [1941], 123). Much as Lincoln did in the nineteenth century, Roosevelt articulated the twentieth century's most consequential and universally inclusive augmentation of the Declaration's meaning in response to historical and political strife.[10] In the context of September 11 memorial services, Roosevelt's rhetoric thus supplied a crucial symbolic bridge, simultaneously heralding the transcendence of the nation's founding principles and their applicability to the exigencies of twenty-first-century geopolitical crises.

On the other hand, the selected portions of Roosevelt's speech provided deftly suggestive terms with which to memorialize not only an unprecedented loss of life but the decimation of the country's most important financial center. Roosevelt's signature identification of economic security, or "freedom from want," as an indispensable means to "secure for every nation a healthy peacetime" (1999 [1941], 123) implicitly addressed the fiscal ramifications of the terrorist attacks in a putatively respectful and nonpolitical vernacular.[11] Americans likely could not recite Roosevelt's "Four Freedoms" speech as they could recite Lincoln or Jefferson's most famous words; but its language nonetheless evoked familiar and widely accepted precepts of modern liberalism. According to these precepts, one takes for granted that foreign threats to U.S. security threaten a uniquely prosperous economic order: American capitalism. In this Rooseveltian logic, equal opportunity for the pursuit of happiness as such should be hailed as a primary civic ideal because economic prosperity allows the community to transcend its other crippling inequities and achieve lasting social harmony. As a central *topos* of neoliberal epideictic, one's private pursuit of economic well-being assumes the status of an unquestioned public good: consumer capitalism honors the loss of innocents by maintaining financial opportunities equivalent to the preservation of American freedom.

Commonplace reverence for the so-called greatest generation only enhanced the allegorical significance of Roosevelt's rhetoric on September 11, 2002. During the final decade of the twentieth century, journalists, film producers, historians, novelists, and politicians all celebrated the World War II generation's defense of pluralist society.[12] In the wake of the September 11 attacks, commentators frequently pondered parallels between those who came to their country's defense following the Japanese raid on Pearl Harbor and the present generation's prospects for responding to violations of American sovereignty at the dawn of the twenty-first century. Thus, the popular memory of World War II recommended fashionable cultural symbols with which to assess the gravity and significance of the September 11 atrocities while invoking the iconic image of a model community unified and mobilized against dire threats to its intertwined democratic and economic institutions. By virtue of these perceived connections, Roosevelt's text offered a form of address understood to have rallied the public around the protection of sacred U.S. liberties during World War II and therefore suited to invoking such a model community once again.

The ceremonial recitation of Roosevelt's speech thus supplied a formally and patriotically satisfying model of virtue where one appeared to be lacking in the wake of the terrorist attacks. By far the majority of victims in the destruction at the World Trade Center, the Pentagon, and in the fields of Pennsylvania were ordinary and defenseless citizens, not soldiers, among them hundreds of foreigners from around the world. Their general anonymity and tragic deaths ironically supplied inapt models of valor for the often militaristic and nationalistic rites staged to commemorate their loss.[13] Hence the memory of the so-called greatest generation provided icons of citizen-soldiers better suited to the formal requirements of neoliberal funeral ceremonies than the individuals who were being memorialized. This weird symbolic substitution demonstrates how the very form of our memorial discourse profoundly structures the medium and content of public memories as well as the models of virtue promoted in their name.

Paired with Roosevelt's address, President Bush's original speech utilized formulaic (and, to that extent, unoriginal) Rooseveltian terms. The similarities between Roosevelt's language and President Bush's were hardly accidental. John Murphy (2003) discerns repeated echoes of FDR's rhetoric in Bush's public statements following September 11, 2001, and Denise Bostdorff (2003) demonstrates that in the same period Bush frequently called upon younger Americans to respond to the terrorist attacks in the spirit of their putative elders, the World War II generation. On the first anniversary of September 11, he similarly eulogized victims of the terrorist attacks by calling on the community, in the formulae of classical funeral orations, to recognize its debt to those who had been lost, to pay them tribute with "the most enduring monument we can build: A world of liberty and security made possible by the way America leads, and the way Americans lead their lives" (G. Bush 2003, 182). Bush's speech accordingly summoned the community to answer "history's call" by rehearsing the defining tropes of wartime rhetoric in the era of modern liberalism, including "a great struggle that tests our strength, and even more our resolve"; an epic battle "between those who believe all men are created equal, and those who believe that some men and women and children are expendable in the pursuit of power";

and a depiction of the United States as the nation that "has defeated tyrants and liberated death camps" and "raised this lamp of liberty to every captive land" (182). With such language, Bush not only echoed Roosevelt's call to the greatest generation but, in doing so, thematically unified the day's orations by recalling the nation's promise to extend equality as first envisioned in Jefferson's Declaration and hallowed in Lincoln's Gettysburg Address. As such, his speech was notable more for its formulaic invocation of modern liberal commonplaces than its original content. Consistent with classical *epitaphioi,* the address's most evident rhetorical novelty was its distinctive rearrangement of conventional *topoi.*

Together with Roosevelt's "Four Freedoms" speech, Bush's rehearsal of familiar commonplaces emphasized not only the triumph of American freedoms over former historical and political conflicts but their inevitable transcendence of present and future calamities. "We will not relent until justice is done and our nation is secure," Bush proclaimed. "What our enemies have begun, we will finish" (2003, 183). In Bush's phrasing, the public— "we"—is an emphatically singular body unified in belief and action. As in the morning recitations of Jefferson and Lincoln's words, these appeals to the transcendence of American freedoms provided an implicit warrant for civic unity in response to the events of September 11 by invoking the iconic ethos of the World War II generation, which allegedly transcended its immediate sociopolitical differences in order to ensure the global propagation of democratic liberties. Indeed, in popular memory this model wartime generation fought to preserve freedom in the form of an economic system under which Americans presumably attained a standard of prosperity unrivaled in modern history. In an era dominated by the military-industrial complex and consumer capitalism, Bush's model of citizenship valorizes equally the armed defense of U.S. liberties and their expression in a culture of individual consumption—or to use his words, in "the way Americans lead their lives." Not coincidentally, in previous statements on September 11 Bush had consistently rehearsed the public in drawing parallels between the country's economic vitality and its armed defense (Murphy 2003).

Such was a fitting resolution to a series of public declamations tailored for mass media consumption. The featured oratory amplified the didactic qualities of conventional epideictic forms to produce patriotic liturgies easily edited for television coverage and composed of nominally universal, self-evident truths. Indeed, such epideictic *topoi* provided serviceable fodder for what one commentator described as "a television event" more "than a political oratory event" (Haberman 2002, B1). This mediated presentation of

Jefferson, Lincoln, Roosevelt, and Bush's words encouraged simultaneously national yet intimately personal, even unspoken, reflection on their truths as an appropriate response to the memory of those killed on September 11, 2001. The epideictic addresses constituted a democratic vernacular of deeply personal emotion disseminated to national and international audiences.

September 11 memorial services in Manhattan demonstrated vividly how corporate media enhance the appeal of neoliberal values through the management of collective pathos.[14] Event planners sought to unify heterogeneous audiences in a public display of mourning that would transcend intervening social, political, and economic divisions. In a period of untold grief and uncertainty, powerful bonds of sentiment would serve as proof of abiding unity. The sacred, personal, affective resonance of the official epideictic therefore called on the public to endorse presumptive beliefs in both the historical transcendence of fundamental U.S. freedoms and its integrity as a civic body.

The September 11 memorial epideictic thus provides a historic example of how contemporary public spectacles increasingly refashion traditional political axioms into expressions of simultaneously personal and universal pathos. Such spectacles provide a virtual civic forum designed for the private spectatorship of a presumably nonpartisan, emotionally charged media event. They call on the public to remember for the simple pathos of doing so. In our so-called society of the spectacle, public events—including political conventions and campaigns, state ceremonies and cultural festivals, and national and international sports competitions—increasingly are organized to unite an otherwise fractured citizenry in a dynamic affective experience.[15] The symbolic rituals of mass mediated spectacles offer an affective idiom that appears to engender a common civic identity from public displays of sentiment during an era of widespread political polarities, conflicting moral paradigms, and heterogeneous cultural traditions. Public address on such occasions provides, as sociologist Michel Maffesoli might put it, "a communication" whose "sole objective [is] to 'touch' the other, to simply be in contact, to participate together in a form of gregariousness" (1996, 57, 62). Offering incantation rather than invention, official epideictic at the site of the World Trade Center and in Battery Park contributed yet one more sound to an ongoing funeral dirge paratactically composed of interwoven texts, music, and other funeral rites (Barry 2002, A1).

The putative effect of public speech in this form is to nullify debilitating sociopolitical differences ordinarily evoked by deliberative speech (such as the political polarization, class and racial disparities, and vociferous debates over social mores that divided the public at the dawn of the twenty-first century). Such nullification, or collective forgetting of outstanding civic differences and difficulties, thereby induces audiences to ritually affirm a tacit yet indelible communal bond. Assured of this bond, neoliberal epideictic does not summon citizens for public advocacy in the presence of others (the essential condition of democratic politics) but excuses them to the preoccupations of private life. Reminded of its civic integrity, citizens may forget their practical responsibility to restore or strengthen the very alloy of that integrity: the agonistic relations that bind them together in political community.

## America's Machiavellian Moment

Even as it offers a form of speech ostensibly denuded of political ramifications, neoliberal epideictic (like all versions of the genre) rehearses audiences in ideal conceptions of governance, civic participation, and social order based on prevailing sociopolitical values. The state eulogies given in New York City on September 11, 2002, vividly illustrated the civic implications of neoliberal epideictic's appeal as a widely embraced medium of public remembrance. Much of the nation experienced the events of September 11 as a violent rupture in time. In their wake, Americans from all walks of life surmised that a halcyon era of prolonged peace and stability had precipitately ended, and that a new epoch of historic geopolitical conflict had begun. The United States entered a twenty-first-century "Machiavellian moment" as J. G. A. Pocock describes it, in which a republic, composed of a potentially unruly mixture of partisan interests, is compelled by the unpredictable fortunes of human affairs to ask how it may "remain morally and politically stable in a stream of irrational events conceived as essentially destructive of all systems of secular stability" (2003, viii). In this moment, the polity is forced to confront the prospect of its inherent contingency, even its temporal finitude, as a sociopolitical body. During such historic episodes of temporal disorientation, officials employ epideictic resources to symbolically incorporate radical ruptures in communal time into the unfolding of central commemorative traditions and thereby assign coherent meaning and purpose to events that seem to defy explanation (Dow 1989; Murphy 1990). Renewal of the public's *vita activa,* in other words, follows from the fitting expression and collective ratification of a revised historical consciousness.[16]

In response to the perceived advent of a new and dangerous era, the public eulogies of September 11, 2002, insisted upon the community's unbroken, or transcendent, connections with its founding liberties. The arrangement and parallelism of Lincoln, Jefferson, Roosevelt, and Bush's words encouraged audiences to view the recent tragedies as yet one more trial in the destined reign of American liberties over the forces of violence, fear, and repression. In this instance, neoliberal epideictic promoted a conception of transcendent, essentially nonpolitical, time rooted in American civil religion. Since the Puritans arrived on the shores of New England in the seventeenth century, Americans of all stripes have mythologized their country as a model community founded to deliver the good news of salvation (whether secular or sacred) to the world.[17] The September 11 epideictic affirmed this article of civic faith by suggesting that the community was witnessing an epic struggle between the forces of freedom and oppression, of good and evil. Yet the outcome of this struggle had been prophesied: freedom will vanquish despotism, good will prevail over evil.

Roosevelt's and Bush's words in particular invoked the messianic themes of Cold War rhetoric in order to prophesy such triumphs. Inspired by Roosevelt's World War II addresses, which depicted an epic contest between Allied and Axis powers over the fate of civilization itself, American officials throughout the Cold War routinely elaborated upon such messianic themes by portraying the United States and its allies as agents of Christian liberty engaged in an epochal struggle against Soviet forces of godless communism. In his Truman Doctrine of 1947, the Cold War's opening rhetorical salvo, President Harry Truman stressed that "at the present moment in world history nearly every nation must choose between" a way of life "based upon the will of the majority" and one "based upon the will of a minority forcibly imposed" (1995, 751). Three years later, Senator Joseph McCarthy notoriously amplified such themes of apocalyptic crisis: "Today we are engaged in a final, all-out battle between communistic atheism and Christianity," he proclaimed. "Can there be anyone who fails to realize that the communist world has said, 'The time is now,' that this is the time for the showdown between the democratic Christian world and the communist atheistic world?" (2000, 173). More recently, President Ronald Reagan implored the public to recognize that "no government schemes are going to perfect man" and "to pray for the salvation of all those who live in that totalitarian darkness" of the so-called Evil Empire (2005, 802).

The September 11 declamations likewise heralded the triumph of U.S. freedoms over cataclysmic historical and political events while imploring the nation to affirm such prophecy in the face of climactic geopolitical conflict. President Bush concluded official memorial services by conjuring the day's most explicit messianic reference, substituting the United States for Jesus Christ (the Messiah) as "the light" to which the New Testament refers in the Book of John: "I believe there is a reason that history has matched this nation with this time. . . . This ideal of America is the hope of all mankind. That hope drew millions to this harbor. That hope still lights our way. And the light shines in the darkness. And the darkness will not overcome it" (2003, 183). Presenting American political principles as prophetic signs and revelations, the September 11 anniversary epideictic thus invoked the conventional messianic symbolism of wartime rhetoric in the era of modern liberal democracy.

The logic of messianic time is ahistorical: it conforms to a divine calendar in which social agents cannot change prophesied ends, only hasten their coming. Speech that affirms such prophecy assigns universal significance to particular events. It encourages audiences to intervene in them only insofar as they may further the arrival of a destined outcome. This epideictic *topos* suggests that the fate of the very freedoms at stake in the present conflict has been destined since their original enunciation. The rhetoric in question calls on the community not to protect or augment those freedoms through sustained civic advocacy, devoted to negotiating profound sociocultural differences and inequities, but by bearing witness to a divine prophecy. The operative appeal is to remember the very idea of historical continuity or destiny, and little else.

Such is a rendition of historical memory that both Nietzsche and Foucault would have found wanting. The seemingly inevitable *telos* that the September 11 declamations assigned to the nation's political past evokes a monumental vision of history, as Nietzsche described it, which "violently" forces "what is individual in it" into "a universal mold . . . in the interest of conformity!" (1997, 69). The lessons of history in this formulation amount to directives, not incitements to critical thought. Foucault, moreover, likely would object that the national traditions symbolized on this occasion seem to have been composed of "profound intentions and immutable necessities" (1977a, 155)—that the past as officially commemorated in such ceremonies, and the story of transcendent freedom it expresses, is designed to appear transparent and unarguable in its basic truth.

Defined as a transcendent achievement, freedom is a gift bestowed by the past rather than a product of civic *agon* in the present—a condition passively received, not actively pursued. This transcendent quality reflects Hannah Arendt's claim that "freedom can so easily be mistaken for an essentially nonpolitical phenomenon" (1993, 169). Event planners for the September

11 memorial services sought precisely to coin a nonpolitical commemorative idiom of freedom and citizenship by appealing to historical transcendence. In this instance, neoliberal epideictic dissociated history from politics by suggesting that the polity's fate lies in a concurrent devaluation of political action and embrace of historical prophecy. By this chiliastic logic, immediate events warrant faith in the foreordained ends of American democracy rather than a rededication to their deliberative enlargement. Hence, the cost of the public's assurance in its destined freedoms is its inattention to collective commitments for their deliberative pursuit in response to immediate sociopolitical dilemmas. Indeed, several commentators noted the September 11 ceremonies' conspicuous lack of explicit calls for public service or civic reform emblematic of leaders' statements on similar epideictic occasions in U.S. history (Haberman 2002, B1).

Neoliberal epideictic therefore reorients the public to its own history in a way that restricts the citizenry's collective capacity to derive resources for speech and action from the terms of civic memory. The public receives from the ceremonial language of such spectacles not a store of inherited wisdom requisite for liberal-democratic judgment, but its mere appearance. This historical disorientation was most evident in the words used to commence memorial services on September 11, 2002: Lincoln's cherished allusion in 1863 to the nation's founding "Four score and seven years ago." In seeking nonpolitical words and rituals, the September 11 memorial services rejected the possibility of codifying contemporary interpretations of historic events that could be remembered, narrated, and reinterpreted by future generations as precedents for political judgment. In remembering so ardently, there is nothing—or no *thing* in the sense of the *res publica,* the public thing or substance—to remember.

This doubtful epideictic mode fails to yield the kind of "strong statement" that Young contends is essential for ensuring that commemorative rituals provide "a basis for political and social action." Citing his own studies of Holocaust memorials, Young argues, "The question is not, How are people moved by these memorials? but rather, To what end have they been moved, to what historical conclusions, to what understanding and actions in their own lives? This is to suggest that . . . the social function of such art *is* its aesthetic performance" (2000, 199). Communal memories are inherently political because public rituals used to formulate and maintain them necessarily condition the community to derive precedents for further speech and action from its remembered past. Bloomberg and his planners' effort to "keep politics out" of official September 11 commemorations diluted this vital civic function of public memory. Remembering the events of September 11 according to the officially prescribed terms constituted an inadvisable forgetting of politics itself.

These considerations confirm the political significance of ritualized epideictic forms—or the notion that, in Young's terms, their aesthetic performance determines their social function. Memory rooted in the unquestioned transcendence of civic tradition can instill tremendous reverence for both its origins and ordained ends; yet it produces dubious public resources with which citizens might speak and act in response to immediate events. Pocock cautions: "Political processes often (some say always) go on within a received and inherited pattern of behavior, and the interpretation of tradition can be a complex and self-conscious political decision. Yet it remains true that a citizen, constantly involved with his [*sic*] fellows in the making of public decisions, must possess an intellectual armory which takes him beyond the perception of hierarchy and tradition, and gives him cause to rely on his and his fellows' power to understand and respond to what is happening to them" (2003, 49). Neoliberal epideictic praises as a public virtue the nominally *a*political decision to refrain from questioning inherited institutional wisdom. It solicits the polity's faith in the continuity of its enabling political processes without articulating conditions for their revitalization in light of immediate sociopolitical conflicts. The genre's failure to do so neglects the requisite capacity for response definitive of freedom itself in Arendt's conception: the distinctly human capacity to begin again, to create something new amid the stream of irrational and destructive events, or Machiavellian moments, to which Pocock refers.

Given advantageous circumstances, *either* formulaic *or* novel speech might draw a constructive "intellectual armory" from the terms of collective memory. The principal issue here is not the originality of an epideictic performance but the discernible institutional ends it serves (or fails to serve) in replenishing the political resources of civic remembrance. Neoliberal epideictic reduces the rhetorical rituals of public memory to discursive forms deprived of deliberative consequence, to mere symbols of tradition. On the eve of the September 11 memorial services, Susan Sontag lamented that when great speeches "are ritually cited, or recycled for commemoration, they have become completely emptied of meaning. They are now gestures of nobility, of greatness of spirit. The reasons for their greatness are irrelevant" (2002, A25). By this account, neoliberal epideictic represents a willful and dangerous aestheticization of politics. It risks confirming the worst fear of classical encomiasts—that epideictic speech amounts to words alone.

To the extent that it conflates the aesthetics and politics of memory, neoliberal epideictic represents a disturbingly unacknowledged form of communal forgetting: a renunciation of politics as a realm of agonistic practices distinct from aesthetic display.

## Conclusion

Neoliberal epideictic vividly reflects an increasingly pervasive culture of memory in contemporary liberal democracies. At present, leaders and ordinary citizens alike assume that public commitments to derive meaning and wisdom from defining events in communal history—the traditional sine qua non of civic memory—can be fulfilled by participating in the choreographed pathos of media spectacles. State eulogies on occasions of national tragedy, patriotic speeches and performances during nationally televised sporting events, and Hollywood historical dramas are among the foremost exemplars of such spectacles. Elaborate rites of public memory flourish, even at this late date, in neoliberal form: in rhetorical adaptations of corporate marketing strategies publicizing ostensibly value-free political slogans.

The widely embraced culture of memory reflected in neoliberal epideictic promotes, as its basic framework of judgment, a morality of memory without an ethics of memory. Margalit differentiates between morality and ethics in relation to memory "based on a distinction between two types of human relations: thick ones and thin ones" (2002, 7). Moral axioms, by this account, originate in thin relations—in our concern for others merely by virtue of the fact that we share a common humanity. Morality is expressed in relatively universal strictures: others are entitled to a minimum degree of respect, compassion, and so forth not because we know them intimately but because we share with them a universal human condition. Ethical conduct originates, by contrast, in our thick relations with particular others, such as "parent, friend, lover, fellow-countryman" (7). The field of ethics concerns relations with others with whom we share complex personal histories and explicitly articulated bonds of loyalty, trust, obligation, and the like. Morality and ethics as Margalit speaks of them ideally should promote balanced, reciprocal goods: a diminishment of our relations with others in one form, thin or thick, would diminish those in the complementary form.

Neoliberal epideictic promotes a conspicuous asymmetry between morality and ethics in the context of memory. Aesthetic displays characteristic of neoliberal epideictic disseminate universally consumable symbols that provide little incentive for attending to the sustained obligations and practices that constitute our thickest political affiliations. Epideictic in this mode implores the public to heed a universal imperative to remember while discouraging explicit consideration of pressing ethical questions, such as how the thick relations of citizenship should be restored or transformed in light of the remembered past, and whether even popularly embraced forms of commemoration undermine such prospects in reproducing a particular culture of memory. These insights are even more troubling in light of Arendt's conviction that the *polis* survives periodic threats to its integrity by virtue of its members' abilities to make and keep promises—to obligate themselves to each other instead of seemingly automatic, ingrained courses of historical and political development (or national destiny, as symbolized by the September 11 anniversary declamations). An ardent morality of memory without a corresponding ethics threatens to diminish the very deed upon which all of politics depends: the act of beginning again.

How, then, may communities reconcile a potential hypertrophy of memory with idioms of forgetting in order to begin again, as Arendt would have it? To adopt a particular rhetoric of public forgetting is, in this calculus, to render a concerted political and ethical judgment on prevailing public perceptions of the past. The remaining case studies analyze specific instances in which communities somehow choose to forget the past as they had previously spoken of it and begin again—not in an effort to negate public memory per se, but as a means to renew its relevance and vitality in matters of communal judgment. Together, the following chapters offer alternative *topoi* according to which one may discern the value of forgetting as a formative and transformative dimension of civic memory, even when passionate and universal appeals to remember appear morally irrefutable, as they appeared on the first anniversary of September 11 and as they continue to appear in myriad liberal-democratic spectacles of remembrance.

HISTORICAL FORGETTING:
JOHN W. DRAPER AND THE RHETORICAL DIMENSIONS OF HISTORY

One logical and patently modern response to the questionable culture of
memory documented in Chapter 3 would be to invoke professional history as a corrective to its aesthetic excesses. Throughout modernity and
late modernity, professional history has maintained its reputation for supplying nominally unembellished historical fact as a means of counteracting
instances of selective revision, obfuscation, or distortion that breed forgetfulness about the past. The present chapter, however, reveals that forgetting
was, and remains, a productive aspect of modern historical culture, and that
institutional history as we know and revere it incorporates forgetting in
essential ways.

Forgetting produces. This claim is meant as an obvious allusion to Foucault's contention that power is productive instead of essentially repressive
or coercive, as colloquial usage would have it. The dominant connotation
of the French *pouvoir* defines power as a creative force: it produces new
forms of knowledge, subjectivity, and politics instead of simply suppressing
or disabling them. "We must cease once and for all," Foucault remarks, "to
describe the effects of power in negative terms: it 'excludes,' it 'represses,'
it 'censors,' it 'abstracts,' it 'masks,' it 'conceals.' In fact, power produces; it
produces reality; it produces domains of objects and rituals of truth" (1979,
194). We may not like all that it produces, and it may be difficult to separate
its desirable from undesirable productions, but power produces a complex
array of effects all the same. Foucault thus eliminates the dialectical schema
that separates presumptively innocent means of resistance from the work-
ings of power. In his understanding, power produces forms of resistance as
internal components of its institutional operations. It is, in Foucault's words,
a "moving substrate of force relations which, by virtue of their inequal-
ity, constantly engender states of power, but the latter are always local and

unstable" (1990, 93). One must therefore evaluate the forms of knowledge, subjectivity, and politics that modalities of power produce by closely analyzing their specific material effects rather judging their merits *a priori* according to categorical moral rules. Modes of power are not good or evil in and of themselves, but their material consequences are indeed worthy of scrupulous evaluation.

Forgetting, this chapter shows, is not merely a repressive, unwanted force in the context of historical memory. In rhetorical terms, forgetting is an intrinsic rather than extrinsic component of communal narratives that, in more refined form, supply the substrate of public history. Michel de Certeau posits that history is not a mimetic representation of the past but a selective enterprise that actively creates the past as we know it. One must distinguish between "the past" and "history" as he defines them: the past occurred and was real but is not contained by or equated with history; history, to the contrary, is a reconstruction of the past—an approximation of the past that takes place in the present (1988, 4). A willed forgetting of the past in its original, unrecoverable form must occur, according to de Certeau, in order to make the past as we know it lucid and uniform (4). Forgetting is a productive, often driving, force in creating the regimes of truth and knowledge that attain the authority of unvarnished historical fact widely embraced by academics and popular culture alike. Supporting this claim obliges one to presume that forgetting, like power, is not good or bad in and of itself but that its specific uses or effects in the formation of historical memory tell a more complex and revealing story about its relative merits than categorical moral axioms would suggest.

The contested and situated nature of historical interpretation indicates the rhetorical nature of history in general. History is a device for producing knowledge through artful interpretation—a way of knowing about the past not to be confused with past events themselves (de Certeau 1988, 4). History is a rhetorical form encompassing reciprocal acts of remembering and forgetting to the extent that it consists in a public, dialogic activity which enables different audiences to perceive temporal reality in contrasting, self-interested ways. Such a premise echoes Kathleen Turner's claim that "the rhetorical process [is] the central epistemic function by which societies constitute themselves" (1998, 6).

John W. Draper's *History of the Conflict Between Religion and Science* illustrates vividly the uses and disadvantages of historical forgetting when the public at large enthusiastically embraces it. Draper's text was the most widely read and influential work within a massive U.S. forgetting that took place during the nineteenth century. First published in 1876, *History of the Conflict* was the most successful text of a polemical nineteenth-century genre that chronicled the history of science and heralded its putative triumph over religion. "Probably no American writer in this tradition," Donald Fleming reports, "was more read in the nineteenth century, in more parts of the world—at home, across Europe, and even in Asia and Latin America" (1950, 140). *History of the Conflict* enjoyed over seventy printings in the United States and abroad, and was translated into dozens of languages throughout the world, thus achieving exceptional international popularity (Fleming 1950, 134; Russell 1991, 41).

Draper's text influentially helped to propagate the familiar flat earth/round earth narrative, which is a sterling illustration of the productivity, in Foucault's sense, of forgetting in public history and modern epistemology (Gould 1995, 44–48; Russell 1991, 38). Christopher Columbus never proved that the earth is round, despite the ubiquity of contemporary scholarly and schoolbook narratives that credit him with doing so; in truth, this copiously documented historical event never occurred (Russell 1991, 3–6, 29, and 35). Medieval scientists and theologians expressed little doubt concerning the spherical nature of the earth (Gould 1995, 42; Russell 1991, 60–70). Columbus never had to convince church officials, King Ferdinand, or Queen Isabella that his ships would not fall off the edge of a flat earth (Gould 1995, 42; Russell 1991, 1–11). In the words of Stephen Jay Gould, "There never was a period of 'flat earth darkness' among scholars" (1995, 42). This tale became both conventional wisdom and historical fact only in the nineteenth century, when science and religion engaged in pitched intellectual warfare. Nineteenth-century scientists and scientific historians inventively characterized the medieval period as an age of ignorance during which Europeans daftly assumed the earth was flat. Such scholars also championed Christopher Columbus as a pioneer who risked his life for science in order to prove the world was round.

This concerted campaign of forgetting produced a now-standard historical narrative that dramatizes epistemic ideals and intellectual values characteristic of modern secular culture.[1] Public historian Daniel Boorstin, in his popular book *The Discoverers,* writes of "a Europe-wide phenomenon of scholarly amnesia, which afflicted the continent from A.D. 300 to 1300," while "Christian faith and dogma suppressed the useful image of the world that had been so slowly, so painfully, and so scrupulously drawn by ancient geographers" (1991, 152). Despite copious evidence to the contrary, even contemporary intellectuals such as Boorstin not only take what Jeffrey

Burton Russell calls "the Flat Error" to be true but appeal to it as a basis for discriminating between better and worse forms of human inquiry and enlightened civilization (Russell 1991). To this extent, the project of forgetting initiated by nineteenth-century scientists and scientific historians remains influential to this day.

Draper's text admittedly was only one of many nineteenth-century discourses that railed against religion for its hindrance of scientific progress.[2] Other widely read treatises of the same period propagated "the Flat Error" as well.[3] But "*History of the Conflict* is of immense importance," Russell writes, "because it was the first instance that an influential figure had explicitly declared that science and religion were at war" (1991, 38). Draper was already an esteemed scientist and popular historian when he wrote this work; he held the public ear like no other advocate for the triumph of science over religion before him. The International Scientific Library series, for which Draper was invited to write *History of the Conflict,* was intended "to contain the best work of every important scientific thinker of the day in all countries" (Fleming 1950, 125). His volume was therefore a pivotal and highly public declaration by an especially esteemed thinker—a declaration that drastically intensified an epistemological crisis profoundly indicative of modern attitudes toward past and present, history and progress, religion and science. Draper's text, according to Russell, "succeeded as few books ever do. It fixed in the educated mind the idea that 'science' stood for freedom and progress against the superstition and repression of 'religion.' Its viewpoint became conventional wisdom" (1991, 38).

To study Draper's *History of the Conflict,* then, is to study the most potent rhetorical means by which a popularly embraced rhetoric of forgetting shaped and intensified the nineteenth-century war between science and religion. The following analysis argues that the artistic appeals in *History of the Conflict* created a form of historical epistemology and a corresponding framework of public judgment that invalidated earlier narratives of a compatible relationship between religion and science. In doing so, Draper's text fixed in the modern *episteme* an authoritative historical discourse that justified presumed incompatibilities between theological and empirical inquiry. Examining the mechanisms of forgetting at the heart of Draper's text is essential to understanding the rhetorical means by which science attained unsurpassed epistemological and cultural authority in Western society.[4]

The following analysis of Draper's text reveals an idiom of historical forgetting that has no use for the musty tropes and figures of oblivion, liquidation, or amnesia. Draper's rhetoric of historical forgetting does not ask the public to honor the usual intellectual, theological, or literary customs of relegating the past to oblivion without substantially changing broader perceptions of historical knowledge and cultural values. He instead implores his readers to adopt a comprehensively transformed understanding of customary historical narratives as well as the evolution of cultural and political identity they relate. One forgets, in the manner that Draper prescribes, not in order to negate discreet portions of the past without meaningfully changing its overall sense and value; one forgets, rather, in order to produce an entirely new and politically transformative understanding of history and its putative lessons—to begin again, so defined.

## Rhetoric, History, Forgetting

Conventional historiography both disavows and depends on its relationship to rhetoric and forgetting alike (or to be more precise, on forgetting as a rhetorical practice). Modern academic history is guided by a sometimes latent, sometimes overt logic of objectivity that strives to catalogue and interpret the events of the past. This conception of history is nonetheless a late nineteenth-century development (Rowse 1963, 63). Modern historiography since this time has labored to suppress its own rhetorical artifice, to obscure the fact that professional history consists in artful narratives, which traditionally were assumed to be integral features of communal history even in highly embellished forms. The notion that modern historiography documents the past as it was belies those acts of forgetting required to produce a persuasive and coherent narrative of former persons, times, and events.

Acknowledging the rhetorical component of modern historiography highlights the epistemic nature of rhetoric itself as a formative ingredient of historical wisdom. One should not confuse knowledge of the past with the past itself: the discursive content of professional history does not hermetically preserve the essence of the past so much as it produces epistemological frameworks that approximate the character of the past in the present.[5] The rhetoric of history, in other words, reflects contemporary epistemological predilections more overtly than it preserves the empirical substance of the past.

The rhetorical, or artfully constructed, dimensions of historical narrative are responsible for the degree of epistemological truth value that such narratives attain. In public debate, Robert Scott argues, we do not give voice to a preexisting truth; the interactive process of debate instead produces those discursive forms of knowledge that achieve the accepted ethos of truth. "Truth is not prior and immutable," Robert Scott explains, "but is contingent." (1967, 13). To the extent that "there is truth in human affairs, it is in time; it can be the result of a process of interaction at a given moment. Rhetoric may be viewed not as a matter of giving effectiveness to truth but of creating truth" (13).[6] Scott demonstrates that rhetoric is epistemic in nature insofar as it creates communally endorsed, conventionally expressed truths. Scott's account of rhetoric mirrors Dominick LaCapra's (1983) contention that the discipline of history consists not in mimetic reconstructions of the past but in contemporary interpretations of it. The dialogic interaction or interpretation that composes the historical record is, in this conception, patently rhetorical in nature.

Every historical interpretation, every discursive fabrication of history, enjoys its own historical character. The rhetorical production of history, involving practices of remembering and forgetting at once, reflects the social and political milieu in which it takes place. "While these discourses speak *of* history," de Certeau explains, "they are already situated *in* history" (1988, 20). The historical character of historical interpretation thus indicates that history is scripted in accord with discernible motivations shaped by existing human relations, that historical wisdom is never an end unto itself but rather a medium of collective decision-making in present-day public affairs. Discourse accepted as history, Ronald Carpenter comments, not only "shape[s] attitudes" but "actions" as well (1995, 1). History is, on this basis, a strategic endeavor tailored for persuasive effect in public deliberations (Benson 1972, 1).

Works of history betray their constitutive rhetorical artifice precisely, as in the case of late nineteenth-century professional history, when they deny the semblance of rhetorical artifice. The rhetorical character of public history, or historical memory, indicates that even apparently objective narratives claiming to preserve the authenticity of former times attain their epistemic veracity by arguing, in light of contemporary needs and interests, for what should be publicly remembered and why—or by the same token, for what should be publicly forgotten. The relationships among rhetoric, history, and forgetting described here are relevant, however, not simply in their more banal forms—in countless minor differences that characterize competing interpretations of the same past. The following sections demonstrate the commanding rhetorical means, vividly illustrated in Draper's polemic, with which nineteenth-century scientific historians persuaded the public to enthusiastically forget large dimensions of its past in order to transform the nature of modern epistemology and cultural values.

Rhetorical Origins of Modern History

It is difficult to overstate the significance of history to U.S. culture during the nineteenth century. Allan Megill and Donald McCloskey call the nineteenth century "the historical century par excellence (1987, 235). John Higham argues that "the historical movement of the nineteenth century was perhaps second only to the scientific revolution of the seventeenth century in transforming Western thought and shaping our modern mentality" (1965, ix–x). Across all disciplines, the nineteenth century was characterized by a faith in the progressive spirit. Enlightenment deists believed that the universe could be known through its intrinsic but impersonal design, which they likened to that of a finely tuned watch; nineteenth-century thinkers believed that human society improved with every sweep of the proverbial watch's hands.

History in the nineteenth century was redefined as the scientific observation of such ineluctable progress. Leopold von Ranke and Auguste Comte articulated influential conceptions of history that operated by virtue of a scientific method and documented the laws that determined the course of human events (Breisach 1983, 17). Ranke argued that history has "an inner connection all its own" (1956, 60), while Comte envisioned a positivist history that revealed this inner connection to be the steady momentum of human improvement (Breisach 1983, 17; Fleming 1950, 59). Charles Darwin's theory of evolution was equally influential to nineteenth-century historians, who reasoned that if nature improved in successive stages by natural selection, then society must likewise evolve over time (Breisach 1983, 17; Higham 1965, 94). Documenting the various stages of social improvement in a scientific manner became the task of "scientific history" (Ritter 1986, 397–401).

Scientific historians generally were not professional or "guilded" researchers but "amateur" scholars who used the enormously popular genre of historical literature to generate public support for their favored causes (Barnes 1963, 298; Higham 1965, 6). To this end, religion became an obvious target for scientific historians. The modern image of the medieval age as a seemingly endless night of theocratic darkness is largely the result of a fervent historical forgetting promoted by nineteenth-century scientific historians (Gould 1995, 42; Russell 1991, 69–77). If science represented the irreversible progress of Western civilization, then the story of such progress had to originate from a period of benightedness. Identifying this dark origin as a religious age served a strategic nineteenth-century purpose: it provided a foundation for the argument that theology should be toppled from its privileged position in Western culture and replaced with science, lest dark-ness reign again (Daniels 1972, vii; Higham 1965, 238). Ultimately, then, the image of medieval religious tyranny also served a nationalist aim of demonstrating the triumph of distinctly American ways of knowing over those of the Christian Old World (Breisach 1983, 14–15; Golinski 1998, 3). The rhetoric of historical forgetting was, to this extent, hugely productive in matters of intellectual, cultural, and even political identity.

Yet scientific historians were not atheists (Higham 1965, 245). Replac-ing theology with science did not amount to an empirical argument against God. They mined history in order to prove that scientific law, the hidden design of progress, was divine, and that theology relied on a false epistemol-ogy that erred wildly in seeking to apprehend such divine law (Knight 1986, 17). Only science could disclose God's blueprint—scientific truth—and render it comprehensible in human terms. Science, according to Draper, "has given us grander views of the universe, more awful views of God" (1897, 234).[7] The nineteenth-century "war" between religion and science (so coined by scientific historians) was a public battle of cultural values and intellectual methods—a clash between diametrically opposed epistemolo-gies and modes of historical judgment (Breisach 1983, 14). The popular appeal of these epistemic frameworks derived not from transparent histori-cal evidence but from the rhetoric of public forgetting that scientific histo-rians such as John W. Draper advocated.

## The Science and History of John W. Draper

Draper's life and work explains his motivations for so forcefully advocating a dramatic historical forgetting and illustrates, in the process, the rhetorical aims of scientific historians more generally. Draper (1811–82) conducted laboratory research during the first half of his career, teaching chemistry and physiology at New York University. His various accomplishments earned him high regard among leading U.S. scientists, particularly the fact that he was the first researcher to photograph a human face, the solar spectrum, and the moon (Reingold 1964, 252–53). He was the first president of the American Chemical Society and received honors from the American Academy of Arts and Sciences and the National Academy of Sciences (Fleming 1950, 138).

Draper was inspired, like many in his circle, by Comte's theory that history is an orderly phenomenon, driven forward by the machinery of scientific law and human progress (Fleming 1950, 58–59). And like other thinkers of his day, Draper was influenced by Darwin's theory of evolution, which raised many questions about natural history (Fleming 1950, 48). One of Draper's essays even served as pretext for a legendary debate on evolution between biologist T. H. Huxley and Bishop Wilberforce—an event remembered as the opening skirmish in the nominal war between religion and science (Brooke 1991, 34; Reingold 1964, 198–99).

Draper felt slighted by European scientists and turned to the practice of history during the second half of his career in order to document the allegedly superior achievements of American science and culture.[8] His most notable historical publications prior to *History of the Conflict* include *A History of the Intellectual Development of Europe* (1863)[9] and *History of the American Civil War* (1867), one of the first accounts of that conflict. By the time Draper was asked to write *History of the Conflict,* he had established himself as a popular and authoritative historian in addition to his existing reputation as one of the foremost U.S. scientists.

Draper regarded himself as a scientific historian and accordingly viewed history as a branch of natural science (Fleming 1950, 58). By documenting the history of science, Draper intended to demonstrate that the modernizing force of scientific progress led away from Europe and directly to the United States (Fleming 1950, 63). "Europe," Draper wrote, "furnishes us with the result of the influences of Roman Christianity in the promotion of civilization," whereas the United States, he contended, "furnishes us with an illustration of the influences of science" (1897, 286). Although Draper repeated these arguments in a number of works, they enjoyed their most elaborate treatment in his enormously successful *History of the Conflict.* Appreciating the significance of this text to modern secular culture requires an examination of the rhetorical appeals to historical forgetting that Draper employed in order to portray recent hostilities between religion and science as a foreordained historical event.

## Forgetting History

*History of the Conflict* is essentially a drama unified by a prophetic narrative that compels readers to view science as the guardian of knowledge and religion as its most baneful enemy. Draper's text is prophetic not in the literal sense of the term—not because he claims to enjoy a covenantal relationship with God. Steely optimism is the source of his inspiration. "In remolding or reformation lies the essential optimism of the prophetic judgment," James Darsey writes (1997, 27). Such optimism embodies the prophetic aspect of Draper's ethos, for he professes an ability to foretell the course of future events. John Clive claims the great nineteenth-century historians habitually "saw themselves as prophets as well as historians" and believed "that their role carried with it the obligation to say what they thought about society and politics of the present and the future as well as the past" (1989, 34). Based on his version of the past, Draper makes strident claims about what the historical conflict between religion and science means in the present, and more important, what it portends for the future. He petitions readers to cast aside the evil ways of religion—to quite simply forget them as respectable subjects of historical inquiry—in order to await the reformation of science. Draper's text therefore indicates a patently modern brand of historical prophecy (or prophetic history) in which the appeal of an authoritative ethos takes precedent over argumentative structure or content, in which fretful visions of future events justify one's forgetting of a more studied and less impassioned past. "At the center of prophetic rhetoric," Darsey submits, "is the prophetic *ethos*" (1997, 27). Draper's ethos is prophetic, then, not because he claims communion with God but because his scientific interpretation of history leads him to perceive its inner design, and so foretell the coming reign of science, however rooted that interpretation may be in a willed ignorance about the past.

Draper's shift from scientific research to a dramatic rendering of history was itself a rhetorical tactic. He felt "hungry for recognition," Fleming explains; a literary version of history would allow Draper to "get in touch with the unscholarly students at New York University and with the whole community of laymen who knew an emotion" if not scientific data (1950, 63). He sought "one of the great publishing houses" and desired "an extensive circulation" for his historical work (75). Draper's choice to write in the fashionable historical genre reflected a desire to reach popular audiences and to sway the public toward an appreciation not only of science but also of Draper himself. In order to achieve these ends, he advocated a radically transformed vision of history in which the content of the past as it had been remembered, in allegedly superstitious and misguided ways, would have to be forgotten.

Draper's preface to *History of the Conflict* makes clear that the text is a strategic use of what the author identifies as history, intended to mobilize support for science in the present. He justifies his study with an appeal to urgency, describing the conflict between religion and science as "the most important of all living issues" (1897, vii). He contends that every individual must take part in the momentous conflict between religion and science: "Can we exaggerate the importance of a contention in which every thoughtful person must take part whether he will or not? . . . The history of Science is not a mere record of isolated discoveries; it is a narrative of the conflict of two contending powers, the expansive force of the human intellect on one side, and the compression arising from traditionary faith and human interests on the other" (vi). The ostensible debate here is not academic: "every thoughtful person" must choose a side—must choose between science, "unstained by cruelties and crimes," and those agents of religion that "have been steeped in blood!" (xi). At stake is nothing less than "the human intellect" itself, which science ensures and religion represses. The nature of the conflict thus lies in the competition between two powerful epistemological traditions—one modern, the other ostensibly ancient. Draper's dramatic rendering of these competing traditions enjoins readers to conscientiously choose between science and religion, between knowledge and ignorance, between good and evil. The self-evidence of this choice obliges readers to enthusiastically forget the fuller complexity of the past in order to embrace an enlightened future.

Draper's work is not a transparent display of historical events but a polemic grounded in quintessentially nineteenth-century intellectual values (Brooke 1991, 36; Fleming 1950, 78). Given the horror of "the intellectual night which settled on Europe," the reader is prompted to affirm that "we live in the daybreak of better things" (Draper 1897, vii). By adopting Draper's scientific worldview, the reader adopts and reproduces the values of that *episteme*—values that place science over religion, America over Europe, the present over the past. Although Draper professed a love of scientific objectivity, his most successful work does not pretend to remain within the boundaries of the historical record. Rather, it enlists the public at large in a partisan crusade against the suppression of human knowledge, which science alone can properly safeguard.

The first few chapters of *History of the Conflict* reveal that, for Draper, there is little difference between the history of Western civilization and the history of the antagonism between religion and science. From the beginning, he reduces the history of religion and science to its slenderest threads. His historical narrative, such as it is, essentially catalogues scientific achievements created within ongoing skirmishes between scientists and theologians. Draper's composition, Fleming observes, is largely a "sorting out of heroes and villains, friends of science and enemies" (1950, 60).

*History of the Conflict* begins with the origins of Western science in ancient Greece. The first six chapters (half of the book) describe the history

of science as it is sometimes encouraged, sometimes repressed throughout early periods of Western civilization, including the Greek, Egyptian,
and Roman classical epochs, as well as the rise of Islam and the Byzantine
Empire. An odious religious power emerges in these chapters, embodied
by the pope, which will cast darkness over knowledge in Europe for centuries.[10] These founding gestures of Draper's discourse suggest the complex,
though often unacknowledged, significance of forgetting as both a catalyst
and an outcome of modern historiography. Draper frames his text as an
effort to correct the historical record by exposing an originally stultifying
repression (or forgetting) of ancient learning. In doing so, he provides an
argumentative ground for eagerly forgetting religion itself as a worthy object
of historical remembrance.

Draper's organizing principle changes halfway through his text. He
continues to chart the major periods of Western history in a more or less
chronological manner but frequently interrupts his chronology with long
descriptions of scientific inventions or processes and random meditations
on the abstract nature of science and religion in general. Draper's prophetic
optimism drowns out any logic of organization when he arrives at the role
of science in the nineteenth century. His descriptions of the "practical appli-
cations" that science has contributed to the overwhelming improvement of
humanity are too protracted to quote here; suffice it to say that Draper
lingers over all that science lends to "the triumphs of the arts of peace—the
industrial exhibitions and the world's fairs" and claims that science "in Russia has emancipated a vast serf-population," while "in America it has given
freedom to four million negro slaves" (1897, 323). Draper completes his
protracted celebration of modern scientific enlightenment and liberation
with a pointed summary: "We have been comparing the spiritual with the
practical, the imaginary with the real. The maxims that have been followed
in the earlier and the later period produced their inevitable result. In the
former that maxim was, 'Ignorance is the mother of Devotion'; in the latter, 'Knowledge is Power'" (326). Draper employs the voice of a modern
secular prophet in reminding his readers that the conflict between science
and religion represents an epochal epistemological battle, a crusade against
religious ignorance on behalf of scientific might.

Draper's final passages offer a prophetic warning meant to hasten his
readers conclusively toward such ends. "No one who is acquainted with
the present tone of thought in Christendom," he cautions, "can hide from
himself the fact that an intellectual, a religious crisis is impending. In all
directions we see the lowering skies, we hear the mutterings of the coming

storm" (327). Although the reign of science has been foretold, Draper counsels his readers, theologians who protect their power by keeping others enslaved to ignorance still desire "a revolt against modern civilization, an intention of destroying it, no matter at what social cost. To submit to them without resistance, men must be slaves indeed!" (367). Readers must join this battle on behalf of science in order to preserve "absolute freedom for thought" (367). Draper declares, with the prescience and conviction of a prophet, that "the time approaches when men must take their choice between quiescent, immobile faith and ever-advancing Science . . . which is incessantly scattering its material blessings in the pathway of life, elevating the lot of man in this world, and unifying the human race" (364). Only by swearing allegiance to science, he implies, will the battle with religion come to its just and prophesied end. Only by forgetting the past as it once was will humanity achieve enlightenment as it should be.

The rhetorical potency of *History of the Conflict* lies in its depiction of fundamental asymmetries between science and religion as bases of sound historical and epistemological judgment. Draper's polemic establishes distinctly nineteenth-century definitions of science and religion that, by the terms of his discourse, veritably require a public judgment in favor of scientific authority. "Science," he writes, "has never been an aggressor. She has always acted on the defensive, and left to her antagonist the making of wanton attacks" (325). Draper conversely offers up chilling metonymies for institutional faith, including the horrors of the Inquisition or a withering body resembling "one of those friar-corpses which we still see in their brown cowls in the vaults of the Cappuccini, with a breviary or some withered flowers in its hands" (260). Traditional associations of death with forgetting operate subtly but persuasively here: corpses should be buried, their deathliness covered over and forgotten, lest the corrosions that consume them affect the living. Hence, the fearsome call of a modern secular prophet replaces exhaustive documentation as the source of Draper's historical authority.[11] Draper achieves persuasiveness as an advocate of historical forgetting through an artful (and not empirically refutable) revision of the past. Such paradoxical historiography reaches its persuasive apogee in Draper's apocryphal account of medieval belief in a flat earth.

## Forgetting the Round Earth

On first inspection, one might be tempted simply to debunk Draper's flat earth narrative—to uncover his misuse of evidence, indict his work as mere rhetorical artifice, and dismiss it out of hand. Professional historians have often distinguished their craft by claiming that sound historiography relies upon hard facts, while rhetoric is at best ornamentation and at worst deception. Attending closely, however, to the richly suggestive example of Draper's flat earth narrative demonstrates the productivity of forgetting, in Foucault's sense. Draper's narrative proves that rhetorical techniques of forgetting, contrary to conventional wisdom, are formative ingredients of those public narratives that attain the authority of unquestioned historical fact.

Draper's polemics offer a version of history that would seem quite foreign to contemporary professional historians, primarily because of its inventive and strategic use of evidence and artistry. An overwhelming amount of historical evidence proves that Europeans never lost Greek astronomical knowledge of a spherical globe; that medieval culture never professed a heedless belief in a flat earth; and that Columbus's journey across the Atlantic was never forestalled because of fears that he would sail over the edge of the earth (Gould 1995; Russell 1991). How, then, could Draper preserve the ethos of a historian and argue to the contrary?

History in the nineteenth century, as previously indicated, was not expected to be a strictly empirical form of knowledge. Washington Irving's fictional works *History of New York* (1809) and *The Life and Voyages of Christopher Columbus* (1837) were precursors to the distinctly American history of Europe that emerged in the later nineteenth century (a genre that includes *History of the Conflict* as one of its landmark texts) (Gooch 1952, 383; Higham 1965, 238).[12] Lowenthal reports that recent historiography represents a deviation from long-standing traditions of historical recollection in which "style and language mattered more than fidelity to historical facts" and "history was read less for what it said about the past than for how it was said" (1985, 225). Draper's readers would have welcomed a gripping narrative in favor of meticulous documentation. Modern academic history largely originated, as a rhetorical practice, in wholesale revisions of the past designed to produce compelling narratives rather than in meticulous efforts to document or preserve it objectively. Even in the nineteenth century, Lowenthal adds, "the historical novel not only made history vivid; it was held a more trustworthy guide to the past" (225). The dramatic energy of *History of the Conflict,* consistent with these conventions, renders any appeal to documentation unnecessary, if not unwise. Its domineering prophetic ethos dictates that readers' only criteria for judgment should be the harrowing image of religion and the emancipatory portrait of science that the text itself inscribes.

The chronology of the flat earth myth enjoys an ethos all its own in *History of the Conflict*. Draper assigns this supposed controversy a crucial role in the development of Western civilization, asserting that it comprises a "great philosophical problem" in the history of science. The belief that "the earth is an extended level surface," he writes, was "the belief of all nations in all parts of the world in the beginning of their civilization" (1897, 152–53). Recall here that Draper's version of history was one in which immutable scientific laws generated human progress with each passing age. The narrative of medieval belief in a flat earth dramatizes the universal ignorance of premodern society and demonstrates the uninterrupted march of scientific progress since that time.

Draper's dramatic rendering of such ineluctable progress simultaneously personifies the villainy of religion. "On the basis of this view of the structure of the world," Draper writes, "great religious systems have been founded, and hence powerful material interests have been engaged in its support" (153). The errors of religion were not only ludicrous, and indefensibly so, but agents of the church "have resisted, sometimes by resorting to bloodshed, attempts that have been made to corrupt its incontestable errors" (153). The development of Draper's discourse here highlights, once again, the complex significance of forgetting as a catalyst for allegedly comprehensive historical knowledge: episodes in religious history revealing the suppression (or original forgetting) of scientific wisdom are of such negative value to human progress that contemporary readers should renounce them as aspects of their cultural inheritance.

Draper emphasizes that the controversy concerning the true nature of the earth was a momentous epistemological conflict. "The authority of the Fathers," he writes, "and the prevailing belief that the Scriptures contain the sum of all knowledge, discouraged any investigation of Nature" (157). Draper claims that "no one did more than [Augustine] to bring science and religion into antagonism" by diverting "the Bible from its true office—a guide to purity of life" and placing it "in the perilous position of being the arbiter of human knowledge, an audacious tyranny over the mind of man" (62). Ignorance reigned for centuries, Draper declares, because the church insisted upon an unscientific source of all knowledge. He offers his readers another epistemology in order to end this putative reign of ignorance once and for all—a scientific way of comprehending both human history and the transcendent design behind all natural phenomena that it reveals.

Draper concedes that there were ancient scientists who relied upon the Bible as a scientific authority. The medieval church invoked the ethos of these scholars, he contends, in order to enforce the alleged European belief in a flat earth. Draper cites Lactantius (c. 265–345), a professional rhetorician who converted to Christianity and authored several Christian apologia and theological expositions (Russell 1991, 32). Lactantius is remembered for his infamous rhetorical question concerning the shape of the earth: "Is it possible," he asked, "that men can be so absurd as to believe that the crops and the trees on the other side of the earth hang downward, and that men have their feet higher than their heads?" (Draper 1897, 64).[13] Draper also cites Cosmas Indicopleustes (c. 540), whose *Christian Topography* was, according to Draper, intended "to confute the heretical opinion of the globular form of the earth" (1897, 65).[14] "For more than a thousand years," Draper declares, "such was the accepted logic, and all over Europe propositions equally absurd were accepted on equally ridiculous proof" (66). "So great was the preference given to sacred over profane learning," he submits, that by the sixteenth century "Christianity had been in existence fifteen hundred years, and had not produced a single astronomer" (157–58). A crucial irony is at work here: the rhetorical force of revelation with which Draper presents his narrative of events obscures the fact that it represents a willful forgetting of the past as it was, as one could find it in the historical record. In rhetorical terms, revelation here is a form of obscurity and forgetting is a form of memory.

Draper claims that Christopher Columbus was the first in over a thousand years to pierce the darkness of European ignorance regarding the shape of the earth (a claim reproduced in today's schoolbook wisdom about the discovery of America). Columbus, not scientists, finally proved the roundness of the earth. "The inciting motives" of the scientific reawakening, Draper tells us, came not from the stunted scientific inquiry of the time but from "commercial rivalries," from the twinned spirits of enterprise and exploration (159). "The circular visible horizon and its dip at sea, the gradual appearance and disappearance of ships in the offing," he explains, "cannot fail to incline intelligent sailors to a belief in the globular figure of the earth" (160). Draper supplies a now-familiar narrative of Columbus's plan to find a faster passage to the Eastern spice trade because of the roundness of the earth, a plan whose "irreligious tendency was pointed out by the Spanish ecclesiastics, and condemned by the Council of Salamanca" (160–61). He declares, however, that Columbus gained sponsorship for his voyage in spite of such resistance and dared to sail on August 3, 1492. Columbus's eventual arrival in the so-called New World meant that "the controversy had now suddenly come to an end—the Church was found to be in error" (294).

With this portrayal of Columbus's adventure, Draper exposes the religious duplicity in a way that links the renaissance of scientific progress with "the discovery of America" (294). His depiction of Columbus's voyage dramatizes the lengths to which the church would go in order to safeguard its fatuous claims to knowledge and demonstrates that the currents of scientific progress lead away from the shores of Europe to those of the New World.

Draper's story of medieval belief in a flat earth is commonly accepted as unquestioned fact, but there is virtually no evidence to support it. Medieval theologians, Edward Grant writes, generally "did not allow their theology to hinder or obstruct inquiry into the structure and operation of the physical world. . . . Biblical texts were not employed to 'demonstrate' scientific truths by blind appeal to divine authority" (1986, 69). "During the Middle Ages," Russell adds, "Christian theology showed little if any tendency to dispute sphericity. . . . Among the uneducated a variety of vague ideas seem to have been common, but among the educated always existed a consensus that the earth was spherical" (1991, 69). The writings of Lactantius and Cosmas Indicopleustes were not representative of medieval wisdom regarding the shape of the earth but wild deviations from scholarly consensus. Lactantius's works were "condemned as heretical after his death," which meant that his writings were "not widely heeded" (33). Cosmas's influence on medieval learning "was virtually nil": "The *first* translation of Cosmas [from Greek] into Latin, his very first introduction into Western Europe, was not until 1706," and for this reason Cosmas "had absolutely no influence on medieval western thought" (35).

A plethora of texts spanning the course of medieval history contradict Draper's account. The following is only a sample of Russell's dense list of medieval intellectual authorities who unambiguously attested to the spherical nature of the earth: Isidore of Seville (d. 636), "the most widely read encyclopedist of the early Middle Ages . . . believed that the earth was round"; Thomas Aquinas (1225–1274) "also affirmed sphericity"; Roger Bacon (1220–1292) "affirmed the roundness of the earth using classical traditional arguments"; and "the greatest scientists of the later Middle Ages, Jean Buridan (c. 1300–1358) and Nicole Oresme (c. 1320–1382), even discussed the rotation of the earthly sphere" (1991, 15–19). Clearly then, "educated medieval opinion was virtually unanimous that the earth was round" (Russell 1991, 70).

The historical record also contradicts Draper's claim that Columbus proved that the earth is round. In Columbus's day, "astronomers, geographers, philosophers, and theologians, far from disputing the Earth's spherical composition, wrote sophisticated treatises based on Aristotle and the 'Geography' of Ptolemy of Alexandria" (Russell 1991, 13). Church officials contested Columbus's plan on several counts, but none of their objections concerned the shape of the earth. Instead, his "opponents, citing the traditional measurements of the globe according to Ptolemy, argued that the circumference of the earth was too great and the distance too far to allow a successful western passage" (8). Columbus met great resistance on the subject of these measurements, not those of the shape of the earth. He finally gained approval for his voyage by misrepresenting nautical distances, estimating "the voyage at about 20 percent its actual length" (10). Proving either the flatness or roundness of the earth was never at stake for Columbus.

*History of the Conflict,* therefore, most prominently illustrates not the transparent recital of preexisting historical fact but artful narrative practices that fashion the semblance of such fact. To this extent, the text illustrates impressively the formative influences of willed forgetting on authoritative historical memory. "Fallacies or myths of this nature take on a life of their own," Russell aptly comments, "creating a dialectic with each other and eventually making a 'cycle of myths' reinforcing one another" (1991, 76).[15] The dialectic of such a cycle explains the repetition of the flat earth narrative in countless textbooks, as well as Daniel Boorstin's invocation of the same myth—a tale that Boorstin presents as historical fact while failing, like Draper, to document any of the copious medieval sources that would disprove it.

Draper's omission of historical evidence that might refute his narrative and emphasis of outlying texts that support his version of events is not an arbitrary mishap easily dismissed as scholarly irresponsibility. His reliance on ethos over evidence creates a prophetically persuasive worldview, the fierce conviction of which supplies its own emotional proof and therefore needs no external evidence. This observation confirms Darsey's claim that "whatever the motives of the prophet, his value lies in his reception, the quality of the *ethos* presented to his auditors [or readers]" (1997, 33).[16] Megill and McCloskey add that nineteenth-century historians modeled their writing on "nineteenth-century novelists," who "strove to create an impression of omniscience, of continuity, of unbroken flow. The 'voice' of professional historians has traditionally been a variant of this novelistic voice" (1987, 226). Marked as it is by these prophetic and novelistic precedents, Draper's text constitutes not so much a narration of events but the construction of an ethos; his prophetic style "exerts pressure to produce a whole and continuous story, sustaining the impression of omniscience, leaping over evidential voids" (Megill and McCloskey 1987, 226). "The prophetic *ethos*," Darsey comments, "becomes its own rhetoric" (1997, 34). *History of the Conflict* illustrates how formal histories incorporate vastly different epistemic elements into an ostensibly coherent and unified ethos through the work of strategic "forgettings," as de Certeau would have it. The prophetic character of Draper's history confirms that such epistemic formations attain self-evidence and transparency—attain the status of *history*, in other words—by virtue of their persuasiveness or utility in response to contemporary questions of political or moral judgment, and not simply because of their conformity to evidence.

## Conclusion

Draper argues for and depicts in *History of the Conflict* a comprehensive revision of the historical record. His contributions to early professional historiography are, in this respect, obviously propagandistic. Draper aspires to not simply redact or rewrite history but to institute a new, rigid, and distinctively modern set of public values in place of the inherited wisdom he so profoundly alters. His most effective persuasive techniques acquire their historical credibility not on the basis of empirical evidence but because of the artfully authoritative ethos that suffuses his work. At first glance, these features might lead some observers to conclude that Draper's historical propaganda and that of modern totalitarian institutions are roughly equivalent exercises in collective forgetting, different in degree rather than kind. Closer inspection, however, discounts this conclusion and suggests broader insights regarding crucial differences among varieties of historical forgetting and the forms of public judgment they commend.

Draper exercised his degree of influence over public understandings of history without enjoying undue political influence, without suppressing or destroying official records, and without the threat of state violence. In totalitarian societies, it is often difficult to separate the semblance, if not the reality, of public enthusiasm for state propaganda and historical revisionism from such repressive measures. But Draper's enthusiastic reading public enjoyed ready access to historical records that easily would have invalidated his account. By endorsing his text with wildly successful sales, moreover, the lay public merely followed the example of Draper's approving scholarly colleagues. In sum, his manipulation of the historical record was wholly transparent. *History of the Conflict* represents a case of public forgetting in which both intellectuals and the public at large embraced, for better or worse, a radical transformation in historical memory based entirely on free will and a belief in the intellectual and cultural goods that would follow from it.

The preceding analysis of Draper's *History of the Conflict* proves the more general claim that acts of public forgetting are not simply repressive in nature. Literal collective oblivion or amnesia is not their *telos*. Such forgetting is highly productive in matters of historical memory and factual authority, regardless of whether or not we endorse the particular memories and facts it produces. The intellectual ideals and cultural values expressed in *History of the Conflict* are highly compatible with those of the current era. Draper's putative historical revelations and moral pronouncements remain (albeit in less hyperbolic form) the stuff of conventional wisdom regarding European and U.S. history, religious dogmatism, and the enlightening (indeed, liberating) powers of modern science. Common threads of optimism run through Draper's time and our own: a faith in progress, a spirit of ingenuity, and above all, an unwavering belief in the power of science. Such optimism justifies divisions characteristic of modern Western culture—between the sacred and the profane, between spirituality and empiricism, between religion and science. In rhetorical terms, Draper provides both a rationale and a public idiom for adopting forgetting as a commendable (albeit counterintuitive) epistemic device with which readers may comprehend the essence and entirety of Western history.

Draper was neither the first nor the last to prophesy the reign of science and to disseminate "the Flat Error." He was, however, "the great popularizer" of such ideas, for *History of the Conflict* was the most popular book of its kind (Fleming 1950, 1). Draper's argument became fixed in the minds of academic and popular readers alike well into the twentieth century (Fleming 1950, 135; Lindberg 1986, 20). Studying the rhetorical dynamics of *History of the Conflict,* and the appeals to forgetting that distinguish them, therefore amounts to studying the boldest discursive patterns of a historic transformation in the nature of modern intellectual authority and cultural values.

The arguments in *History of the Conflict* are not matters of abstract intellectual opinion. To the contrary, Draper was responding to an ostensibly urgent crisis of *episteme* in the nineteenth century. He designed his polemic to enlist readers in a moral and epistemological war and motivate them to take action on behalf of science. Close textual analysis of *History of the Conflict* reveals how emerging public epistemologies in the late nineteenth century established an opposition between religion and science deeply characteristic of modern U.S. culture. Such analysis also reveals that these seemingly unquestionable oppositions, which remain so characteristic of modern secular values and historical memory writ large, were produced by artful appeals to historical forgetting.

Yet the prophetic nature of Draper's rhetoric indicates that his particular appeal for public forgetting paradoxically reproduces, rather than abolishes, the alleged intellectual errors of the past. *History of the Conflict* argues vigorously that religion is founded upon a specious criterion of proof. Religion, Draper claims, has no basis as a source of knowledge. Hence he labors to create a way of knowing diametrically opposed to it. To this end, Draper castigates theological belief, based solely on the signature criteria of modern scientific inquiry. Science in his narrative becomes the singular arbiter of all knowledge, especially religious insight.[17]

But the logic of Draper's argument reflects a telling irony: his discourse on the virtues of science constitutes a faith not in the scientific method or reproducible results but in the essence of science itself, a faith in the intrinsic divinity of scientific law. Draper's unwavering faith in the essential goodness of science creates a religion out of science itself, despite his stated intention to identify moral and intellectual incompatibilities between faith and empiricism. In this sense, Draper commits the very epistemological crime for which he indicts religion. Nietzsche skewers the historical culture of nineteenth-century Germany, a close cousin to that of scientific historians, for this very reason: "What, are there no longer any living mythologies?" he mocks. "What, are the religions dying out? Just behold the religion of the power of history, regard the priests of the power of the idea and their battered knees!" (1997, 105). Draper's elaborate appeals for historical forgetting produce remarkably complicated results: he attempts to establish a new sense of public time and history, a new present and future, in which empirical fact eradicates theological belief; yet his rhetoric of historical forgetting establishes new versions of the reputed intellectual prejudices he rails against. The novel history he labors to inaugurate contains a dubious remainder of the one he seeks to terminate—a new "religion of the power of [scientific] history," as Nietzsche might say.

Draper's text is a dramatic and decisive means of publicly forgetting and beginning again, but a conceptually flawed one for all that. His rhetoric of historical forgetting, despite its considerable productivity, offers a relatively weak mode of judgment by the standards that Nietzsche sets. Nietzsche's doctrine of critical history presupposes a transvaluation of all values, including those commemorated and expressed in customary forms of history, from the monumental to the antiquarian. Simply expunging a large dimension of the past from historical recollection while nevertheless duplicating the faulty values that allegedly defined it (in Draper's case, mistaking a form of faith for empirical certitude) represents something other than the soberly critical justice Nietzsche advocates when he asserts that an unjust remainder of the past "deserves to perish" (76). Draper's rhetoric of forgetting fails, by this criterion, to heed Nietzsche's admonition that forgetting in the sense of termination (as the standard tropes and figures of the *ars oblivionis* would have it) may seem appealing in light of a dogmatic past, but it overlooks the fact that vast portions of the history we would deny have somehow contributed to who we are in the present. To boldly negate the past as such would be to negate defining parts of ourselves. From this vantage, Draper's nominally professional historiography, and the rhetoric of forgetting that permeates it, appears ironically naive; it supposes that one can adopt a truly enlightened understanding of one's own history (or at least crucial parts of it) by seeking to transcend that history altogether.

Draper's rhetoric of historical forgetting therefore occupies an ambiguous middle ground: his comprehensive manipulation of the historical record is not equivalent to totalitarian historical revisionism; but neither does it facilitate the sort of strong historical criticism and judgment that Nietzsche envisions. This insight suggests a more general principle useful for evaluating other efforts at public forgetting: one must measure the value and utility of such forgetting to public affairs not simply in terms of its sheer productivity but according to the prospects for informed critical judgment that it encourages. Draper's rhetoric of forgetting is, by this measure, enormously productive but unable to produce a robust framework of public judgment.

Draper's faith in science explains much about the historical forgetting he advocates; but another act of faith is equally germane to this study. The public may act on a measure of faith by accepting popular works of history as authoritative. Formal histories attain the status of unquestioned historical memory when their spokespersons persuade the public into recognizing their scholarly efforts as perpetually relevant to present-day affairs. History is important, according to Roger Wilkins, because "we argue a lot about who we are on the basis of who we think we have been, and we derive much of our sense of the future from how we think we've done in the past" (1995, 410). Such a universally uncontested view of history emphasizes belief, not fact, which suggests that history has more than one function beyond simply getting the facts right. History, in Higham's phrasing, "lend[s] itself to all the cross-purposes of life" (1965, xi). Rhetorical techniques allow formal works of history to speak to these "cross-purposes" without *a priori* facilitating the manipulative jettison of historical truth. Every history implicitly or explicitly argues that the public should remember some elements of the past and forget others, all the while supplying a ready idiom with which it may do so. Every history thus labors to create its own epistemology—its own truth. The relative value of that epistemology lies not only in its conceptual or evidentiary coherence but also in the integrity of the political and moral judgments that its signature rhetorical appeals produce—including those which implore the public to forget the history it has always known.

CULTURAL FORGETTING:
THE "TIMELESS NOW" OF NOMADIC MEMORIES

When the shadow of the sash appeared on the curtains it was between seven and eight oclock and then I was in time again, hearing the watch. It was Grandfather's and when Father gave it to me he said I give you the mausoleum of all hope and desire; it's rather excruciating-ly apt that you will use it to gain the reducto absurdum of all human experience which can fit your individual needs no better than it fitted his or his father's. I give it to you not that you may remember time, but that you might forget it now and then for a moment and not spend all your breath trying to conquer it.
—WILLIAM FAULKNER, *The Sound and the Fury*

Thus begins Quentin Compson's existential sojourn in William Faulkner's *The Sound and the Fury,* a literary masterpiece whose true subject, more than any character, may be the poignant influence of memory on the experiences of its several narrators. Faulkner's plot is comprised of four sections, each with a different narrator relating the events of four different days. The echoes of the past suffuse the various narratives, as if the nature and meaning of the present only coalesced out of memory's reverberations. Quentin cannot hear the ticking of his grandfather's watch without remembering the words his father spoke upon giving the heirloom to his son. He recalls his father's lugubrious commentary on the significance of time to one's mortality whenever he touches or thinks of this small but momentous memento, "the mausoleum of all hope and desire." With this gift, Quentin's father lends prophetic meaning to his son's entire life, resounding endlessly in Quentin's consciousness and distressing his every passing moment with their gravity. Quentin remains acutely aware of the watch's unstoppable progression, which transforms his days into "the reducto absurdum of all human experience": the knowledge that time is finite and therefore futile, that even the most carefully measured life will culminate in a timeless end. Despite constant efforts, Quentin never honors his father's admonition, which was not to "remember time" by carrying the timepiece but to "forget it now and then for a moment and not spend all your breath trying to conquer it." For Quentin, attempting to forget time only reminds him of its inevitable consequence, even as he tries to repress his awareness of its passage. Such repression merely stimulates memory anew while renewing its potency. Quentin wanders in and out of past and present according to the repeated interplay of time forgotten and the rush of memory this forgetting provokes.

The senses of time, memory, and forgetting explored in *The Sound and the Fury* are not overtly public. They are, in fact, intensely personal and even resistant to public expression. Yet a "fictional technique," Jean-Paul Sartre wrote in an essay on *The Sound and the Fury*, "always relates back to the novelist's metaphysics" (1955, 79). Faulkner's work offers no explicit meditation on *public* memory, but it nevertheless dramatizes what Sartre called "a metaphysics of time" (79)—a system of values and ideals concerning the interrelated meaning of past, present, and future—which allows one to reconsider common assumptions underlying modern ideals of public memory, particularly those concerning its alleged antipathy with forgetting.

*Repetition* offers the most provocative organizing principle of such metaphysics. Olga W. Vickery observes that, although they "appear quite unrelated," the discrete sections of *The Sound and the Fury* "repeat certain incidents and are concerned with the same problem" (1964, 29), namely, the plight of Caddy, the oldest Compson sibling. "Thus," Vickery elaborates, "with respect to the plot the four sections are inextricably connected, but with respect to the central situation they are distinct and self-sufficient. As related to the central focus, each of the first three sections presents a version of the same facts which is at once the truth and a complete distortion of the truth" (29). Vickery's account suggests that distortions intrinsic to repeated acts of recollection shape the complex truth of memories as much as any original or authentic perception. In this context, according to Cleanth Brooks, "the sense of enlightenment" that the novel produces "comes simply from the fact that we are traversing the same territory in circling movements" (1963, 326). The novel's repetition of frequently cryptic and disjointed recollections, or "circling movements," paradoxically induces a sense of lucidity and linearity, a kind of "enlightenment."

These observations suggest a host of conceptual questions: What is being repeated here? Does such repetition preserve the authentic truth or meaning of past events, or merely the value and pathos coincidentally associated with it? Is the defining function of memory to preserve a truth when that truth may be engendered only by its "distortion," by discursive mutations inherent in every attempt to narrate the past? To what extent are the apparent lucidity, linearity, and perdurance of memory related to the inevitably incoherent, fragmentary, or ephemeral nature of recollection? To what extent, moreover, does memory depend upon forgetting, or a repeated inducement of amnesia such as that which Quentin's father prescribes for his son? And in what manner does further meditation on the centrality of repetition to memory warrant closer inspection of the privileged ideals of public memory, including the objectivity of the past, its conformity with historical representation, and the ability to express memory in normative or canonical forms? To raise such questions is to ask about the degree to which forgetting, in its various manifestations, represents a formative dimension of entire cultures of memory.

This chapter addresses such issues by exploring the apparently vast difference between conventional Western ideals of public commemoration and a form of communal memory distinguished by complex proclivities for repetition (as defined with reference to Faulkner's novel). The analysis turns from Faulkner's temporal metaphysics to a set of cultural practices that exemplify such metaphysics, and the modes of repetition intrinsic to it, in the idiomatic or symbolic formation of communal memory. The discussion draws, more specifically, from a variety of studies focusing on Eastern European Gypsies in order to delineate the defining features of their communal memory, which one might also describe as a form of self-conscious communal forgetting. Gypsies' embrace of memory *work* (or the ritualized revision and reinventisi of memory) exemplifies their characteristically unorthodox proclivities for repeating—and thus reinventing—their own memorial practices. Repetition, so defined, reveals the pervasive work of communal forgetting in producing cultural forms of memory and the material practices that perpetuate them. Gypsy folklore appears to exhibit a sense of time, memory, and community dramatically different from modern Western forms of public commemoration. For the Gypsies, forgetting often represents an advantageous, albeit atypical, form of preservation. The rhetorical practices that most vividly illustrate Gypsy ideals of communal memory (or more accurately, forgetting) therefore suggest an unusually revealing alternative to both traditional and contemporary Western cultures of memory, which characteristically cultivate abiding fidelity to the past, often with great earnestness and expenditure.

In this respect, the present chapter furthers the overall aims of this book by examining idioms and ideals of organized forgetting that contradict conventional Western tropes and figures coined in order to lament the evils of forgetting in communal life. The conviction that persecuted peoples may counteract evils done to them by bearing witness for the sake of future generations, and that those generations are sworn to remember such testimony in turn, has been embraced by moderns and ancients alike as a justification for opposing the forces of forgetting. But Gypsies often respond to their own long-standing persecutions by contravening this very imperative, choosing to defiantly forget the injustices they have suffered. Forgetting, in Gypsy folklore, is not attributable to isolated and dreaded instances of oblivion, liquidation, amnesia, and the like; it constitutes one of the primary formative principles of Gypsy heritage in general. As such, Gypsy communal forgetting suggests an ethic of communal nonrecollection that produces not merely formal artifacts of public history but an entire cultural identity and the informal yet no less consequential practices that sustain it. By this measure, Gypsy proclivities for forgetting reflect not merely unorthodox commemorative tropes and figures but an equally unorthodox mode of communal judgment—one in which the community is deemed pragmatically wiser and freer for leaving much of its own past behind in order to begin again.

This is not to conclude, however, that Gypsy practices of memory (or forgetting) *a priori* constitute a conceptual or practical antithesis to those of Western communities. The final argument of this chapter is that examining Gypsy folklore provides grounds for recognizing how recurrent patterns of forgetting help to produce iconic and seemingly static commemorative forms—even those expressly dedicated to combating communal forgetfulness. In doing so, the analysis concludes that public memories in general function *nomadically*. The nomadic character of communal memory is analogous to the often extraordinary capacity for adaptation characteristic of individual memory. We wander, like Quentin Compson, in the landscape of memory. We may remember the same events over and over again, but we remember according to fluctuating conditions, in different times and places, in response to changing needs and desires. Acts of recollection invariably transform the nature of memory because the changing incitements and purposes of recollection ensure that we remember in different ways, even if we remember the same event.

This principle implies a natural connection to the often quiet but no less consequential work of forgetting in various cultures of memory. Communal or public memory is nomadic insofar as it encompasses a landscape of recollection shaped not by stability but by ongoing redistribution—or *re*membering—in which forgetting is an unavoidable and oftentimes productive catalyst.

The ensuing analysis probes the deep intimacy of memory and forgetting by examining both the rhetorical practices of communal *re*membering that transpire in forgetting and the modes of forgetfulness that help to produce apparently constant and uniform symbols of public memory.

## The Permanent Present

Public memory scholars have long recognized the fundamental relationship between place, historical memory, and communal heritage. Western ideals of remembrance presume that the stability of communal tradition depends, in large part, upon the preservation of historically significant places in which those traditions first began. Gypsy collective memories, however, evince markedly different notions of place, history, and heritage. Some scholars believe that the Gypsies became itinerant not by choice but because they were repeatedly driven away from whatever land they came to occupy (Fonseca 1995, 178). This trend continues today in the volatile topography of postcommunist Eastern Europe (Crowe and Koltsi 1992). The ethnic and geographic origins of the Gypsies remain unproven because of their perpetually displaced status (despite compelling evidence tying them to northern India) (Fonseca 1995, 83–112; Fraser 1992, 10–22; Liegeois 1986, 34–38). This fact raises the question of how one might preserve and profess the distinctive character of one's people without recourse to a transparent civic origin, to a common locus of memory.

It also raises the more comprehensive question of how such a people would value (or not) the very idea of organized remembrance rooted in a synthesis of place, history, and community. "Origin" is an especially appropriate term for this synthesis. Conventional wisdom holds that the apparent unity of communal recollection reflects the authority of an unmediated historical origin, which ostensibly regulates the nature and scope of collective memory in its historical unfolding. Cultural reproduction so conceived exemplifies the Platonic logic of an ideal model approximated by a lineage of diminished copies, for what is repeated is always the same: the ideal and original form that transcends the mottle of every repetition and retains its essence in doing so. Repetition, in Gilles Deleuze's words, occurs "in relation to something unique or singular which has no equal or equivalent. This is the apparent paradox of festivals: they repeat an 'unrepeatable.' They do not add a second and a third time to the first, but carry the first time to the 'nth' power" (1994, 1). The festival commemorates an origin through ceremonial repetition, and thereby preserves its sense and value; the origin, which cannot be repeated but merely symbolized in memory, transcends the very ritual, or repetition, that renews its institutional power and dominion.

Despite whatever conflicting testimony they might provide, the Gypsies lack the unity of memory, place, and community that would legitimate such a repetition, and thus preservation, of their culture. This observation does not mean that specific places are unimportant to Gypsies as loci of memory. But Gypsy folklore is marked by the conspicuous absence of a distinct common origin from which they emerged and to which they may ritually return as a source of wisdom or solidarity. In Angus Fraser's estimation, "If a people is a group of men, women and children with a common language, a common culture and a common racial type, who can be readily distinguished from their neighbors, it is a long time since the Gypsies were that" (1992, 1).

The Gypsies' lack of an objective ethnic origin likely explains the instability of myth as an organizing principle of their culture. "Gypsies have no myths about the beginning of the world," Isabel Fonseca explains, "or about their own origins; they have no sense of a great historical past. Very often their memories do not extend beyond three or four generations" (1995, 243). Michael Stewart highlights the radical juxtaposition between Judeo-Christian and Gypsy figurations of time and remembrance. He contrasts Walter Benjamin's vision of "an angel of history, with his face turned toward the past, helplessly observing the debris of historical events as it accumulates skyward" with the Gypsies' comparatively striking ambivalence to passing time and the prospects for recollecting it: "For the Gypsies, there is no history, nor is there a past to be redeemed. They live with their gaze fixed on a permanent present that is always becoming, a timeless now in which their continued existence as Rom is all that counts" (1997, 246).

Gypsies possess their distinctive histories and memories because they purposefully forget and therefore continually reinvent them, not because they remember the past in canonical or uniform ways. Gypsies do not repeat the past in order to remember it; they forget the past in order to repeat its mythic invention. A given repetition, an ostensible reproduction of Gypsy culture, repeats only the novelty of "a timeless now." Gypsies' attitudes toward history and memory presuppose that the past only comes into being as it suits the changing needs and desires of the present. The act of beginning again by consciously interrupting or altogether reinventing customary memorial practices is a normative, and not merely elective, aspect of Gypsy folklore. Counter-memorial forms are the rule, not the exception, in their commemorative practices.

Gypsies regard the archives of official memory, with their stores of authoritative documents, as barren edifices. The Gypsy taboo against writing, against documentation, is illustrated by the story of "Papusza," who was "one of the greatest Gypsy singers and poets ever and, for a while, one of the most celebrated" (Fonseca 1995, 3). But her people quickly turned on her when, in 1950, Papusza allowed the Polish poet Jerzy Ficowski to publish some of her works (7–9). There are no native Gypsy words for "to write" or "to read," Fonseca notes. "Gypsies borrow from other languages to describe these activities" (11). Gypsy culture is largely maintained by the unfettered license of their oral practices, which remain open to constant embellishment and revision. Writing is nonsensical to Gypsies and carries a stigma of arresting or pinning down. They have no use for graphic memory, for the reassuring existence of official records or institutional memory as such. Thus, "Papusza was put on trial," and with "little deliberation, she was proclaimed *mahrime* (or *magherdi* among Polish Roma), unclean: the punishment was irreversible exclusion from the group" (9).[1] Committing Gypsy narratives to writing objectifies the memories they recount by establishing a fixed interpretation of the past. Many Gypsies would regard the civic archives, a prized institution in Western communities, as a house of dead letters. Papusza's crime was to reduce the changeable repetition of Gypsy culture—a repetition invested in difference and mutation—into a repetition of the same, of an official document.

The Gypsies are remarkable storytellers, despite a lack of empirical evidence or coherent oral history concerning their origins. Gypsy folktales, although they purport to account for such origins, often raise more questions about the past than they answer. Konrad Bercovici recorded a rendition of perhaps the best-known such tale by Macedonian Gypsies in the 1920s (1928, 41–46). Legend has it that Roman soldiers searched for blacksmiths to forge the nails used to crucify Jesus. After two Jewish blacksmiths and a Syrian refused to make the nails for this purpose, a Gypsy apparently agreed to do so. The soldiers commissioned four nails, but before the last nail cooled, they rushed out of the Gypsy's tent (recall that Jesus was crucified, according to the gospels, with only three nails). The nail continued to glow, no matter how much water the Gypsy poured on it; no matter where he went, the nail followed him. Thus, the legend concludes, "that nail always appears in the tents of the descendents of the man who forged the nails for the crucifixion of Yeshua ben Miriam. And when the nail appears, the Gypsies run. It is why they move from one place to another" (Bercovici 1928, 46).

Three features of this legend in particular illustrate the baffling character of Gypsy folktales in general. First, its apparent account of the Gypsies' nomadic ways accounts for very little. The Gypsy in the story is named as a Gypsy, but inexplicably so; the tale begs the question as to how his people came to be even as it purports to account for their origins. Second, the symbolism of the nail is certainly evocative, but one wonders what, exactly, it means outside of its normal significance in the Christian gospels. Why is this paramount New Testament event of any importance to the Gypsies? Third, the elliptical nature of this legend reflects its susceptibility to adaptation, its accommodation of strategic forgetting far more than pious preservation. When Fonseca rehearsed the tale for modern-day Macedonian and Bulgarian Gypsies, she learned that some characters had changed over time to include Communist dictators from those regions. Like all myths, the story lends itself to variations in which the general plot stays the same while select elements change; but the story is also characterized, unlike other myths, by scarce information concerning the history and genealogy it is supposed to preserve. Indeed, the story identifies its main character, the Gypsy, almost as an afterthought. As such, the tale conjures not the authenticity of Gypsy origins but a simulacrum of authenticity itself. It is, with respect to memory, a better vehicle of communal forgetting than historical recollection.

The simulacrum that typifies so many Gypsy narratives belies the fact that Gypsies lack a common sense of identity, and thus of culture and memory. This claim is not meant to suggest that Gypsy communities evince no sense at all of a defining identity, culture, or memory. Recalling his time among Hungarian Gypsies, Stewart writes: "For them, identity was neither primordial nor essential, though it was no less deeply felt for that" (1997, 58). Nonetheless, the Gypsies' demonstrated lack of a transcendent origin, their distrust of archival memory, the highly mutable and often elliptical nature of their cultural folktales, and above all their proclivities for forgetting prevent Gypsy identity, culture, or memory from achieving the stable or uniform sense and value that such phenomena acquire in Western conventions of remembrance.

Romani, the language of the Gypsies, reflects the long and complex chronology of such fragmentation and dispersion. Among a dearth of recorded events, Romani provides crucial clues about the Gypsies' wanderings throughout the landscape of time. Scholars have identified in Romani a number of ancient Indian roots, several Persian elements, a smattering of Turkish, a peppering of Armenian, and various Greek inclusions dating back to the Byzantine Empire (Fonseca 1995, 93–96; Fraser 1992, 10–22;

Liegeois 1986, 17–47). The sheer variety of Gypsy dialects stemming from these diverse linguistic seeds offers an index of the Gypsies' difficulty in forging and professing the transparent ethos of identity, culture, and memory so esteemed in the Western tradition. Jean-Pierre Liegeois fittingly illustrates the difficulty in question: "There is no single word for 'Gypsy' in all Romany dialects. In some dialects, the word 'Rom' is a noun meaning 'Gypsy,' its plural being 'Roma.'" But not all Gypsies call themselves Roma, and to complicate matters there is a sub-group of Gypsies who do call themselves Rom (in the singular and plural alike), but use the designation to set themselves off from other Gypsy groups" (1986, 16). The meaning of being Gypsy resists signification: as a group, Gypsies lack a proper name and therefore a proper history—a confidently shared past that binds them together. Some scholars contend, in light of such lacunae, that it makes no sense to refer to the Gypsies as a common cultural group. Gypsy culture and memory accordingly lack the semblance of a transcendent cultural logos characteristic of Western traditions. At best, Gypsies aspire only to the semblance of such logos and the authenticity it confers on their shared identity and perpetually dissimilar memories.

For these reasons, the slander of outsiders has played an oddly influential role in the development of Gypsy cultural heritage. Much of the familiar lore about Gypsies purports that they are liars and swindlers by trade. Gypsy stereotypes "of wanton women, of carrion-eaters, and even those among them who had a 'relish for human flesh'" (Fonseca 1995, 88; Hancock 1987; Liegeois 1986, 87–141) circulated in European folklore from medieval times through the early modern periods. The lingering memory of such tales accounts, in large part, for the continued persecution of Gypsies today. Gypsies, however, seldom offer a competing narrative in response to such folklore. On the contrary, the oral culture of Gypsies and the slander of outsiders throughout the centuries appear as different sides of the same tapestry: identifying where one ends and the other begins seems impossible. Perhaps this common tapestry helps to explain the doubtful legend of the Gypsy blacksmith, a time-honored folktale in which the forefather of one's people participates in the death of another culture's central religious figure.

Adaptation in the form of mimicry has long been a vital principle of Gypsy survival. Fonseca well describes their talents in this regard: "When they first appeared in Europe in the fourteenth century, the Gypsies presented themselves as pilgrims and told fortunes: two winning professions in a superstitious age. Their leaders called themselves Counts and Princes and Captains. These were not expressions of Gypsy values so much as further evidence of their (often underemployed) talent for adopting local moods and hierarchies in order to sustain their ever-precarious prestige" (1995, 14). Gypsies often sustain their communities by testifying to the authenticity of a counterfeit heritage instead of demanding recognition for a unique and unbroken legacy. The public pronouncement by Yugoslavian Gypsies, in the late 1980s, of an ancient Egyptian ancestry exemplifies the political utility of such cultural forgery. When the Serbs came to power after the fall of the Soviet Union, Wim Willems records, the so-called "Yugo-Egyptians" reached back to "reclaim an old, alternative identity" (1997, 3). This declaration of an alleged Egyptian heritage provided the Gypsies with an alternative fate to either assimilation or expulsion. As "Yugo-Egyptians," they were able to contend that their ancient Egyptian heritage must be protected. It was likely a tactical decision for the newly classified Egyptian descendents to reclaim this ancestry by appropriating Westerners' habitual, yet erroneous, attribution of an Egyptian past to the Gypsies (a misconception phonetically crystallized in the very term "Gypsy"). The opportunism of Gypsy collective memories dramatizes Young's distinction between ostensibly uniform collective memory and more randomly assorted collected memories, or "the many discrete memories that are gathered into common memorial spaces and assigned common meaning" (1993, xi). The striking inventiveness of Gypsy memories accordingly evinces a community's nomadic accumulation of memory in the face of changing social and political exigencies rather than the institutional retention of a stable and continuous tradition.

The Gypsies' very lack of a coherent and unified historical consciousness (insofar as they claim to be unburdened by the past) enables them to adapt to the burdens of the present. Such adaptation, however, carries a heavy price: the indifference of many Gypsy communities, despite repeated persecutions, to systemic political organization. To be sure, certain Gypsy organizations have initiated nationalist and human rights movements in recent decades. These organizations have even established archives and museums housing Gypsy art, history, and folklore, especially in Eastern Europe. But without the consolidating power of a commonly embraced past, without the sense of meaning and destiny signified by common memories, a transnational and politically viable Gypsy consciousness apparently has yet to emerge.

Gypsy communities accordingly lack a collective investment in the evidentiary power of the past—a manifest politics of remembrance, in other words. Even the horrors of the Holocaust apparently failed to inspire a lasting commemorative consciousness in Gypsy culture. The Gypsies were the first population slated for extermination by the Nazis specifically on the basis of their race and lost a higher percentage of their people than any other such population (Fonseca 1995, 243; Fraser 1992, 269; Hancock 1987, 61–87).[2] But Fonseca reports that Polish Gypsy survivors of what they call the *porraimos,* or "the devouring," today expend minimal effort attempting to shelter or pass on collective memories of the Nazis' genocidal programs. "The Second World War and its traumas are certainly within memory," she writes, "but there is no tradition of commemoration, or even discussion" (1995, 243). What Stewart calls the "timeless now" is such a dominant component of their commemorative economy that many Gypsies find no benefit in reliving their harrowing past; the compulsion to forget appears to offer greater rewards than institutional remembrance.

This is not to deny, once again, that certain organizations have taken measures to preserve evidence, and thus memory, of Nazi atrocities against the Gypsies in select archives and museums. As a whole, however, Gypsy communities exhibit little aspiration to establish a uniform memory of their wartime past. Their manner of judgment concerning the moral and political vitality of communal memory is noticeably at odds with that of modern liberal-democratic states. A simple contrast makes the point: unlike the epic relationship that Jewish Holocaust survivors have established with that past, the massive symbolic weight of which is quite literally concretized in their many public monuments, little more than diaphanous recollections connect the Gypsies to the same harrowing events (Fonseca 1995, 275). Gypsies traditionally have placed a premium on breaking with the past as a means of escaping its trials rather than modeling their communal ethic and social agenda on a continuity between former and present times—even times of persecution or unspeakable atrocity (Liegeois 1986, 54–55).

One should not interpret this Gypsy proclivity for forgetting, however, as a form of resignation, a renunciation of the duty to bear witness extolled in modern liberal-democratic institutions of remembrance. Such forgetting reflects a pragmatic politics of memory, or a dogged commitment to the communal goods of counter-memory, invested in something far more fragmented and transitory than democratic consensus sanctioned by the lessons of history. "Among Roma," Fonseca writes, "forgetting does not imply complacency: its tenor is one of—sometimes buoyant—defiance" (1995, 275). Forgetting is, for the Gypsies, a commendably active, productive practice. In their case, it produces not merely formal histories (as in the case of John Draper) but the ethos of one's cultural heritage or communal identity writ large.

Perhaps this defiance in forgetting appears less complacent in light of the obstacles that some Gypsies have faced while working for recognition of the *porraimos* in international Holocaust commemorations. True to their legendary flair for adaptation, Gypsy practices of forgetting suggest an unconventional political response to the prevailing liberal-democratic politics of memory, which, in laboring to remember the past so as not to repeat it, reproduces familiar forms of exclusion by endowing particular kinds of remembrance with political priority. Consider: not one Gypsy was called to testify in the Nuremburg Trials; only one Nazi has been convicted for crimes of genocide against Gypsies since the end of World War II; those Gypsies who petitioned the U.S. Holocaust Memorial Council for involvement and representation in its museum met with prolonged resistance and dubious results; and violence against Gypsies has only increased in the newly democratic regions of postcommunist Eastern Europe. All these facts and more may warrant some Gypsies' defiant forgetting, if this is what liberal-democratic commitments to the equitable representation of diverse commemorative interests will make of memory.[3] In short, perhaps the fact that the Gypsies' victimization prior to, during, and after the Holocaust is so little remembered by those Western alliances pledged to the preservation of its fatal lessons is proof enough that Western institutions habitually mistake a necessarily partial and privileged account of the past for its transparent and universal truth. The repetition of *difference,* or an investment in the politics of forgetting and the incorporation of new folkloric elements, appears to sustain Gypsy memories as well as the unorthodox brand of political judgment they reflect; conventional Western institutions of public memory, in contrast, remain invested in a putative repetition of *the same,* in a historical logos whose pretensions to transparency and universality obscure its fundamental debt to strategically selective commemorative values and politics.

Despite their reputation for wanderlust, the nomadic travels of Eastern European Gypsies were dramatically and sometimes violently curtailed during the twentieth century. Gypsies were forced to settle and assimilate under Communist regimes. Romantic tales of a bucolic Gypsy life in which, as Bercovici muses, "The Gypsy has locked himself out of the gates of modern civilization and roams freely on the highways and byways of the world" could not be more misleading (1928, 3). Stewart advises us to "forget romantic notions of the careless freedoms of caravans and campfires; the Gypsies' lives were hard and sometimes brutal" (1997, 1). The sudden eruptions of ethnic hatred in postcommunist Eastern Europe form a tragic contrast with "romantic notions" of their culture and history (Crowe 1994, xi-xvi; Liegeois 1986, 44, 56).

Yet in the landscape of memory the Gypsies remain essentially nomadic. Rather than a repetition of the same, of static and transparent recollections, Gypsy memories evince the continual repetition of difference, a "timeless now" in which the Gypsy past is conjured and reinvented according to the changing needs and desires of the present. The eternal recurrence of this timeless now is even symbolized on the Gypsy flag in the figure of a wheel: the emblem of a people who experience a unifying past only in their travels away from it. In every repetition of their culture—of its apparent sameness—difference returns, eternally.

## Mnemonic Nomads

The apparently idiosyncratic nature of Gypsy commemorative practices suggests grounds for reconsidering conventional ideals of remembrance. Their artfully invented cultural heritage raises the question of whether, and how, the very obfuscation or substantial loss of memory can help to produce seemingly transparent or monolithic memorial forms and artifacts. The following discussion provides evidence for this claim by consulting yet another disciplinary perspective on the interrelated subjects of memory, repetition, and forgetting. The addition of this perspective will yield further conceptual terms with which to reconsider the value of forgetting as a formative component of communal reminiscence and cultural heritage.

### Remembering by Forgetting

Although it concerns individual memories, psychologist John Kotre's research on autobiographical memory provides an additionally instructive perspective on the metaphysics of time and memory surveyed in this chapter.[4] Kotre's work on autobiographical memory entails a dispersion of individual memory as such and an affirmation of its inherently collective, nomadic, and forgetful character. The terminology featured in his research also helps to delineate principles of repetition inherent in the nomadic formation of memory not only in seemingly unique cultures of memory but as a recondite feature of cultural memory in general.

Kotre posits that we often remember not on the basis of stable and transparent recollections but by virtue of forgetting. A "commonplace" phenomenon known as cryptomnesia refers to recollections in which "you remember *what* someone told you but you forget *that* you were told" (1995, 36).[5] Our most intimate memories, shaped by processes of forgetting, might be implanted components of someone else's life experience: "An individual starts to remember what he heard in a hallway conversation or a group meeting, but he forgets where he heard it, and even that he heard it. An old idea becomes his original creation" (36–37). Renowned psychologist Jean Piaget once wrote that he grew up with a vivid memory of narrowly escaping a kidnapping when he was a toddler. Throughout his later childhood and adolescence, Piaget recalled his nurse at the time heroically fending off the would-be kidnapper; he even remembered that his nurse's face was scratched during the attack. The nurse, however, wrote to Piaget's parents when he was fifteen and admitted that the story was fabricated (1962). "The clarity with which Piaget had seen the event in his memory," Kotre remarks, "and the personal conviction that he had about its truth, was no proof that it ever happened" (1995, 36). Even the visceral transparency of memories related to personal trauma (which ostensibly preserve raw, unmediated experience) occludes the fact that such memories may well exist in a state of translation, migration, or even comprehensive reconstruction from one locus of memory to another. "Because of cryptomnesia," Kotre concludes, "it's possible to believe that a picture actually planted in your memory by a photograph, a film, or someone else's words originated in a direct experience of your own. Nor can you tell if a memory has been cryptically implanted by the way it looks or feels. Unreal memories look and feel like real ones" (37). This account even prompts one to consider whether or not categories such as "real" and "unreal" prevent deeper understanding of the nomadic character of memory, of its formation and function in ongoing processes of adaptation from one context to another.

Cryptomnesia is merely one common form of mnemonic reconstruction. "Memories don't sit inertly in our minds the way they do on an audiotape or the shelves of a library," Kotre remarks. "They are constantly refashioned" (37). The irony here is profound: memories from which we derive our most fundamental sense of self may simulate the memories of others, attain a significance completely altered from their "original" import, and even refer to a different time and place than they once did. The vividness and coherence of such reconstructed memories is predicated upon scattered instances of forgetting. Memory does not repeat an ideal and original impression of the same "unrepeatable" event *ad infinitum;* it repeats a series of performative differences and transformations that supply the mere semblance of such an "unrepeatable" origin. Quentin Compson's efforts in *The Sound and the Fury* to forget the defining episodes of his past merely stimulate his memories anew, renewing their potency and lending them new sites of investment. Gypsy collective memories reveal that forgetting comprises an essentially productive aspect of memory rather than its unfortunate repression or erosion. Such illustrations demonstrate, together with Kotre's insights, that various gaps in recollection and the processes of reconstruction they entail are not exceptions to either individual or collective memory but one of their formative principles.

It is appropriate, then, to say that memories subsist rather than exist. "Where is the great Cartesian Theater," Kotre asks, "the place where the chemical messengers of memory become actors before our mind's eye?" (25). Memories subsist in a state of dispersion but do not exist in the form of a unified or stable presence. "We cannot say that memory as such 'is,'" Charles Scott concludes. "Memories are already 'there' when we speak or think, not as an origin, but as inheritances, structures, associations, inevitabilities, possibilities, forms of enactment" (1999, 12). The activation of a memory, depending on its age and significance, involves several areas of the brain, a host of neuronal firings, and any combination of senses or "associations." We activate the fickle and nomadic character of memory whenever we discuss our memories with others, whenever we preserve them in writing, images, or sound, thereby ensuring that our memories subsist in more than one place and form, in multiple "inheritances" or "forms of enactment" at once.

These conditions portend scattered, unavoidable occurrences of forgetting as much, or more, than the preservation of mnemonic continuity. The memories of Benjy Compson, the first narrative perspective in *The Sound and the Fury,* consist of only a few traumatic fragments, repeatedly invoked by the smell of trees, the voices of golfers teeing up on the course across from his house, or the feel of his sister's worn and dirty slipper. Quentin's recollections, like those of his brother Benjy, do not lie dormant in some fixed cognitive nook but are stimulated by the sound of his father's watch, the smell of honeysuckle, or the sight of his own shadow. Memories, like the Gypsies, lack a proper home—a stable ground or transparent origin. They connote radical multiplicity instead of unity. Recall, for instance, how the same incessantly repeated memories, with each narrator "traversing the same territory in circling movements,"[6] pervade the novel's different narrative perspectives. "The families, neighborhoods, and nations that envelop us," Kotre muses, "all have memories of their own that transcend any one individual's. So do the memories in the vast cultures we call Art and Science and Religion. We grow up in the context of collective memory, and over the course of life we breathe it in and breathe it out" (1995, 221). The memories of individuals, collectivities, or even entire cultures thus evince an inherent capacity to subsist in multiple forms and appearances, precisely as a consequence of minor or major operations of forgetting.

This multiplicity is equally germane to the formation of public memory. Scholars since Halbwachs have taken for granted that communal, religious, and national memories are composites of individual recollections, and that individual recollections necessarily embody such collective frameworks of memory (1992). Young economically summarizes this premise: "A society's memory . . . might be regarded as an aggregate collection of its members' many, often competing memories. If societies remember, it is only insofar as their institutions and rituals organize, shape, even inspire their constituents' memories. For a society's memory cannot exist outside of those people who do the remembering—even if such memory happens to be at the society's bidding, in its name" (1993, xi). Forgetting, as described in the preceding passages, constitutes an intrinsic, formative dimension of such simultaneously individual and social remembering. Both Kotre's research and the examples of memory traced throughout this chapter warrant the conclusion that memories are not chosen, possessed, or preserved by individuals or publics, at least not in the conventional senses of those terms. Such memories may appear to open a transparent window onto the past; but their semblance of transparency reflects, as in Gypsy communities, patterns of forgetting, fragmentation, and discontinuity elemental to their formation. Individuals as well as publics derive their sense of identity by attempting to remember with continuity, to symbolically or discursively fashion a meaningful relation between the past and present; but individuals and publics attempt to do so within the radical mnemonic alterity of what Kotre calls "the immense ecosystem" of memory (1995, 217)—or by the same token, of forgetting.

By this reasoning, the dynamics of forgetting and remembering characteristic of Gypsy collective memories are not fundamentally different from the interplay of revision and preservation that motivate conventional Western rites of remembrance. Kotre and other researchers provide compelling evidence that disparate and fragmentary recollections that refer to no certain referent, only discontinuity, combine to produce the perceived authenticity and continuity of communal memory writ large. Even the most traditional, seemingly uninterrupted forms of public memory may conceal episodes of shared cryptomnesia. "Once we assign monumental form to memory,"

Young posits, "we have to some degree divested ourselves of the obligation to remember" (1993, 13). The frequency with which Western communities erect public monuments may indicate merely the frequency with which we have unwittingly substituted (or "divested ourselves of") one monumental version of the past for another. The abiding expression of Western public memory according to such forms suggests how widely and officially sanctioned this cryptomnesia may be.

The accounts of memory featured in this chapter accordingly suggest that evaluating public memories according to whether they accurately represent the past or even aspire to a transparent communication of its meanings or lessons indicates an investment in analytical principles contrary to the formation and perdurance of memory itself. The operative concern here is not with the preservationist ethic that motivates a good deal of self-described social, collective, or public memory projects. This line of thought is meant to question, instead, the forms of commemorative enforcement sometimes established in the name of that ethic. Preserving the past by mandating institutionally correct and incorrect ways to remember—even in adherence to seemingly progressive historical wisdom—curtails the degree to which groups and individuals may adapt established commemorative resources in response to changing needs and desires. Reducing public memory to the repetition of a static, ideal image of the past and domesticating it in a proper home elides the fact that the nomadic and perpetually unfinished memory work of groups and individuals is ingredient even to the most apparently monolithic public memories. Gypsy collective memories illuminate this feature of public memory in general: it would not "exist" in its representative forms without a capacity for variation and even dissolution. Nominally public memories depend for their relevance and coherence upon some principle of modification, distortion, or loss. The basic ethical question in this context is not whether these outcomes occur but to what ends one manages such deep commemorative indeterminacy.

Hence, one may value the nomadic character of collective (or collected) memory by cultivating its abundant relevance to diverse social interests instead of safeguarding its allegedly essential and unchanging content or meaning. One may do so by embracing, rather than laboring to counteract, its aptitude for new sites of application and the establishment of new sociopolitical relations—"as a basis for political and social action" (Young 1993, 13). Conceiving of memory as a repetition of difference rather than a repetition of the same enables one to value the productive capacities of forgetting and mutation elemental to even the most apparently monumental forms of public memory. To regard public memories in this way is to regard them, with both Schacter and Foucault, as inherently adaptive and counter-memorial in nature.

This is not to say that all public memories should be equally valued, or certified as equally authentic, thus excusing irresponsible and dangerous programs of historical revisionism. Saying that memories are nomadic, devoid of fixed empirical referents, does not warrant the conclusion that they are all morally innocent and interchangeable. Communal memories display nomadic characteristics to the extent that they subsist in constellations of dissimilar material practices, which reflect their ambulatory careers as symbolic resources of communal judgment in response to ever changing needs and interests. Customary practices of memory, which evince the sociopolitical relevance or utility of particular recollections to a given community, are never invented *ex nihilo*. They are shaped, rather, by mnemonic conditions—including pervasive modes of forgetting—that influence what can be publicly remembered, and how. Even counter-memories, such as those of Gypsies who trace their heritage to the archetypes of other cultures, derive sociopolitical significance from existing discursive and historical precedents, from established forms of memory. The erection and maintenance of public memory often involves considerable labor, born of constraint rather than fancy. On this basis, one may measure the ethical and political implications of collective memories by the quality of the sociopolitical relationships they establish or sustain, as both Arendt and Margalit would have it, rather than the transcendent truth or undiminished authenticity of memory itself. "Instead of stopping at formal questions, or at issues of historical referentiality," Young submits, "we must go on to ask how memorial representations of history may finally weave themselves into the course of ongoing events" (1993, 12).

The labor of memory as such involves the repetition of forgetting as much as the repetition of a static memory. Or rather, every attempt to preserve a static memory, in whatever form, occurs in relation to some form of forgetting. To attest that a memory is engendered and maintained according to an essential unity is to forget the inherent partiality and mutability, the intrinsically nomadic character, of any recollection. Memories are neither forgotten nor preserved: the labor of memory requires forgetting, and acts of forgetting make possible new memories.

Affirming public memory as such requires an affirmation of public forgetting. Assigning this value to forgetting admittedly runs counter to the conventional Western rhetoric of memory and forgetting. The familiar injunction that we must not forget the past so as not to repeat it tells only half the story. This injunction treats forgetting as an irretrievable subtraction from a complete and objective apprehension of the past. Public memories retain rhetorical influence by appearing essentially unchanged, and thus authentic, from their origins to their present incarnation. But there is no semblance of such memory without collective memory work, without the imperfect—and productively forgetful—practices that engender its transparent ethos and sustain its social value or utility. The two forms of mnemonic repetition surveyed in this essay—repetition of a static, uniform memory and repetition of the differences or transformations essential to its evolution—are not antithetical. Even those public memories which announce themselves with an apparently homogeneous voice are merely the aggregation of multiple and oftentimes mercurial recollections.

There is more at stake here than a simple opposition between static or uniform memories and those subject to mutation or fragmentation. Something distinctively *un*public—the disparate memory work of collectivities and even individuals—helps to engender public memories, including their semblances of permanence and uniformity. This is not to deny that public memories display an ethos of objectivity, uniformity, or permanence; indeed, that ethos is part and parcel of their rhetorical sense and value as symbolic resources of communal judgment. But such memories derive their monumental ethos from the codification of multiple commemorative practices, from the manifold memory work that sustains it. *In principle,* if not in appearance, public memories attain their sense of objectivity, uniformity, or permanence by virtue of partiality, fragmentation, and forgetting.

Observing that even the most monumental forms of memory lack an essential home or transparent origin underscores the fundamental difficulty of defining memory itself as categorically public, collective, or private. The imbrication of collective and individual memory within public commemoration holds considerable explanatory force for the study of public memory in general. Such study, however, primarily concerns not the authenticity of public memory but the discursive practices, the diverse memory work and formative acts of forgetting, that help to instill public memories with their rhetoric of authenticity, with their authoritative ethos as guides to the past and the wisdom it holds. "Public," "collective," and "private" refer less to hermetic categories of memory and more to the changing value and significance it acquires throughout its nomadic life span—in the permanent present or timeless now, in simultaneous recollection and forgetting, in continually ending and beginning anew.

## Conclusion

Faulkner's *The Sound and the Fury,* like Gypsy collective memories, suggests that memories are most at home when they travel. Benjy, the handicapped Compson sibling and the novel's first narrator, erects a piteous monument, which other characters refer to as his graveyard. It consists of two blue glass bottles containing withered jimson weed placed in the Compsons' yard. This public memorial holds an impenetrably private meaning: it undoubtedly anchors Benjy's loosely connected memories of his estranged sister, Caddy, but none of the other members of the household comprehend its significance. Benjy treats the least disturbance of these markers, despite their vagueness, as a desecration. Benjy's intense effort to preserve the past reflects his understanding of commemoration as "an inflexible pattern which he defends against novelty or change with every bellow in his overgrown body" (Vickery 1964, 35).

One risks the onset of mnemonic atrophy by treating novelty and change—even forgetting—as antitheses of memory, by insisting on rigid invocations of essential commemorative form and content. "It is not that the bottle has any intrinsic value for Benjy," Vickery observes, "but merely that it forms part of the pattern which must not be disturbed" (1964, 35). The memory itself, like the jimson weed in Benjy's memorial, has withered. This unyielding effort to preserve an authentic memory foreshadows an unwanted and destructive act of forgetting, for it imposes a pallid and inflexible commemorative form on the memorial's robust and suggestive meaning. Benjy is "momentarily shocked into silence . . . overwhelmed with horror and agony" (Vickery 1964, 35) when this sacrosanct pattern is disturbed, when novelty and change defile his ideal and original memory, as they always will. The fossilization of memory results in an incapacitation, or even dissolution, of its possessor.

Benjy's trauma over the least disturbance of his memorial suggests the importance of distinguishing between *what* publics remember and *how* they remember it. Dictating how communities should remember, uniformly and authentically, promotes a culture of public memory that threatens the ability of marginal communities to sustain their unconventional memorial practices and to vie for public recognition of their professed heritage (including those characterized by a heritage of forgetting). Communities that fail to appreciate the reciprocity of public remembering and public forgetting might mistake faithfully maintained commemorative norms and rituals for comparatively adaptive and inventive cultures of memory. Collective allegiance

to the bare authenticity or traditionalism of public memory does not produce automatically deeper communal bonds. Such allegiance might even
foster superficial ideals of citizenship and public judgment that leave the
community unprepared for future calamities in the ways that both Nietzsche and Arendt indicate. Learning to value the nomadic character of public
memory, to conceive of such memory as the crucible of communal remembering *and* forgetting, presupposes that one regard the occluded provinces
of the past not as unwanted constraints but as malleable resources of ethical
and political possibility for the present and future. The Gypsies' culture (or
cultures) of collected memory showcase this often unnoticed principle of
public memory more generally.

Gypsy proclivities for forgetting as a memorial ideal indicate a difference
in degree rather than kind from conventional ideals of public memory—but
they represent an extreme difference nonetheless. Promoting Gypsy cultures
of forgetting as a theoretical or practical model for communal memory in
general would risk replacing one reductive antithesis with another, trading
the primacy of memory over forgetting for the primacy of forgetting over
memory. Gypsy practices of forgetting illuminate the prevalence and value
of forgetting as a feature of communal memory writ large; yet the forms of
memory (or better, counter-memory) addressed in this chapter indicate that
the prospects for developing a viable mode of long-term political advocacy
in light of one's shared past appears tenuous when forgetting has become
the central fount of communal memory. "Sometimes," Nietzsche advised,
"this same life that requires forgetting demands a temporary suspension of
this forgetfulness" (1997, 76). Nietzsche's maxim concerning the need for
judiciously balanced forgetting and remembering furnishes the essential lesson in this context: "*The unhistorical and the historical are necessary in equal
measure for the health of an individual, of a people and of a culture*" (63; emphasis
in original). Forgetting, as it operates in Gypsy communities, helps to foster
the immediate and transitory goods of mobility, mutation, and adaptation.
But it apparently fails to assist in forging new, more durable social and
political customs founded, as Arendt would have it, on the inaugural power
of the remembered past. By embracing ritual forgetfulness to the exclusion
of institutional remembrance, one may substitute the productive intimacy
of public memory and public forgetting, or the two forms of repetition
addressed throughout this chapter, for yet another version of their supposed
practical or moral incongruity.

Abraham Lincoln's rhetoric of moral and political forgetting in his signature wartime addresses, the Gettysburg Address and the Second Inaugural, resolve lingering questions raised by the examples of public forgetting previously analyzed in this book. Lincoln's speeches evince a more refined framework of historical judgment than John W. Draper's ambitious program of historical forgetting. They also inaugurate, in contrast to the Gypsy ethic of forgetting, a quietly revolutionary set of normative political relations and, with them, a decisively transformed culture of memory. The present chapter brings the subject matter of this book thematically full circle by demonstrating how a mature rhetoric of public forgetting, in contrast to the neoliberal epideictic offered on the first anniversary of September 11, can furnish a viable and restorative mode of moral and political judgment in times of national crisis. It illustrates how leaders may employ idioms of forgetting as moral and political resources in order to profoundly rejuvenate the content of formal public history, informal ideals of cultural identity, and the quality of sociopolitical relations they celebrate—to begin again, that is, in moments of civic tragedy or instability.

Lincoln's most renowned wartime addresses also show how public forgetting can operate as a productive force within established commemorative or historical practices. The idiom of public forgetting that Lincoln fashioned during the calamities of civil war avoids the tropes of oblivion, liquidation, and amnesia. He calls on the public to forget, rather, in the spirit of rededication, reconciliation, restoration, and renewal: there is something fundamentally conservative, preservative—indeed, commemorative—in Lincoln's rejection of customary reminiscence, which may explain why his legendary public statements are more commonly described as sacred articles of national memory.

Volumes of encyclopedic commentary could not document in full Abraham Lincoln's prodigious influence on U.S. public memory. Don E. Fehrenbacher observes that "Lincoln's words have acquired *transcendent* meaning as contributions to the permanent literary treasure of the nation" (1987, 285). He is, in Merrill Peterson's words, "a hero, a religion, an industry" (1994, 374). Peterson's sweeping study of Lincoln as depicted in myriad forms of reminiscence reconfirms the enormity of his mythic stature in U.S. academic and popular memory alike. Hegemonic perceptions of Lincoln and U.S. national history share the same cloth. According to Barry Schwarz, he quite simply "personified the substance of America's sense of itself" (2000, xi).

Lincoln's mythic persona thus functions synecdochically, as a lens through which contemporary Americans instinctively perceive and assign meaning to their national past (and by extension, to their present and future). The imagined persona of Lincoln is a ubiquitous cipher of public memory. Frequent reductions of U.S. history to Lincoln's legendary vision of it are among the most resounding effects of his distinctive rhetorical talents. Garry Wills proposes that Lincoln remade normative perceptions of U.S. history in his Gettysburg Address by gathering disparate historical events into expressions of a single national mission. "For most people now," Wills opines, "the Declaration [of Independence] means what Lincoln told us it means, as a way of correcting the Constitution itself without overthrowing it" (1992, 147). In this respect, he concludes, "Lincoln's Address created a political prose for America" (52), a form of public speech (indeed, of remembrance) uniquely adapted to preserving the transcendent meaning of essential U.S. political ideals.

Lincoln applied the same unifying logic concerning the Union's past, present, and future in numerous public statements, especially throughout the Civil War. James McPherson argues that Lincoln won the war with metaphors to the extent that his uncanny use of figural language endowed the Union cause with a meaning and purpose worthy of crucial public support (1992, chap. 5). Peterson additionally proposes that Lincoln's rhetoric, or "the spiritual capital of his words," is more indispensable to his sanctified presence in U.S. public memory than the actual facts of his life: "Were everything else about him forgotten, and only his writings together with some of his talk survive, he would stand revealed as an extraordinary human being, as one who in the terrible crisis of the nation's history recreated the promise of its origins and thereby secured its destiny" (1994, 396). Academic wisdom of this sort presumes that Lincoln's rhetorical genius is central to understanding not only his preeminence in the pantheon of U.S. public memory but also the origins and evolution of such memory writ large.

Lincoln's rhetoric has exerted a controlling influence on modern historical memory in part because he frequently spoke of history and memory in
his speeches as paramount tests of judgment. The concluding paragraph of
Lincoln's annual message to Congress in 1862 illustrates his frequent appeals
to the burdens of historical conscience and the scrutiny of popular memory
as precedents for political judgment: "Fellow-citizens, *we* cannot escape history. We of this Congress and this administration, will be remembered in
spite of ourselves. . . . The fiery trial through which we pass, will light us
down, in honor or dishonor, to the latest generation" (1989c, 415). Lincoln
resolutely kindled the "fiery" glow of historical memory throughout his
wartime proclamations. But he also maintained that such light depended
for its luminescence on the historical and memorial shadows surrounding
it. Lincoln's succeeding comments in the same speech reveal his equally
ardent belief that historical memory can burden present-day deliberative
judgment: "The dogmas of the quiet past are inadequate to the stormy
present. The occasion is piled high with difficulty, and we must rise with
the occasion. As our case is new, so we must think anew, and act anew. We
must disenthrall our selves, and then we shall save our country" (415). Lincoln's reasoning here broadly resembles Nietzsche's contention that normative forms of historical recollection can stifle rather than nurture life in the
present. Juxtaposing these final passages of Lincoln's address demonstrates
that he balanced his widely admired sensitivity to the wisdom of civic tradition and historical conscience with an understated ambivalence toward (and
even occasional rejections of) tradition, history, and memory in present-
day political judgment.

From this vantage, Lincoln's public statements on the relevance of historical memory to political judgment convey a more puzzling attitude to the
remembered past than is typically appreciated either in Lincoln scholarship
or in public memory studies. Lincoln charges Congress to recognize that
the dogmatic past is a hindrance to contemporary political decision-making,
that legislators should "disenthrall" themselves from it in order to "think
anew, and act anew"; yet he also urges the same body to recognize its servi-
tude to "history," to accept the weighty knowledge that future generations'
memories of its actions will serve as final judgment of its members' "honor
or dishonor." Lincoln's charge to Congress consists of an apparent paradox:
he argues that it should break with the past in order to "save our country," which requires the Congress to affirm its obeisance before historical
memory precisely as a means of maintaining the nation's political continuity.
Lincoln's artfully expressed ideal of historical disenthrallment thus reveals

his unusually nimble grasp of the profound yet elusive intimacy between memory and forgetting as grounds of political judgment.

The strange juxtaposition of these passages exemplifies a recurrent tendency in Lincoln's most celebrated evocations of historical memory. In seeking to enlarge the scope of U.S. public memory, Lincoln's rhetoric frequently conveyed an unease with residues of the past that inhibited clear political and moral insight in the present, a reluctance to accept artfully fabricated memorial symbolism as a natural or universally inclusive medium of historical experience, and a principled unwillingness to engage in substantive ceremonial reviews of recent historic events. Remarkably, however, Lincoln's professions of discomfort with the past's symbolic encroachment upon immediate affairs curiously aided rather than undermined his repeated pleas for the public to think and act with the judgments of history and memory ever in mind. Lincoln's meditations on historical memory suggest complex rhetorical and political strategies, but not inconsistent ones. His appeals to public forgetting, his occasional expressions of dissatisfaction with sometimes burdensome remainders of the past, complement rather than contradict his better-known calls for historical responsibility and commemorative fidelity. For Lincoln, public forgetting constituted an effective rhetorical tactic with which to instill in Northerners and Southerners alike a more balanced, dramatically revised orientation to historical memory intended to moderate feverish fixations on past offenses. Doing so, he ventured, would help to restore political accord in the present.

This chapter shows how Lincoln's rhetorical and political appeals for *mercy* as president were critical factors in his efforts to persuade Union and Confederate states to disenthrall themselves from their recent wartime past. In doing so, he developed a civic idiom that harmonized appeals to historical memory as well as national forgetting into a coherent and politically transformative vision of the nation's past, present, and future. Unlike Radical Republicans such as Thaddeus Stevens (2005), who sought to punish the former Confederacy for its loathsome crimes against the Union, Lincoln believed that instilling a public morality of mercy amongst Northerners and Southerners, orchestrating scenes of mutual forgiveness for their shared sins against the Union, was imperative for successful reconciliation. "From the Amnesty of 1863 to the last grand chord of the Second Inaugural Address," Peterson writes, "he sought to make the seat of power a seat of mercy" (1994, 103). The ritual of forgiving and forgetting in this context does not imply a complete disavowal of public history, only those select elements whose remembrance would hinder charitable relations in the present. By this logic,

Lincoln's many public expressions of mercy, and the rhetoric of forgetting that shaped them, vitally supplemented his efforts to forge a harmonizing interpretation of U.S. history and a redemptive culture of national memory.

This chapter supports such claims by offering a counterintuitive interpretation of Lincoln's rhetorical influence over U.S. public memory and national history.[1] Lincoln undoubtedly expended "the spiritual capital of his words" in order to influence normative memories of the American experiment in popular government; yet his attention to the limits of memory—his rhetorical inducement of strategic forms of public forgetting as just and propaedeutic elements of our defining commemorative traditions—are seldom appreciated or substantively examined in those terms. The following analysis therefore argues that Lincoln's most cherished contributions to U.S. public memory, such as his Gettysburg Address and the Second Inaugural, are equally noteworthy as masterful acts of public forgetting. They constitute sterling examples of the complementary moral and political work that artful appeals to forgetting can accomplish. Closely examining the formative influence of forgetting in these rhetorical touchstones of national memory ultimately warrants the conclusion that, in favorable circumstances, one may embrace public forgetting as a judicious instrument of political restoration and as a revitalizing moral force in the democratic culture of memory that facilitates it.

## Forgetting, in Argument and Expression

The Gettysburg Address and the Second Inaugural vividly reflect Lincoln's sundry invocations of national memory as a source of moral and political wisdom in moments of public crisis. Briefly considering antecedent forms of public forgetting in Lincoln's oratorical career will situate these later wartime speeches in an optimal interpretive context: as Lincoln's most mature and significant expressions of public forgetting, as highly refined moral and political axioms inspired by his persistent reflections on the civic merits of customary memorial rituals. Lincoln advocated public forgetting throughout his political career in alternately explicit or implicit ways—in explicit pleas to omit select aspects of communal history from public deliberation or in his implicit performance of such omissions in artful turns of phrase.

In the former case, Lincoln occasionally argued for the value of collective forgetting as a desirable aspect of communal memory. In his July 10, 1858, speech in Chicago, while campaigning for the U.S. Senate, Lincoln characteristically ponders the memory of the nation's founding. "We run our memory back over the pages of history for about eighty-two years," he muses, "and we discover that we were then a very small people in point of numbers, vastly inferior to what we are now" (1989g, 455). Lincoln extends this contrast between the country's humble origins and its present bounty by underscoring the importance of national anniversary celebrations. "We hold this annual celebration," he declares, "to remind ourselves of all the good done in this process of time, of how it was done and who did it, and how we are historically connected with it" (455). To this point, Lincoln offers commonplace memorial *topoi:* the Union's present vigor and expansiveness recall its early aspirations, and our dedication to ritual commemoration betokens continued preservation of its enriching traditions.

More remarkable, however, is Lincoln's ensuing admission that such memory is inherently limited in scope. He cautions: "We have besides these men—descended by blood from our ancestors—among us perhaps half our people who are not descendents at all of these men, they are men who have come from Europe. . . . If they look back through this history to trace their connection with those days by blood, they find they have none, they cannot carry themselves back into that glorious epoch and make themselves feel that they are part of us" (456). Lincoln urges his audience to recognize that traditional historical remembrance may circumscribe the boundaries of political identity. He emphasizes that, for some, inclusion in the country's defining memorial traditions is highly qualified, if not precluded.

New U.S. citizens cannot share in organic memories of the Revolution, but they can lay claim to something at once more vital and transcendent: the civic principles that inspired it. Lincoln argues:

> But when they look through that old Declaration of Independence, they find that those old men say that "We hold these truths to be self-evident, that all men are created equal," and then they feel that that moral sentiment taught in that day evidences their relation to those men, that it is the father of all moral principle in them, and that they have a right to claim it as though they were blood of the blood, flesh of the flesh of the men who wrote that Declaration, and so they are. (456)

Lincoln defies epideictic conventions in this striking passage by proposing that naturalized Americans' lack of communal memory can be profitably forgotten, that the present-day "moral sentiment" the Declaration inspires may compensate for their lack of a flesh-and-blood relation to the nation's founders. Lincoln's juxtaposition between anniversaries of the Union's founding and the present composition of its citizenry warrants an enthusiastic affirmation of public forgetting. In his peroration, he implores: "Let us discard all this quibbling about this man and the other man—this race and that race and the other race being inferior, and therefore they must be placed in an inferior position—discarding our standard that we have left us. Let us discard all these things, and unite as one people throughout this land, until we shall once more stand up declaring that all men are created equal" (458). Lincoln contends that ritual commemoration of the Revolution is not enough; we must actively "discard," forget, or disenthrall ourselves from sociopolitical divisions inherited as part of routine remembrance in order to achieve national unity, and hence the civic equality that the Declaration originally promised.[2] The persuasiveness of Lincoln's appeal to historical forgetting on this occasion lies in clear logical demonstration far more than the stylistic adroitness of his language.

On other occasions, however, Lincoln did not simply advocate public forgetting on argumentative grounds but performed it in artful speech. The difference here is subtle but crucial: the difference between analytically describing or critiquing a particular culture of memory, including its formative limitations and lacunae, and symbolically bringing it into being in one's discourse. Lincoln's celebrated closing passages in his First Inaugural Address succinctly illustrate this rhetorical and commemorative distinction. For the vast majority of the speech, Lincoln traces the genesis of sectional conflict and advances a detailed constitutional argument in support of his contention that secession is legally impossible. Immediately prior to his peroration, however, Lincoln enacts (instead of simply arguing for) the logic of public forgetting he described in July of 1858. He bars the very fact of secession and the seemingly permanent state of disunion it created from even entering into his language. He refers to the self-described Confederates not as members of a separate nation, much less as antagonists, but as "my countrymen, one and all." "In your hands, my dissatisfied fellow-countrymen, and not in mine," Lincoln pleads, "is the momentous issue of civil war" (1989e, 223). Lincoln's rhetoric in these passages is itself a medium of forgetting: refuse to acknowledge even the existence of the Confederacy, prevent its name from so much as entering into public speech, and the Union may be restored as if secession never occurred. To argue *for* public forgetting in argumentative terms would be to paradoxically acknowledge and thereby validate the existence of the Confederacy; in doing so, one would have to identify the very thing that must be forgotten. Lincoln instead adopts a nomenclature in which debilitating sociopolitical controversies are already forgotten, in which the Union is already ceremonially and seamlessly restored—"one and all."

In the final paragraph of his First Inaugural, one of the most beloved passages of U.S. political address, Lincoln rhetorically performs such forgetting in order to preserve the semblance of a harmonizing national memory. He continues to deny the Confederacy even the slightest acknowledgment precisely as he directs his closing comments to its members: "I am loath to close. We are not enemies, but friends. We must not be enemies. Though passion may have strained, it must not break the bonds of affection" (224). The adamant phrasing here conveys firm conviction: we *are not* enemies; we *are* friends. Destabilizing animosity, or "passion," between the states is already forgotten in this discourse. Lincoln identifies a present, indisputable state of being instead of arguing for a reality more imagined than actual, a moment of reconciliation desired but not yet achieved. His civic benediction thus culminates in an image of commemorative continuity and fraternal affection unblemished by the specter of secession: "The mystic chords of memory, stretching from every battle-field and patriot grave to every living heart and hearthstone all over this broad land, will yet swell the chorus of the Union when again touched, as surely they will be, by the better angels of our nature" (224). Lincoln preserves such binding lineaments, or "mystic chords," of memory through a sly but resounding act of forgetting: by excising the very fact of secession from the national political vocabulary. Indeed, he promotes this scene of national reconciliation in predictive but not propositional terms. Such a reality is *certain*—"mystic chords . . . *will yet swell* the chorus of the Union when again touched, as *surely they will be,*" by our "better angels"—without being *conditional*. In his discourse, the divisions that would make it so are already rescinded.

Prior to the Civil War, then, Lincoln's oratory featured sporadic inducements to public forgetting. Such forgetting, in his strategy, would initiate political reform or restoration not by rejecting the country's memorial traditions but by reinventing them. The foregoing synopsis nonetheless demonstrates that Lincoln had yet to integrate these dissimilar, alternately direct and indirect, appeals to public forgetting into a unified and refined public idiom by the eve of civil war. To that point, public forgetting played a relatively discrete role in his chief rhetorical tactics.

In fact, memorable imagery and meticulous historical detail overwhelmingly characterize Lincoln's speeches during the late antebellum era. His overriding rhetorical tactic at this time (of which his 1858 "House

Divided" speech and 1860 Cooper Union Address are excellent examples) was to arouse Republican support by imploring audiences to recognize and remember every offense against the Constitution committed by proslavery conspirators and to prove in arresting detail the political recklessness of popular sovereignty.[3] The unprecedented exigencies of the Civil War, however, moved Lincoln to craft, in his Gettysburg Address and Second Inaugural, a commemorative vernacular of public forgetting in which the rhetorical form and function of such forgetting are one and the same.

## Moral Forgetting and Rededication

Much has been made of the stark contrast between Edward Everett's grandiloquent oratory and Lincoln's comparatively curt, plainspoken remarks at Gettysburg on November 19, 1863.[4] Everett's encomium (1870) to the cause of the Union and its fallen defenders was the main attraction for an estimated fifteen thousand spectators assembled to witness dedication ceremonies at the site of the Union army's most important victory to date. Presidents at the time appeared at public events infrequently, and in late 1863 growing antiwar sentiment made Lincoln an unpopular chief executive, despite recent Union victories. Organizers were therefore surprised when he accepted their last-minute, courtesy invitation to attend. Everett's orotund address lasted two hours; true to the epideictic conventions of the day, he narrated the battle of Gettysburg in epic fashion, patriotically argued that secession was illegal, and dismissed fears that the Union would not survive civil war. Lincoln's terse and homespun eulogy lasted merely two minutes, providing a surprising anticlimax to Everett's ornate panegyric. What became the most famous oration in U.S. history (if not in the English language) and an object of reverent commemoration in its own right began as an ambivalently received rhetorical curiosity, stylistically idiosyncratic for its time and an apparent failure, according to many, in the art of ceremonial address.[5]

The rhetorical eccentricity of Lincoln's speech, according to conventional wisdom, is the very reason for its unrivaled veneration by later generations. Everett's speech was a consummate product of the time, and therefore destined not to outlive it; Lincoln's was visionary, secreting a genius appreciable only in historical hindsight. Everett's speech was a quintessential example of rhetorical overstatement and embellishment; Lincoln's was austerely understated but pregnant with meaning, requiring the interpretative efforts of later generations to ascertain its densely packed significance.

Everett's oratory sought to document the thick and variegated texture of the era; Lincoln's evoked a seemingly ageless meditation on the transcendent essence of events rather than their ephemeral veneer. Wills distills from such antitheses the following evaluative distinction: "Classicism of Everett's sort looks backward; but the classic *artifact* [Lincoln's] sets standards for the future—for a whole rank (*classis*) of efforts it makes possible" (1992, 52).

Such scholarly lore concerning the relative fortunes of Everett's and Lincoln's Gettysburg orations suggests that one may judge the artistry of the two addresses according to a single, objective conception of public memory itself, as if both speeches were designed to achieve the same memorial end. Everett's oft-quoted confession, in personal correspondence to Lincoln, that "I should be glad, if I could flatter myself that I came as near to the central idea of the occasion, in two hours, as you did in two minutes" (Wilson 2006, 229), provides compelling support for the notion that Lincoln succeeded where Everett failed. Commentators equipped with historical hindsight thus meticulously delineate artistic differences between the two addresses in order to laud Lincoln's speech as a vastly superior fulfillment of an identical commemorative exercise. But notable differences between the orations, remarkable as they are, extend further than stylistic asymmetries alone.

Everett's and Lincoln's addresses embody antithetical conceptions of the form and substance of public memory itself. The speeches are stylistically irreconcilable because Everett and Lincoln fashioned them in pursuit of irreconcilable commemorative ends. Everett's discourse allows no substantive role for public forgetting as a formative dimension of national memory. Its breadth and depth of historical detail typify a monumental work of memory, as Nietzsche defined it—a permanent resource of authoritative preservation and public instruction meant to withstand the erosions of time. In contrast, Lincoln affords public forgetting a central, even indispensable, commemorative function. His Gettysburg Address admonishes listeners to disavow the rituals of memorialization precisely because monumental memory is woefully insufficient as an alloy of political community in times of civic crisis. Nonetheless, the signal effect of Lincoln's admonishment in this context is supremely ironic: recasting U.S. political principles as transcendent ideals and fitting objects of reverent commemoration. The claim here is not that Everett embraced commemoration, and thus a vigorous culture of memory, while Lincoln shunned it. Lincoln's stunningly counterintuitive approach to the very act of commemoration, in which forgetting plays an indispensable part, reveals his visionary apprehension of the moral insights that commemorative rituals can generate when their ceremonial language promotes public scrutiny of the typically unacknowledged boundaries and blind spots of national memory.

At Gettysburg, Lincoln once again lingers over the boundaries of memory, as he did during his 1858 senatorial campaign speech in Chicago. But the presence of memory itself is radically diffuse compared to his earlier invocations of this *topos*. Lincoln previously spoke of memory as a tangible and organic substrate, regardless of its practical limitations. In his senatorial campaign address, memory of the Revolution was palpable and accessible, at least to those who possessed ancestral recollections of it ("We run our memory back over the pages of history for about eighty-two years"); in his First Inaugural, "mystic chords of memory" connoted a cohesive force securing the continuity of America's past, present, and future—a subterranean presence impressed upon graves, hearths, and hearthstones.

In Lincoln's remarks at Gettysburg, however, memory connotes a ponderous absence rather than a natural and abiding presence. He frames his address by separating historical time from the rites of memory. Such rites lose their organic ethos and appear oddly transparent when estranged from historical chronology. In performing this separation, his opening statements contrast sharply with his invocations of memory prior to the war:

> Four score and seven years ago our fathers brought forth on this continent, a new nation, conceived in Liberty, and dedicated to the proposition that all men are created equal.
>
> Now we are engaged in a great civil war, testing whether that nation or any nation so conceived and so dedicated, can long endure. We are met on a great battle-field of that war. We have come to dedicate a portion of that field, as a final resting place for those who here gave their lives that this nation might live. It is altogether fitting and proper that we should do this.[6]

This terse historical chronology is not an incitement to purposeful remembrance. It merely relates facts in brisk temporal succession. "Four score and seven years ago our fathers" founded the nation in the name of equality; "now" that nation and the principle of equality is tested by civil war; "we have come," the public has already gathered, to conduct "fitting and proper" dedication ceremonies. Lincoln withheld divisive topics in the peroration to his First Inaugural, yet the "mystic chords of memory" retained a robust and self-animating presence therein. Memory lacks autonomous content as Lincoln first speaks of it in the Gettysburg Address. All that remains is the bland and routine fact that citizens have assembled for customary memorial proceedings. It is "fitting and proper" to dedicate the battlefield, but ordinary and unremarkable as such. Commemoration here is not a source of inspiration, instruction, or reassuring historical continuity; it is merely something that happens from time to time.

This line of reasoning becomes more purposeful as Lincoln's discourse unfolds. He not only insinuates the arbitrariness of memorial rites but, more significantly, reverses the customary impetus to memorialize. Conventional ceremonial address performs the act of commemoration in language, yet Lincoln's words abruptly interrupt such rituals and thus the continuity of memory itself: "But, in a larger sense, we can not dedicate—we can not consecrate—we can not hallow—this ground. The brave men, living and dead, who struggled here, have consecrated it, far above our poor power to add or detract. The world will little note, nor long remember what we say here, but it can never forget what they did here." Lincoln employs "the densest array of negatives we find in the extant speeches" (Briggs 2005, 309) to insist that the language of commemoration cannot commemorate—it cannot "dedicate," "consecrate," or "hallow." Only the flimsiest vestige of durable memory survives in his statement that "the world . . . can never forget" the soldiers' valorous deeds (which faintly echoes the classical axiom that those who perform heroic acts should be awarded fame and immortality in communal lore). Such remembrance, however, lacks substantive agency or commitment in Lincoln's phrasing. The fact that "the world" will "never forget" the soldiers' deeds ascribes only the vaguest, most passive agency to this honorific gesture. If "we," actual citizens gathered for purpose of commemoration, cannot effectively dedicate, consecrate, or hallow "this ground," then by implication we cannot effectively preserve memory of the heroism that transpired there. The soldiers' own actions, rather than our memorial agency, ensures that their valor will be *not forgotten,* so to speak, more than we will effectively remember it. Lincoln's stated conviction that forgetting will not occur paradoxically emphasizes the disquieting transience of memory far more than the undesirability of its passing.

As such, Lincoln does not simply solicit an interruption of memory but, more decisively, performs it in language. His dedicatory remarks reveal the speciousness of memorial dedication. His ceremonial words reject the prudence of ceremony. His commemorative language refuses to name a proper object of commemoration. Lincoln's peculiar transmutation of memorial rites spurs something very different from commemoration traditionally conceived. If remembrance is an essentially impotent activity mired in the past, in death and decay, then we the public should forget the traditional rites of memory in order to undertake effectual action in the present and future. Memory, Lincoln insists, is not our aim:

> It is for us the living, rather, to be dedicated here to the unfinished work which they who fought here have thus far so nobly advanced. It is rather for us to be here dedicated to the great task remaining before us—that from these honored dead we take increased devotion to that cause for which they gave the last full measure of devotion—that we here highly resolve that these dead shall not have died in vain—that this nation, under God, shall have a new birth of freedom—and that government of the people, by the people, for the people, shall not perish from the earth.

Lincoln ennobles not memory but the "unfinished work" of the fallen soldiers, which they "have thus far so nobly advanced" but tragically left undone. We cannot memorialize this "work" because it continues in the present, because it is not yet a thing of the past. Forgetting customary and unreflective imperatives to memory, he suggests, prepares the community to uphold its truly consequential civic duty: the urgent labor of preserving the Union. In doing so, Lincoln does not merely identify a fitting alternative to commemorative rites; his language enacts the necessary transference from one object of "dedication" to another. Instead of memorial exercises, the charge to "us the living" is to "be here dedicated to the great task remaining before us." Lincoln notably expresses such dedication in a middle-voiced construction: his repetition of the phrase "It is" (for us to be dedicated) lacks a clear referent. Our dedication to action instead of memory "is"—it simply exists, and irrefutably so. Lincoln does not provide an ordered rationale for such an act of public forgetting; his words accomplish it by evoking the political reality it would create as an event that has already occurred.

Lincoln's phrasing renounces the conventional meaning of commemoration and dedicates his listeners to a purpose shorn of its rituals. To this end, his wording reassumes an active tense when he identifies the desired outcome of his encomium. He does not entreat listeners to commit themselves to a course of action but simply proclaims that "from these honored dead we take increased devotion." "We," in Lincoln's portrayal, do not recollect—we *act,* "we take." He does not *argue for* such activity as a desired goal; his discourse symbolically brings into being a united citizenry already dedicated to it, unburdened by commemorative trappings. Discarding ceremonial ritual consequently produces a result as self-evident as our dedication. Lincoln states as unambiguous fact that "these dead shall not have died in vain"; that "this nation, under God, shall have a new birth of freedom"; that "government of the people, by the people, for the people, shall not perish from the earth." He thus concludes his paradoxical commemorative discourse by bestowing upon spectators a morally binding reality rather than an object of commemoration—the prophesied achievement of a nation permanently free, unified, and redeemed where none had existed before.

This claim to such expansive rhetorical effect is not an overstatement. Scholars credit Lincoln's rhetoric, particularly the political dicta intoned in his Gettysburg Address, with comprehensively redefining U.S. national identity. On the brink of the Civil War, Americans routinely spoke of the United *States* in a plural sense, describing it as "the Union" with an emphasis on voluntary confederation. Lincoln himself adhered to such rules of ordinary usage at the time; he spoke of "the Union" twenty times in his First Inaugural but never of "the nation" as a singular entity. Lincoln's wartime promotion of a resolutely inclusive vocabulary of national identity, however, created much of what Peterson calls the "spiritual capital" of his words. By late 1863, Lincoln described the severally defined United States as "this nation," the *United* States—a resolutely singular construction. Lincoln referred to "the nation" five times in his Gettysburg Address without speaking of "the union" once (Bryson 1994, 80).[7] His performance of public forgetting at Gettysburg abrogated traditional idioms of memory in which the United States was conceived as a loosely connected plural entity and coined a new vernacular of universal and univocal civic identity. "Because of it," Wills states, "we live in a different America" (1992, 147).

In this respect, Lincoln's performance of public forgetting in the Gettysburg Address produces the speech's most admired rhetorical achievement: its transformation of political principles first proffered in the Declaration of Independence, with specific relevance to the events of 1776, into transcendent articles of liberty applicable to all people everywhere. Lincoln's interpretation of the Civil War as an epic test of the Declaration's validity endowed internecine strife in a fledgling republic with a significance as transcendent as the global fate of popular government itself. Scholars often marvel at Lincoln's use, in the Gettysburg Address, of almost painfully simple impersonal pronouns to reinterpret the meaning and purpose of inaugural U.S. political ideals and bequeath to ordinary Americans a revised collective memory of their common origins unadorned with historical particulars. The foregoing analysis suggests, however, that this account tells an incomplete story concerning the memorial ramifications of Lincoln's conspicuously impersonal language.

The impersonal pronouns that make Lincoln's Gettysburg Address such a readily available cipher of historical memory succeed as such because they operate as permanent instruments of public forgetting. Lincoln's deceptively simple phrasing accomplishes a weird rhetorical slight of hand: his language is unrelentingly vague even when he appears to identify specific people, places, and events. In the first sentence, for instance, every means of identification is at once clearly phrased but unavoidably obtuse: "Four score and seven years ago our fathers brought forth on this continent, a new nation, conceived in Liberty, and dedicated to the proposition that all men are created equal." Temporally, listeners must not only perform a convoluted mathematical exercise (determining the numerical equivalent of a "score," multiplying it by four, adding seven, and then subtracting that sum from 1863) but also infer that the historical referent in question is the unnamed year of independence. The identity of "our fathers" is more assumed than stated. They are known not by personal identification but as an impersonal group, which also implies another impersonal group: the "we" that remains equally indistinct but claims such fathers as *ours,* as common ancestors. Geographically, the United States is similarly named and unnamed as "a new nation"; this designation would have been even more unusual in 1863 because, once again, the country at the time was commonly known as a plural entity. The only noun in this sentence to warrant a proper name is "Liberty," a hopelessly broad construct nonetheless. This pattern holds true throughout Lincoln's subsequent descriptions of the Civil War, the Gettysburg battlefield, and the fallen soldiers as, respectively, "a great civil war"; "a great battle-field of that war"; and "those who here gave their lives," "brave men," or simply "they."

Lincoln's language intricately performs the suspension of memory, or public forgetting, which his stated conviction that "we can not dedicate," "consecrate," or "hallow" "this ground" conveys as the basic argumentative premise of the entire Gettysburg Address. His steadfastly impersonal descriptors evoke a liminal sense of time, place, and personality, retaining the impressions of dates, places, and names remembered, but mere impressions all the same. His pronouns mimic the gesture of identifying discernible eras, events, and individuals while simultaneously lightening the memorial speech of all historical particulars. Such descriptors are, in effect, placeholders for historical referents, adaptable to countless memorial occasions after the fact.

In this address, the past is both preserved and relinquished. Lincoln's impersonal language transforms a commemorative ritual intended to conserve a surfeit of historical detail into a rhetorical sieve through which it passes, a conduit of perpetual forgetting. To invoke the Gettysburg Address in future commemorative situations, as so many have done, is to perform yet again the unburdening of historical particulars and the dispersal of existing memory that defines its wily memorial logic. Lincoln's rhetoric dictates that it is not merely conductive but *necessary* for the public to forget virtually all historical aspects of the events at Gettysburg in order to remember their essential meaning. Or conversely, one can memorialize the fundamental moral lessons of the war, in the terms that Lincolns establishes, without acquiring any substantive knowledge of its historical or political development. The fact that this essential meaning turns out to be nominally transcendent in nature—to exceed the boundaries of historical experience, and thus the customary foundation of public memory—only compounds the acutely ironic nature of Lincoln's commemorative speech.

The Gettysburg Address most poignantly produces transcendent meaning out of historical forgetting by transmuting wartime history into an essentially Christian parable. The soldiers to whom Lincoln refers occupy the sacrificial focal point of this parable. They, like Jesus, died for a universal principle: the equality of "all men." They knowingly sacrificed themselves to redeem the nation, to ensure a "new birth of freedom" in which "government of the people, by the people, for the people, shall not perish from the earth." It is incumbent upon the citizenry to ensure that the soldiers "shall not have died in vain," that its wicked violations of the nation's founding principle will be redeemed by imitating the feats of its soldiers, just as it was incumbent upon the disciples of Jesus to honor his supreme sacrifice by dedicating themselves to his unfinished work.

A subtle but resounding tenor of forgetting runs through this allegory of political sacrifice and redemption—or more to the point, of forgiveness. Lincoln uses consistently impersonal pronouns in referring to the slain soldiers, once again, only as "those who here gave their lives," "brave men," or "they." "They," in his unadorned but telling word choices, are neither Union nor Confederate combatants but citizen-soldiers who bravely sacrificed themselves—"who here gave their lives." Lincoln's wording quietly enacts a forgetting of national division and violent discord analogous to Jesus' instruction that his followers must forgive even those who do them gravest harm, a lesson embodied in his own gruesome death. Union and Confederate identities dissolve and enemies share in a common sacrifice on behalf of the nation.

The specter of these soldiers as Lincoln conjures it constitutes a public model of forgiving by forgetting, of granting mercy through disenthrallment from the past. The nation, in order to ensure that its soldiers did not die in vain, is morally obligated to forget its present-day cleavages and reconcile as one political body unburdened by animosities, as a community of forgiveness whose members have been cleansed of their shared sins—indeed of the very past in which they transpired—and released to perform good deeds in the future. To disavow inflammatory elements of the nation's past is to pledge its members, in the strongest moral terms, to a refurbishment of political fidelity in the present. Lincoln's appeals to forgetting and forgiveness do not amount to a call for public obliviousness toward the past (unlike traditional and modern forms of the *ars oblivionis* documented in Chapter 2). They constitute, rather, a mechanism of civic restoration, as Arendt envisions it, in which members of the *polis* interrupt the course of seemingly automatic, irreversible events (in this case, the overwhelming carnage of civil war) by adopting a transformed set of sociopolitical relations—or simply put, by beginning again.

## Political Forgetting and Reconciliation

Lincoln's Christian allusions in the Gettysburg Address suggest a fundamental principle of justice: the death of its soldiers is the price the nation must pay for political redemption and rebirth. The path to justice lies not in conventional memorial rites but in ascetic forgetting. A comprehensive review of the bloody past at this juncture would merely preserve in public discourse the debilitating divisiveness that defined it. But why, necessarily, must the nation pay this heavy toll? Why does it suffer under this heavy moral burden in the first place?

Lincoln's Second Inaugural Address provides convincing answers to these queries. It does so, moreover, by notably amplifying the confluence of justice and forgetting that Lincoln displays at Gettysburg. As such, the Second Inaugural represents an equally vital stage in Lincoln's prolonged effort to coin an idiom of public forgetting conducive to political restoration. The following section examines how the Second Inaugural augments the Gettysburg Address's rhetorical performance of moral forgetting in order to demarcate a comparatively stringent ground of political judgment and reunification between North and South.

Scholars understandably express admiration for Lincoln's rhetorical ability in the Gettysburg Address to derive nothing less than a revolutionary reinterpretation of U.S. history in a spare 272 words. Lincoln's Second Inaugural represents an equally masterful demonstration of his uncanny talent for conveying a wealth of meaning in highly compressed language. The shortest inaugural address in U.S. history, it contains only four efficient paragraphs and a tight 703 words; it falls far short of tripling the rhetorically tiny Gettysburg Address. Lincoln's glaringly concise Second Inaugural constituted a more brazen defiance of ceremonial expectations and situational constraints than did his elegy at Gettysburg. The president's inclusion in the proceedings at Gettysburg was a polite afterthought in an age when presidents rarely made public appearances; the inaugural platform, however, was reserved solely for marking his return to office in decidedly public fashion. Dedication ceremonies at the site of a crucial Union victory undoubtedly represented a significant civic event; but the public at the time of Lincoln's Second Inaugural eagerly anticipated the surrender of the Confederacy as well as the president's statements regarding his agenda for national reconciliation (R. White 2002, 22–23). Lincoln's response to these unique situational and generic factors—a markedly clipped public statement unadorned by customary invocations of national memory and civic tradition—was an unusually bold rhetorical choice.

In the Second Inaugural, Lincoln again assumes a persona located weirdly outside the ceremonial rites over which he presides. This detached persona acquires paramount significance during the course of the address as part of Lincoln's effort to influence the spirit of national reconciliation. The provisional effect of such a stance, however, is once again to reveal, from an incongruous perspective, the arbitrariness of public rituals in which commemoration normally plays a vital role. Lincoln's use of this technique upon entering his second term in office arguably exceeds his suppression of communal memory from the dedication ceremony at Gettysburg. As before, he does not symbolically endow his audience with political will and agency through collective remembrance of a common heritage (which standard inaugural conventions would dictate) but portrays the nation as feebly subject to the whims of a divine dramaturgy in which even he, the president, lacks the agency to implement his political will, particularly one rooted in the wisdom of historical recollection. The public forgetting of both ceremonial tradition and wartime history that Lincoln stages in his Second Inaugural thus provides a stark but powerful symbolic enactment of national reconciliation in a forum more conducive to its practical pursuit than that of the Gettysburg Address.

Lincoln's opening paragraph performs a decisive rejection of routine memorial customs. This rejection invalidates the public's recourse to those customs as a source of collective agency over the vicissitudes of history:

At this second appearing to take the oath of the presidential office there is less occasion for an extended address than there was at the first. Then a statement somewhat in detail of a course to be pursued seemed fitting and proper. Now, at the expiration of four years, during which public declarations have been constantly called forth on every point and phase of the great contest which still absorbs the attention and engrosses the energies of the nation, little that is new could be presented. The progress of our arms, upon which all else chiefly depends, is as well known to the public as to myself, and it is, I trust, reasonably satisfactory and encouraging to all. With high hope for the future, no prediction in regard to it is ventured.[8]

The passive voice dominates Lincoln's curiously detached reflection on the propriety of his own utterances. John Channing Briggs pinpoints the striking rhetorical effect Lincoln achieved with this technique: "The strange mingling of his resolute energy with an almost alarming passivity allowed Lincoln to persuade while withdrawing into his audiences' world, like a profound dramatist who spoke elliptically through others" (2005, 302). Lincoln does not choose to speak briefly; rather, "there is less occasion for extended address." He did not decide on the prudence of "a statement somewhat in detail" for his previous inaugural; instead, it merely "seemed fitting and proper." The notion that one could present "little that is new" on this occasion is not his personal conviction, but merely a fact. He does not argue against predicting whether the country's "high hope for the future" will be satisfied but flatly states that "no prediction in regard to it is ventured," utterly denying his or anyone else's ability to foretell the fate of the nation based on a ceremonial review of its past. Lincoln's only reference to himself as an agent in these circumstances—"I trust"—is semantically passive if not grammatically so; it expresses little more than a wish that the public is sufficiently informed of the "progress of our arms," meaning the military force that he leads as commander in chief. His intricately wrought passive grammar emphasizes the apparently staid nature of the inaugural ceremony, including its customary displays of intertwined political and memorial continuity. Not even Lincoln, as president, can change the fact that artful appeals to the nation's past will be of little help in the present conflict.

Lincoln's wording inverts the standard memorial logic of inaugural ceremonies. Presidents on such occasions conventionally recall signal features of the national past as sources of public instruction. But Lincoln's tactic is the inverse: historical review is undesirable ("there is little new that could be presented") and, as such, provides no indication of the country's impending fortunes ("no prediction in regard to it is ventured"). Lincoln flatly asserts as self-evident fact the impropriety of formal appeals to a national past instead of securing public legitimacy by asserting his policies' continuity with political tradition. Instead of consolidating public support by invoking the guidance of history, Lincoln blankly dismisses its validity as a warrant for the exercise of political will. His rhetoric reduces the inaugural ceremony to its scantest ritualistic remainder. Its paradoxical purpose is to announce the current futility of such ceremony in its customary forms, to justify the polity disenthralling itself from (or forgetting) its normally unquestioned confidence in the moral and political destiny that those forms allegedly foretell.

Lincoln commences his inaugural remarks with a remarkably elliptical review of the events that led to war. His language in these passages strangely places the public at an even further, less empowered remove from the bloody history through which it has so recently lived. As in his remarks at Gettysburg, Lincoln does not pretend to summon a palpable sense of the historical past but merely presents a litany of limpid facts. "On the occasion corresponding to this four years ago," he intones, "all thoughts were anxiously directed to an impending civil war. All dreaded it, all sought to avert it." The past that Lincoln describes is curiously drained of subjectivity. His phrasing separates the "thoughts" of "impending civil war" at that time from any agent who possessed them; they simply exist on their own. His wording implicitly ascribes affect and intent to an inclusive body—"All dreaded it, all sought to avert it"—but fails to draw any resemblance between that former constituency and the public he now addresses. Lincoln's opening remarks in the Second Inaugural provide a logical rationale for state forgetting; but he rhetorically enacts such forgetting by withholding personal identity from the past he relates. In symbolic terms, the public cannot remember a past of which it has been dispossessed. Neither, by implication, can the public take that past for granted as an exemplum of praiseworthy conduct in the present.

The political advantages of public forgetting as such become clearer in Lincoln's ensuing report of how the Civil War began. Lincoln circumvents the epideictic procedures of praise and blame characteristic of inaugural ceremony by continuing to excise all traces of identity and agency from his account of Southern secession and its aftermath. He thereby transmutes a formerly divisive national past, including the animosities that fueled it, into an oddly unifying interregnum: "While the inaugural address was being delivered from this place, devoted altogether to *saving* the Union without war, insurgent agents were in the city seeking to *destroy* it without war—seeking to dissolve the Union and divide effects by negotiation. Both parties deprecated war, but one of them would *make* war rather than let the nation survive, and the other would *accept* war rather than let it perish, and the war came." The appellations "North" and "South" and "Union" and "Confederate," seemingly unavoidable political designations at the time, have already been forgotten in Lincoln's discourse. His language consequently deprives both entities of causal agency, whether positive or negative. He, as president, did not deliver the inaugural address four years ago in an attempt to prevent secession and civil war; rather, the address was merely "delivered from this place" and "devoted" of its own accord "to *saving* the Union" (a statement which implies a public forgetting of the crucial fact that many Southerners as well as their Northern sympathizers viewed Lincoln's inaugural address as the spark that ignited the flames of war). Lincoln vaguely describes "insurgent agents" who sought to "*destroy*" the Union but fails to further identify them.

This public forgetting of subjective agency is *partially* redemptive. Despite the desire of one side to save the Union and of the other to destroy it, both endeavored to do so "without war" because they "deprecated" war alike. Northerners and Southerners bitterly divided by irreconcilable aims prior to the war are now reconciled as one, in Lincoln's retrospection, through their mutual abhorrence of armed strife. Lincoln's language achieves an uncanny rhetorical balance in preserving the reality of mortal conflict without levying blame for it on any one party. One unnamed entity made war and the other accepted it, but above all, "the war" simply "came," an event visited on both parties for which neither was responsible. "'War,'" Ronald White Jr. observes, represents "the subject rather than the object" of this speech (2002, 63). In Lincoln's version of events, making and accepting war were not even willful decisions: the idea that one side "would *make* war" and "the other would *accept*" it implies reluctant acquiescence to an unalterable *telos* rather than a zeal for its completion.

Lincoln's delicate phasing enacts his overarching rationale. A detailed survey of the wartime events that dominated his previous administration would preserve in public record the rancor that so vehemently divided the country. Such a survey, moreover, would perpetuate that rancor by arousing competing attributions of blame among its various sections. To deny obvious manifestations of sectional discord even the slightest entrance into one's language, to portray the recent past as if they were already forgotten, is to cultivate a ground of mutual political commitment in the midst of manifold damage to U.S. national identity.

This is not to say that Lincoln fails to identify a cause of the bloody conflict; he merely does so in a manner that furthers the process of public forgetting and redemption begun in his allusions to its origins. The cause, in Lincoln's retelling, is neither Northern aggression nor Southern belligerence but the mere existence of slavery in the United States. "One eighth of the whole population was colored slaves," Lincoln states, "not distributed generally over the Union, but localized in the southern part of it. These slaves constituted a peculiar and powerful interest. All knew that this interest was somehow the cause of the war." Lincoln continues to eradicate all traces of historical agency and political will, whether Northern or Southern, in his rendition of past events. His language suggests that slavery was the cause of enmity between the states by the fact of its mere presence in "the southern part" of the Union. Prolonged efforts to either protect and extend or impede and abolish the institution are forgotten in this account. Slavery simply existed, in and of itself, as a cause of animosity.

Lincoln maintains this interpretation even as he concedes that partisans adopted antagonistic policies regarding the existence of slavery. "To strengthen, perpetuate, and extend this interest," he observes, "was the object for which the insurgents would rend the Union even by war, while the Government claimed no right to do more than to restrict the territorial enlargement of it." Notice, however, that Lincoln does not identify "the insurgents" of which he speaks, who "would rend the Union" in defense of slavery, as the Southern states or their representatives. Rather, slavery simply existed before the war in its "southern part." The Union is counterintuitively whole even in Lincoln's account of its initial fragmentation, a single polity undivided into opposed Northern and Southern partitions. Lincoln's performance of public forgetting omits the fact that, for many Northern partisans, "the insurgents" who rent the Union were obviously Southern secessionists bent on achieving decisive political and territorial separation. He conversely performs the same procedure of public forgetting for those who would identify Northern aggression against states' rights as the cause of civil warfare. In Lincoln's phrasing, neither the federal system nor he as president could exercise significant agency concerning slavery. Instead, "the Government"—a construct as faceless as the aforementioned "insurgents"— claimed only an allegedly modest right to "restrict" the "territorial enlargement" of slavery, not curtail its existence. Lincoln's development of this *topos* suggests that the bare existence of slavery "constituted" such a "peculiar and powerful interest" that it alone incited hostilities among the warring parties rather than their conscious designs or impulsive actions. These reciprocal erasures of historical agency and political will accomplish the peculiar rhetorical feat of absolving both North and South of blame for the war while nevertheless preserving in state remembrance the putative essence of that bitter conflict. As in the Gettysburg Address, one forgets virtually all historical and political details pertaining to the causes of war in order to understand clearly its radical moral significance.

Lincoln's rhetorical performance of public forgetting, in which bloody discord and oppositional identities are written out of the past, subsequently moves from intimations of mutual blamelessness to a subtle granting of forgiveness. In this respect, it extends the political logic of forgiving by forgetting that he initiated at Gettysburg. Lincoln's account in his Second Inaugural of how the Civil War began places both Union and Confederacy in a state of apparent innocence: neither is at fault for the war because neither willfully instigated it. North and South indeed fought the war—but innocently, unaware of the destruction it would cause. "Neither party," Lincoln maintains, "expected for the war the magnitude or duration which it has already attained. Neither anticipated that the *cause* of the conflict might cease with or even before the conflict itself should cease. Each looked for an easier triumph, and a result less fundamental and astounding." Distinctions between Union and Confederacy are once again forgotten, along with the otherwise obvious agency and accountability of both parties, as evinced in Lincoln's repetition of impersonal collective pronouns ("Neither" and "Each") to describe the two sides as one in their helplessness amid the bloody conflagration. The war, including its "magnitude and duration," was not the result of something either North or South did; it was something done *to* them, an idea accentuated by the fact that bloodshed continued even after "the cause of the conflict" was removed (a deed accomplished, in Lincoln's logic, by the Emancipation Proclamation of 1863).

This portrait of reciprocal innocence, induced by a public forgetting of shared culpability and omnipresent discord, is central to the motif of mutual forgiveness that Lincoln crafts. His insinuation of such forgetting in this context furthers his purpose of attaining a symbolic ground of political reconciliation. He poignantly locates this ground when both sides of the dire conflict are helpless to arrest its course: "Both read the same Bible and pray to the same God, and each invokes His aid against the other. It may seem strange that any men should dare to ask a just God's assistance in wringing their bread from the sweat of other men's faces, but let us judge not, that we be not judged. The prayers of both could not be answered. That of neither has been answered fully." Lincoln identifies a source of commonality (indeed, of communion) in the hour of fiercest acrimony among Northern and Southern states: their mutual faith in the same higher power. Even when pitted against one another, asking "a just God's assistance in wringing their bread from the sweat of other men's faces," they nevertheless pray desperately to the same God. Distinctions between Union and Confederacy are forgotten in the tragic recognition that the prayers of both "could not be answered," that the pleas "of neither have been answered fully" by their common savior. No longer divided, they are spiritually joined in this despairing state.

God, in Lincoln's reasoning, does not grant forgiveness for the war. Forgiveness comes from both sides' forgetting of their seemingly intractable differences in favor of recognizing their common despondency. In Lincoln's account, the fact that God has not answered the prayers of either North or South reveals the futility of attempting to discern the designs of the supreme deity in historical events as well as the fruitlessness of our efforts to steer them toward favorable resolution. Lengthy public recollections of a divisive past would only obscure this vital insight. Such a fate recommends, instead, the wisdom of not judging—of not preserving detailed public memories rife with malevolence—so "that we be not judged." North and South are reunited as a political body in this vision through the only source of historical agency and spiritual redemption they have left: forgetting the malice that permeates their remembered past in order to release one another from blame and thereby begin to restore the Union's integrity—to begin again as such. As before, Lincoln's professions of forgetting and forgiveness involve an effort not to blot out the past entirely (in the manner of Judeo-Christian tropes) but to persuade a violently fractured public to regard its contested past in a radically different way and to adopt dramatically altered sociopolitical relations as a result.

This secular derivation of forgiveness allows Lincoln to cultivate a rationale for national reconciliation as politically obligatory as it is symbolically idealistic. His rhetoric of public forgetting compels the nation not to linger over the vitriol of a past emblazoned in collective memory but to anticipate an ominous future in which divine (not earthly) judgment awaits North and South alike. In the secular realm of public affairs, the separateness of those entities formerly known as Union and Confederate are forgotten, thus allowing human forgiveness of mutual sins; but God has not forgotten such iniquities, and ultimate judgment has yet to be delivered. "The Almighty has His own purposes," Lincoln declares. He invites listeners to "suppose that American slavery is one of those offenses which, in the providence of

God, must needs come, but which, having continued through His appointed time, He now wills to remove, and that He gives to both North and South this terrible war as the woe due to those by whom the offense came." This passage features Lincoln's only identification in his Second Inaugural (or in the Gettysburg Address) of North and South as separate entities; yet their nominal distinctness in this context is nugatory to the extent that Union and Confederacy are manifestly one in their joint culpability for the scourge of slavery and in their suffering as a result of the holy retribution that God visits on them for having condoned it.

Lincoln thus locates (as he did at Gettysburg) the essential meaning of the Civil War neither in memory nor in history but in a transcendental realm ungoverned by such human constructs. In so doing, Lincoln interrupts the ordinary tendency to inspect our collective past for patterns of regularity with which to predict the course of historical events. He recasts the war as an event determined "in the providence of God," "through His appointed time." Secular memory and historical perception are meaningless in those timeless domains. Conventional recourse to memory or history as sources of political wisdom and resolve are forgotten in Lincoln's prophetic vision. The nation is now restored as one in its very lack of historical agency, in its pitiable but universal hope for a speedy end to the odious war that God has inflicted on it: "Fondly do we hope, fervently do we pray, that this mighty scourge of war may speedily pass away." Lincoln does not entreat the public to embrace its past as a source of national continuity and restoration; he admonishes them to anticipate, with fear and trembling, divine judgment in an apocalyptic future.

Lincoln's vivid rendering of God's protracted vengeance engulfs the feckless prayers for a quick and merciful end offered up by Northerners and Southerners alike:

> Yet, if God wills that it continue until all the wealth piled by the bondsman's two hundred and fifty years of unrequited toil shall be sunk, and until every drop of blood drawn with the lash shall be paid by another drawn with the sword, as was said three thousand years ago, so still must be said, "The judgments of the Lord are true and righteous altogether."

Lincoln again inverts standard inaugural conventions of praise and blame rooted in prominent appeals to national memory. Instead of commending the nobility of civic traditions, he identifies one such tradition—"American slavery," which extends back to the country's prenational origins—as shameful proof of the nation's transgressions against God. Lincoln invokes the national memory of slavery not as a device for galvanizing public will but in order to reveal that the country's long-standing wickedness, its traditional tolerance for slavery, has placed it in a state of powerlessness before God, who undoubtedly will deliver "true and righteous" judgments. Comprehension of worldly history, in this eschatological vision, merits uncertainty rather than confidence in the course of an indeterminate future.[9] God may will that the war continues, Lincoln reveals, "until all the wealth piled by the bondsman's . . . unrequited toil" is repaid in blood. His prophecy imparts no historical calculus according to which such a fearsome debt would finally be satisfied. Historical memory, by implication, fails pathetically as a resource for judgment in the face of such overwhelming debts, the momentousness of which shatters ordinary perceptions of historical order and regularity. The meaning of the present conflict and the destiny it holds lie in a divine realm unmoved by human desires or calculations.

The substantive political advantage of Lincoln's prophecy, aside from its popular theological resonance, is that it provides a motivation for the protracted work of social and political renewal beyond conciliatory gestures of forgetting and forgiving. Displaying such conciliation is only a provisional and largely ceremonial step. What deeper motivation, beyond officially orchestrated gestures of goodwill, might secure a compulsory commitment between North and South to the more demanding and prolonged work of national reconciliation? Lincoln's implicit answer is that such commitment constitutes our only hope of *divine,* rather than human, forgiveness. Granted, we must first forgive one another in order to at least commence it, and do so by willfully forgetting our initially bellicose separation. But true and righteous justice, in this conception, involves reparation of a mammoth collective debt that one can never be sure of having repaid. The spiritual debt is so extensive that our efforts at justice through the penitence of political restoration must be even greater.

Lincoln's rhetoric additionally suggests that the nation's hope for salvation as such lies in the aforementioned higher-order form of public forgetting rather than that of worldly forgiveness. Both the form and content of his Second Inaugural attest that the unhistorical, immemorial, and thus incomprehensible calendar of divine judgment exposes the arbitrary influence of ritual public commemorations over the work of political unification. Forget not only immediate hostilities and bitter sectional discord, Lincoln asserts; forget, as well, the trained habit of memorializing iconic figures or events and attend to the colossal moral debt yet to be paid for the country's offenses. The Second Inaugural's formal brevity and avoidance of ceremonial language embodies this premise, while its oft-quoted peroration explicitly affirms it: "With malice toward none, with charity for all, with firmness in the right as God gives us to see the right, let us strive on to finish the work we are in, to bind up the nation's wounds, to care for him who shall have borne the battle and for his widow and his orphan, to do all which may achieve and cherish a just and lasting peace among ourselves and with all nations." Lincoln's benediction models the dispersal of commemorative custom that he identifies as a fundamental condition for restoring the integrity of the Union. In doing so, this brief concluding statement efficiently constellates the Second Inaugural's major *topoi*. With charitable forgiveness, Lincoln implores, let us forget our differences, let us attend to one another's basic and undeniable human needs, let us set aside trivial ceremonies that distract us from those solemn obligations, and let us remember all the while that only the grace of God determines our ability to discern right conduct. The abbreviated form of the peroration reinforces such explicitly stated premises by performing the very disinclination for state remembrance that Lincoln rejects in the Second Inaugural's opening passages. Following the zealousness of the divine prophecy immediately preceding it, such ostensibly simple and unembellished sentiments resolve the address in an abrupt anticlimax that soberly dismisses listeners to their urgently waiting duties.

The rhetoric of public forgetting in Lincoln's Second Inaugural thus improves upon the Gettysburg Address in one crucial political sense: it delineates a comparatively decisive principle of justice, presented as motivation for Northerners and Southerners to relinquish their fractured national identities and mutually dedicate themselves to restoring the integrity of the Union. Despite its brilliantly concentrated and prismatic turns of phrase, Lincoln's essential message in the Gettysburg Address—dedicate yourselves to securing the promises of the Declaration so that these soldiers will not have died in vain—is unoriginal among classical *epitaphios logos,* which commonly extolled fallen heroes as models of civic conduct. Lincoln admittedly endows the classical eulogistic form with Christian significance and imagery; but he does not substantially alter that form itself. The logic of forgetting and forgiveness in the Gettysburg Address is also reassuringly familiar and harmonious, reflecting a Christian conception of grace. The fallen soldiers sacrificed themselves so that unified popular government would be reborn. Lincoln's repetition of insistent, unequivocal future tenses in his famed closing lines expresses this idea as a certainty: "We here highly resolve that these dead *shall not* have died in vain—that this nation, under God, *shall have* a new birth of freedom—and that government of the people, by the people, for the people, *shall not* perish from the earth" (emphasis added). The president's remarks at Gettysburg therefore suggest, perhaps unwittingly, that the nation's moral debt to providence has been paid—tragically, by the grave sacrifice of its soldiers, but paid nonetheless. In Christian theology, Jesus redeems the sins of humanity in the sacrificial act; his death is the price paid for the sins of humankind. Lincoln's closing in the Gettysburg Address implies an analogous secular assurance in the wartime deliverance of divine grace: the sacrifice of Union and Confederate soldiers ensures that popular government will endure perpetually, that justice is done and we are released to good works in the future, knowing we have been redeemed. Justice so conceived resembles a *fait accompli* as much as a task awaiting completion.

In his Second Inaugural, however, Lincoln fashions a criterion of justice that characterizes the work of national reconciliation as an unheeded civic imperative. Here, he insists that justice for North and South alike requires the repayment of a potentially infinite moral debt, and warns that even complete repayment of this debt will not guarantee the public's salvation. Lincoln's depiction of justice as such reconciles what one might initially interpret as a theological inconsistency in the Second Inaugural suggested by his portrayal of forgetting and forgiveness. Lincoln absolves both Union and Confederacy of ultimate responsibility for the conflict, at least in the world of secular affairs, by banishing their separate political identities from public discourse; he seeks to establish a transformative amity among military foes by arguing that their mutual culpability renders them blameless to one another ("Let us judge not, that we be not judged"). Neither foe may indict the other because sin imbues them both. If "the war came" because of the mere existence of slavery (and not the passions or intent or either party), and if both sides suffered it as a result of their shared sins, then they began and ended the war in a state of comparable innocence. By this logic, divisive elements of the national past deserve to be forgotten because remembering them impedes the ability of each party to forgive the other in the present. Hence the potential inconsistency: if both sides are innocent to each other, and deserving of mutual forgiveness, then why does the country still face the terrible prospect of God's wrath for the sin of slavery? Why does it await redemption still?

Lincoln avoids inconsistency, and provides a compelling imperative for political reunification, by underscoring a distinctive criterion of justice.

The Gettysburg Address features an essentially Christian conception of justice in which our sins are absolved and forgiveness is granted in the sacrificial act; but Lincoln withholds divine absolution and forgiveness in the Second Inaugural's prophetic, Old Testament conception of judgment. Suffering and sacrifice provide scant hope for redemption in this latter circumstance. God has not answered either Union or Confederate prayers, despite the "magnitude" and "duration" of death and destruction that both sides have endured. In Lincoln's narration, such death and destruction may proceed interminably, at God's behest, according to an eternal calendar that crushes our beliefs in the efficacy of commemorative rituals or historical predictability. North and South may forget their acrimonious past and forgive one another, but forgetting and forgiveness as such is unequal to divine justice. For this reason, the immediate conciliation (or forgiving by forgetting) that Lincoln seeks among North and South is necessary but lamentably limited to secular affairs. At Lincoln's urging, Union and Confederate listeners may at least set themselves back on the path to ultimate justice when they collectively ratify a higher order form of public forgetting: when they disenthrall themselves from naïve beliefs in their ability to steer worldly events toward a just end based on the alleged wisdom of their selectively remembered past.

The pivotal revelation of Lincoln's Second Inaugural is that the Civil War confirms, in Old Testament fashion, that the nation has inherited its forebears' sins, and that such wickedness pervades it still. For Lincoln, the fact that Union and Confederacy continue to battle against one another proves the accuracy of this revelation. In his Gettysburg Address, the sacrificial death of Union and Confederate soldiers removes the sins of the nation and confers grace upon it; in the Second Inaugural, the nation was born and will remain fallen from grace, for sin burdens the country in all its incarnations. Recognition of this inexorably fallen state reveals the absurdity of seeking to draw inspiration from a nostalgic past or a roseate future. Lincoln's invocation of such theology for political purposes mirrors that of Old Testament prophets who delivered news of impending apocalypse: our only hope of salvation, according to God's distribution of justice, lies not in maintaining continuity with a past steeped in iniquity but in the social justice we model in the present, in the merciful and charitable acts we perform for one another, especially the meanest and lowest among us.

On these grounds, however, one may raise understandable objections to the claim that Lincoln's Second Inaugural culminates in a politically transformative act of public forgetting. Isn't the address devoted to fixing in listeners' minds an image of their unmitigated vulnerability before divine retribution?

Doesn't Lincoln essentially prompt the public to remember constantly this fearful prospect? Affirmative answers to these questions prove, rather than contradict, the thesis that interrelated forms of public forgetting explain the radical political significance of Lincoln's Second Inaugural.

Lincoln indeed implores his listeners to anticipate God's wrath; but he does so precisely by rejecting customary rituals of public ceremony, and the collective past they reputedly preserve, as immaterial to the labor of national reconciliation. He urges his listeners not to derive meaning or purpose from a stable and replenishing past (to remember as such) but to merely remind themselves of the terrifyingly uncertain future they face. The national fate revealed in Lincoln's prophecy confirms the arbitrariness of secular history and public memory, the significance of which are overshadowed by an eternal calendar recording the infinity of divine justice. Lincoln's appeals for historical disenthrallment through displays of mercy illustrate W. James Booth's postulation that "lessening" the burdens of communal history and memory can desirably redefine citizenship as "a condition where the possession of the past is (mostly) irrelevant. This political forgetting is meant to allow for an identity that nurtures impartiality, a neutrality as between citizens, a condition in which the only relevant fact about their status is that of their shared citizenship" (2006, 151). Employing timeless prophecy in order to dispel public enthrallments with history is politically beneficial to the extent that it accentuates the enormity of the public's waiting civic duties, even as war continues, instead of seeking to ameliorate the hardships they pose with the illusion of an ideal, virtuous, and reassuring past. Whatever remembrance Lincoln consequently induces in his audience is a source of ever-renewing commitment to the ills of the nation's present, to the massive work of moral atonement that defines its future, to the common ideals of citizenship that such work requires, rather than a reliable and restorative connection with its sinfully divided and divisive history.

## Atonement for the Past, Mercy in the Present

Lincoln's Gettysburg Address and Second Inaugural richly illustrate the multivalent politics of public commemoration. Lincoln authors a plaintive but decidedly Union-friendly revision of recent wartime history by rejecting the evidence of the brutality that riddles it. He most exerts the authority of his office to define the essential meaning of national strife when speaking in a public idiom that feigns to expunge all forms of agency, including his own, from the state record. Lincoln refuses to engage in customary rites of memory precisely as he presides over them; he delivers orations intended to add nothing of significance to worldly affairs, yet fated (as we now know) to become benchmarks of historical and political eloquence. Without question, then, Lincoln's displays of political impotence function as instruments of sociopolitical control. His professions of a transcendent, nonpartisan national destiny mask a deeply partisan interpretation of the war's meaning, and his pleas for relinquishment of the past provocatively refurbish and magnify its contemporary significance. Multivalent, indeed: forgetting animates rituals of remembrance, and displays of political powerlessness consolidate political power.

Lincoln's public gestures of forgetting thus function as incitements to altered, and hopefully transformative, patterns of memory. They seek to dissociate the nation's present affairs from corrosive dimensions of its past in order to inaugurate a new and redemptive vision of historical memory, albeit one no less deeply held than the divisive past it replaces. By the same token, Lincoln's performance of vitally important national rites of memory does not simply encourage willful forms of public forgetting; it *requires* them as indispensable moral and political resources with which to restore the civic relevance and efficacy of such ceremonies. His enactment of public forgetting posits a rejuvenated culture of public memory as its ideal outcome, just as the culture of public memory he envisions requires public forgetting as the means to produce it.

Lincoln's ceremonial invocations of mercy—of forgiving by forgetting—form a subtle but decisive counterpoint to modern spectacles of state memory likewise conceived to achieve a measure of sociopolitical redemption. Barry Schwartz and Horst-Alfred Heinrich (2004) perceive the emergence of a new ritual of public memory in the recent proliferation of official state apologies for past injustices offered by representatives of democratic governments. Such exercises in apologia proliferate in both literal and symbolic forms. The South African Truth and Reconciliation Commission, for example, is one of the most celebrated instances in which a modern state solicited detailed public testimony regarding the very injustices it once sanctioned. U.S. federal as well as state agencies have, in recent years, offered a variety of explicit apologies related to matters of racial justice, from presidential proclamations apologizing for U.S. participation in the transatlantic slave trade and the internment of Japanese-Americans during World War II to a spate of legislation in southern states apologizing for their former tolerance of slavery. The German government's controversial Memorial to the Murdered

Jews of Europe in Berlin, moreover, represents one of the most elaborate symbolic gestures of state apologia. But these are only a few examples; Schwartz and Heinrich note that "the list of regrets seems endless" (114). With these literal and symbolic displays, present-day leaders ceremonially profess that previous generations of their government committed, or at least condoned, past atrocities and offer formal apologies to the descendents of those who were unjustly persecuted in former times. Such state representatives might even express public pleas for forgiveness from those called upon to act as surrogates for their victimized forebears.

The ideal political goal of such spectacles is to establish improved relations in democratic states among members of a common citizenry who remain divided by memories of injustice. Contemporary state apologies acknowledge injustices formerly suppressed from public discourse and symbolically transform them into occasions for state ceremony, into objects of public commemoration in their own right. Schwartz and Heinrich observe that rituals of this sort "are particularly useful" for practical sociopolitical purposes, such as legitimating "new distributional policies," "new civil demeanor and discourse," or "new interpretations of minority contributions to history" (116). Rhetorically, that which was shrouded in shame and silence is now an officially recommended subject for public dialogue. Morally, that which was denied as a potentially incendiary *topos* of state remembrance now occupies its focal point. Politically, constituencies divided by historical animosity now cohere as a stronger polity through their orchestrated public remembrance, and thus mutual recognition, of past injustice.

Lincoln's ceremonial invocations of forgiveness pursue a similar moral and political end but employ a qualitatively different set of rhetorical and commemorative techniques to accomplish it. He voices a model of public judgment regarding memories of internecine violence and national tragedy strikingly different from that involved in contemporary rituals of state atonement. As illustrated in his Gettysburg Address and Second Inaugural, Lincoln both argues for a redaction of past antagonisms from present-day civic dialogue and performatively enacts it in public speech. Here, the deepest shame lies not in listeners' all too vivid and painful recollections of recent events but in the fact that a divided public has not yet learned to banish its bitterly held memories to the shadows of time. Late twentieth-century democratic state apologies produce forgiveness by recovering and validating memories in danger of being forgotten, and thus seize the opportunity for public atonement that would have been lost with them. Lincoln, however, models atonement and forgiveness precisely through public forgetting, through willfully denying that specific dimensions of historical memory hold moral value or political utility in the crucible of national reconciliation. The former is a more democratic form of forgiveness in that it seemingly ratifies the public's existing, informally acknowledged recognition of injustices once committed in its name; a democratically elected leader's ability to apologize for past injustices on behalf of ordinary citizens implies their tacit approval of such sentiments. The latter form of forgiveness, however, is more aristocratic in nature to the extent that it unilaterally rejects citizens' innate and widespread desire to clutch tightly their destructive perceptions of past injustices, going so far as to excise traces of recent internecine conflict from official statements without the slightest modicum of debate. Rituals of modern state apologia suggest that the community, having confronted condemnable episodes in its history and learned from the lessons of its past, now stands a better chance of intervening constructively in the course of future affairs. Lincoln, however, never wavers from the quasi-theological principle that the course of future events lies not in democratic decision-making but in divine will, not in remembrance of secular history but in remembrance of God's unknowable designs.

This comparison provides final insight into the question of when and under what circumstances public forgetting may be a viable instrument of political improvement in contrast to more traditional forms of public commemoration. Recent spectacles of state atonement reflect preoccupations with recording, archiving, preservation, and testimony so prevalent in our turn-of-the-century culture of memory. Much of the *pathos* of such official apologia comes from the fact that it implores the public to remember regrettable acts and events at a historical remove, to preserve remaining but tragically incomplete traces of the past long after they should have been appreciated in greater detail. Leaders call on citizens in such circumstances to remember injustices formerly perpetrated in their name as a mechanism for strengthening political bonds.

At other times, however, the proverbial record of public events may be overflowing with politically volatile recollections. Lincoln uttered his most powerful appeals for public forgetting in much closer proximity to the events that inspired embittering historical memories. Instead of addressing audiences that can only act as moral surrogates for their forebears, Lincoln addressed a nation still engaged in brutal civil war, a public not yet able to forget the crimes it committed firsthand or the offenses that inspired them. To create a public climate in which such forgetting could take place would be a politically transformative, if not revolutionary, act. In this case, stronger political bonds come not from enhanced remembrance of past injustices committed by previous generations but in a willful forgetting of mutual hatreds and violent deeds perpetrated by members of the present generation upon one another—indeed, of hatred and violence that continues apace. Contemporary state apologists urge the public to ponder ruins as tokens of a fading past—from a temporal, if not emotional, distance. Lincoln speaks to a weary public living and laboring in the fresh wreckage of war; he implores his listeners not to attend to the wreckage itself but to join together in erecting new houses of memory and political accord on their very remains.

## Conclusion

Lincoln's rhetoric of public forgetting is the most successfully refined model of such forgetting addressed in this book. The language of Lincoln's Gettysburg Address and Second Inaugural illuminates the customarily unacknowledged arbitrariness of memorial rituals. Lincoln's memorial speeches transform both the past as a seemingly natural, obligatory object of commemoration and its moral or political meaning for contemporary audiences. The rhetoric of forgetting featured in these addresses does not negate the past but, true to the deep intimacy of memory and forgetting, crafts for public audiences an extensively altered and arguably worthier moral and political vision of it. The signal effect of this rhetorically transformed past is to engender a new sense of public time and a novel array of sociopolitical relations—to begin again, in Arendt's intertwined temporal and political senses.

Lincoln's rhetoric of public forgetting produces a revised version of public history as expansive as Draper's narrative of scientific progress. But it does so with the added advantage of delineating a comparatively stronger, less passionately enthralled framework of historical judgment truer to Nietzsche's doctrine of critical history. Draper expressed forceful confidence in historical patterns as augurs of scientific progress, in modern historiography as a portent of the future. Lincoln, however, expressed a lack of confidence in the predictive wisdom of ceremonial recollection and a disdain for the romantic prophecies that such recollection promotes. The president's ample skepticism regarding the limitations and lacunae of traditional commemorative rituals, rather than any putative mastery over past and future that they signify, provides grounds for pursuing humbler, pragmatically oriented political relations in the present.

Lincoln's rhetoric of public forgetting also features a rich idiom, like that of Eastern European Gypsies, useful for transforming collective identity as a means of securing communal survival or restoration. But it does so precisely in order to establish a newly rejuvenated culture and politics of memory. The Gypsies' distinctive culture of forgetting emphasized the apparent value of forgetting as an antithesis to more enduring orders of memory and the political institutions they typically inspire. But Lincoln implored the public, in his Gettysburg Address and Second Inaugural, to disenthrall itself from the past in order to transform traditional boundaries of political community, to found a new and merciful politics of memory itself. The fact that Lincoln's orations contributed so extensively to basic U.S. idioms of historical and political identity is testament to his success in this regard.

In this light, finally, Lincoln's rhetoric of public forgetting reveals that commemorative redactions can hold salutary political and moral value, when judiciously conceived and articulated, in the wake of unprecedented national tragedies, from the deep enmities of the Civil War to perhaps even communal sentiments of helplessness before historical destiny in the wake of September 11. Skillfully managed appeals to public forgetting can provide a politically transformative idiom of public memory as a resource of communal deliberation and, with it, a novel spectrum of civic relations, even in those times of national crisis when the liberal-democratic imperative to remember seems irrefutable. Public forgetting so defined constitutes a vital symbolic medium of moral rededication and political reconciliation in circumstances when the collectively remembered past hinders a polity's ability to make promises, to establish and maintain thick sociopolitical relations, to affirm the character of civic life in the present in equal measure to that of the past.

Forgetting has a bad reputation. The worry that it typically inspires is a product of the language that ancients and moderns alike have used to describe it. The disconsolate trope of oblivion is a common linguistic denominator spanning the many troubling depictions of forgetting in historical as well contemporary discourses on memory, history, and mortality. One of Shakespeare's most haunting uses of this trope, in *As You Like It,* is paradigmatic of the trend. The bard's famous soliloquy likening the span of mortal life to a role played on the stage culminates in this chilling finale: "Last scene of all, / That ends this strange and eventful history, / Is second childishness and mere oblivion, / Sans teeth, sans eyes, sans taste, sans everything" (II.vii.163–66; 1969). An apposite portrait of oblivion: the "second childishness" of dementia, of our inevitable decrepitude, which not only ends all personal "history" but also decomposes our "eyes," our "taste"—indeed "everything"—to the point of death. The trope of oblivion has lost none of its powerful currency since Shakespeare's day as a standard designation for forgetting. In *Austerlitz,* one of the most celebrated meditations on the transience of memory in our time, W. G. Sebald invests the prospect of forgetting with formulaically dark significance when he ponders "how little we can hold in mind, how everything is constantly lapsing into oblivion with every extinguished life, how the world is, as it were, draining itself, in that the history of countless places and objects which themselves have no power of memory is never heard, never described or passed on" (2001, 24). To equate forgetting with oblivion, whether in the Elizabethan past or the liberal-democratic present, is to invoke a vocabulary that disparages it many times over: as a symptom of absence, lack, or loss; of apathy, neglect, or inaction; of ruin, destruction, and death.

This is not to deny that customary venerations of memory have nonetheless inspired unorthodox affirmations of forgetting throughout biblical, Greco-Roman, and modern Western history. But modernist rejections of ancient regimes and the postmodern penchant for historical pastiche show that orthodox conceptions of memory shape even ambitious attempts to upend its traditionally dialectical superiority over forgetting. Anxiety over, and worried attention to, the destructiveness of forgetting is a prominent feature of both modernity and late modernity; but such anxiety and attention do not amount to an affirmation of forgetting in particular social and political circumstances. To promote oblivion, liquidation, and amnesia as cardinal tropes or figures of forgetting is to equate it with forms of negation all the same (and also, by implication, to reaffirm the categorically positive status of memory).

This book has investigated the value of forgetting by pursuing a different path, exploring its rich and revealing intimacy with memory instead of simply inverting, and thereby reproducing, hierarchies of value in which memory and forgetting have long been opposed. Presence and absence, production and destruction, fertility and barrenness, and life and death comprise the most common and enduring antitheses of this sort. The book has advocated an alternate *public* conception of forgetting and, with it, an alternative vocabulary for determining its value as an available resource of political and moral judgment.

The organizational structure of this book performed its basic argument about public forgetting as a rhetorical phenomenon—as a communicative, discursive, or symbolic activity fashioned to achieve persuasive effect. The chapters in Part 1 answered the question of how and why we have come to speak of forgetting in such ardently negative terms, demonstrating that parallel venerations of memory and denigrations of forgetting form a significant part of the Western heritage extending back to biblical times. These early chapters also showed how contemporary public and scholarly commitments to institutional memory strongly partake of the putative moral or political wisdom expressed by historically influential tropes and figures of forgetting. The case studies collected in Part 2 of this book put such long-standing wisdom to the test, investigating forgetting not as a categorically negative and passive phenomenon but as a rhetorical and communal activity that may contribute positively to the content of formal public history, the evolution of informal cultural heritage, and transformative political leadership in periods of national crisis. In doing so, the case studies displayed alternate rhetorical resources for assessing the relative merits of forgetting as a form of public judgment regarding the lessons and dilemmas of the communal past.

None of this is to suggest that one should adopt an unqualified acceptance of forgetting in public affairs. The road to a more affirmative treatment of forgetting in communal deliberation and decision-making is fraught with political and ethical difficulties. But an inherently capacious attitude toward memory as a resource of public judgment can be equally fraught with theoretical and practical conundrums. Fittingly, then, the whole of this book does not advocate a simple rejection of memory in favor of forgetting. It argues instead for the value of public forgetting in both forming and transforming particular cultures of memory as well as the civic institutions and sociopolitical relationships legitimated in their name. For this reason, the case studies in Part 2 of this book demonstrated how practices of organized forgetting operate productively in historical or commemorative endeavors central to the study of public memory in general: in public history, in communal heritage, and in the moral and political uses of memory during times of national crisis.

The remainder of this conclusion further contends that modes of public forgetting concern far more than idiosyncratic instances of counter-memorial rhetoric and politics. Public forgetting also provides more general insight into a dilemma characteristic of both modernity and late modernity: the dilemma of how social and political bodies can most auspiciously end the regimes of old and bring into being new and ideally freer forms of community. Arendt superbly captures the sense of profound uncertainty that characterizes such pregnant hiatuses in public time, which require inventive judgment concerning dispensable and indispensable portions of a community's past; she writes of "the odd in-between period which sometimes inserts itself into historical time when not only the later historians but the actors and witnesses, the living themselves, become aware of an interval in time which is altogether determined by things that are no longer and by things that are not yet" (1993, 9). The following passages explain how the analyses of public forgetting in this book offer valuable insights into the rhetoric and politics of public time and communal reinvention occasioned by the sort of "odd in-between period" or "interval" that Arendt describes. The chapter accordingly closes by identifying essential criteria, generated across the previous case studies, for determining the relative value of public forgetting as either a pernicious or prudential means with which communities may choose to rhetorically and politically begin again.

## Ending and Beginning Again in Modernity

Defining public forgetting as a strategically commendable ideal does not amount to an affirmation of any and every consequence that may follow in its wake. Foucault, Nietzsche, and Arendt offer useful cautions in this regard. Foucault proclaimed the oft-quoted dictum (which is consistent with Nietzsche and Arendt's treatments of history and memory) that "everything is dangerous" (1994, 256)—that even ostensibly enlightened and liberating political paradigms are not immune from internal contradictions or unexamined premises that could potentially thwart their reasoned, emancipatory goals. For Foucault, the work of counter-memory does not involve dialectically replacing repressive versions of history with certifiably liberating reconstructions of it. Nietzsche, moreover, does not anticipate that critical history can effectively sever one from the heritage of which one is a part, however disagreeable it may appear. Arendt, finally, affirms natality not as a utopian condition that brings the *polis* into civic harmony once and for all but as a faculty of political transformation that communities should practice whenever the works, words, and deeds of their own communal past impose constraints on present-day thought and judgment.

The conception of public forgetting advanced in this study heeds such words of caution by striving to be affirmative but not roseate about the political and moral prospects of organized forgetting. The value of such a rhetorical and political practice to public affairs lies in its capacity for transmutation, not culmination—in its capacity to transform the nature and scope of existing cultures of memory, of public time itself, without presuming to arrest such cultures in ideal, unchanging forms. This outcome would signal the demise of memory as a viable ground of social and political action. Public forgetting constitutes a mode of public judgment whereby communities articulate in speech, language, or other symbolic forms the advent of a radically new set of attitudes, beliefs, or customs concerning the meaning of their own past. Judgment of this sort goes far beyond acknowledging mundane differences in historical interpretation. The value of public forgetting so conceived lies not in achieving ideal ends, some form of permanent order, but in the strategically invoked ideal of beginning again—an inauguration accompanied neither by naïve negation of the past nor by utopian anticipation of an untroubled future.

Some might ask more of such definitional work. Some might request a strict formula for determining when public forgetting reliably resolves the dilemmas and injustices of the past. But even the heartiest appeals to conventional forms of public memory cannot promise such ends (or are misguided if they do). Young's disdain for museum installations that preserve only evidence of horrific atrocities, that force us to remember Holocaust victims from the standpoint of their killers, demonstrates that even forms of public memory motivated by stalwart intentions can go horribly wrong. The complex politics of public memory and its sometimes strange career in various rhetorical forms prevents one from translating its lessons into categorical political formulas. The same caveat applies to public forgetting, even if one endorses it as a strategically vital element of public culture writ large.

This is not to say, however, that investigations of public forgetting hold only speculative or retrospective value. The case studies in this book have shown that public forgetting affords communities a practical and elective procedure conducive to the very existence of political freedom as Arendt defines it: the capacity to begin anew. Public forgetting may not cut an inevitably clear path to a harmonious communal future. But communities that seek to render appropriate judgment on encumbering portions of their past, that attempt to revise or even reject inherited wisdom in light of current affairs, practice a form of political realism rather than speculative theory or historical retrospection.

The heuristics of counter-memory, critical history, and natality implemented in each of the preceding case studies allow one to address with admirable honesty a thorny sociopolitical problem characteristic of Western modernity: the momentous prospect of ending and beginning anew, the great hope and irreducible uncertainty it carries in equal measure. David Harvey identifies the beginnings of modernity in economic paralyses that swept through Great Britain and Europe during the late 1840s, followed by the eruption of coincident political revolutions across the continent. "After 1848," he writes, the "progressive sense of time" characteristic of the Enlightenment, in which history supposedly foretold the reign of reason and human achievement, "was called into question," such that "the question 'What time are we in?'" became an urgent philosophical issue (1990, 261). (Late nineteenth-century German philosophies, which remain obligatory fodder for contemporary continental thought, pursued characteristically deep and influential examinations of this issue.) Modernity subsequently witnessed a series of cataclysmic geopolitical events, namely World Wars I and II, which appeared to bring entire histories to violent ends and induce massive experiences of historical dislocation. Perhaps more significant, global warfare in the early twentieth century implemented new technological capabilities by which governments and armies, rather than God's will or the unseen hands of history, could bring about those ends.

Foucault, Nietzsche, and Arendt's philosophies reflect profoundly conflicted attitudes in modernity toward the sometimes indistinguishable rewards and hazards of historical ends and beginnings. Applying their philosophies to an investigation of public forgetting accordingly suggests that communities and their leaders must carefully negotiate trials of public judgment in which forgetting extends the prospect of substantial political transformation. Modernity has been shaped, in large part, by unprecedented irruptions of change, which incited efforts to end prevailing traditions of historical memory and inaugurate new ones that resulted in the reality of liberation and subjugation alike. On the one hand, the ideal of throwing off the burdens of tradition, rejecting dogmatic ways of old, motivates many of modernity's most famous intellectual, socioeconomic, and political projects. Time and again, however, revolutionary vanguards have burst the shackles of history only to find themselves without bearing amid dizzying historical developments, leading them to embrace dangerous or repressive political doctrines for the appearance of security and stability they afford. On the other hand, modernity is inconceivable without the passionate summons of writers, artists, laborers, and politicians to a new and better future in which human society is comprehensively transformed and its long-standing ills are no more. Marxist and Hegelian doctrines of history, which appeared to clear the way toward such an emancipatory future, inspired many revolutionary movements in the late nineteenth and early twentieth centuries. Time and again, however, the state-sponsored pursuit of such a future merely created a horrific present in which the rule of law was sacrificed and basic human rights were suppressed, often by means of state violence, in obedience to a prophesied social or political order.

Walter Benjamin's "Theses on the Philosophy of History" conveniently illustrates the profoundly ambivalent modernist perspective on historical ends and beginnings. Thesis XV approvingly interprets a political movement's rejection of master historical narratives, dictated by ruling classes, as a revolutionary act: "The awareness that they are about to make the continuum of history explode is characteristic of the revolutionary classes at the moment of their action. The great revolution introduced a new calendar" (1968, 261). To introduce a "new calendar" is to liberate oneself from "the continuum of history" in its commanded versions. Benjamin's approval for such revolutionary endings is also evident in his contrast between the logic of "universal history" and "materialist historiography": "Universal history," he writes, "has no theoretical armature" (262)—no theory, that is, with which one may inspect patterns of historical development in order to discern the arrival of a revolutionary upheaval in historical time itself. The "method" of universal history, he continues, "is additive; it musters a mass of data to fill the homogeneous, empty time. Materialistic historiography, on the other hand, is based on a constructive principle. Thinking involves not only the flow of thoughts, but their arrest as well" (262). Universal history merely accumulates data, unreflectively and without end; the "constructive principle" proper to materialist historiography requires an awareness of the need to "arrest" such accumulation as a revolutionary act, to end it in order to begin the work of emancipation.

Benjamin's optimism for the revolutionary forging of new calendars, however, chafes against his equal or greater pessimism concerning the dreams of permanent future progress that they often inspire. Benjamin's oft-cited angel of history (inspired by Klee's *Angelus Novus*) bears out his pessimism as such. The angel beholds the ceaselessly accumulating "wreckage upon wreckage" of the entire past and desires to "awaken the dead, and make whole what has been smashed" (257). Yet, in Benjamin's vision, a storm has "got caught in his wings with such violence that the angel can no longer close them. This storm irresistibly propels him into the future to which his back is turned, while the pile of debris before him grows skyward" (258). The angel of history cannot intervene in cycles of historical decay, restoring life and wholeness to the past; a terrible force preserves the past in its entirety as "wreckage upon wreckage" relentlessly impinging on the present. "This storm" Benjamin mordantly surmises, "is what we call progress" (258). Fascism exploits to dogmatic ends the modern fervor for progress. "Social Democratic theory, and even more its practice," Benjamin writes, "have been formed by a conception of progress which did not adhere to reality but made dogmatic claims" (260). When progress is proclaimed in the style of fascist regimes—as "the progress of mankind itself," as "boundless" and "irresistible" (260)—then the allure of such chimerical goods can be used to justify the enhancement of state power to potentially horrific ends. Hence, the future of the regime and the inexorable march of historical progress appear as one.

Benjamin's theses thus distill generally ambivalent modernist attitudes toward willed forgetting and the new formations it makes possible. Exploding "the continuum of history" (253) as it has been dictated by ruling classes is indeed a revolutionary act; but to assume that such acts by themselves complete the work of liberation, or are immune to violent exploitation, is dangerous folly. Fascist regimes prove, to the contrary, that modern obsessions with breaking from the past in order to pursue dreams of "boundless" progress may only further the accumulation of historical ruin that Benjamin's angel of history beholds. One may describe modernity in this regard as an epochal scene of historical and memorial tragedy: bringing history as it has been recorded and remembered to a purposeful end in order to propagate new forms of culture, economics, or politics is a guiding dream of modernist freedom, the grand hope of which is often exceeded by the unprecedented repression and violence that peoples and governments have used to instantiate those ends and beginnings. An affirmation of public forgetting in its most desirable forms must be candid about, and responsive to, not only the uses but also the disadvantages that have attended revolutionary endings and new beginnings throughout modernity. Such candidness obliges one to ask the daunting question, prevalent in modern thought and practice, of how publics can bring historical memories and the traditions that embody them to constructive ends.

## Violence or Deliberation

Forgetting emerges in arguably its most frightful and potentially destructive forms when it operates unnoticed, or is even popularly accepted, as a form of memory. The Holocaust is, of course, commonly and understandably interpreted as modernity's most horrifying use of widespread forgetting against memory, of death against life in those forms. The Nazis themselves proudly advanced this interpretation. In a 1943 speech to the SS, Heinrich Himmler proclaimed the Nazi program of genocide "a glorious page in our history which has never been written and which will never be written" (Bartov 1993, 112). In an obvious sense, forgetting was both the method and aim of the Final Solution.

Young, however, suggests that the Third Reich's terrifying program of forgetting was equally one of remembrance, in ends no less than means. His insightful remarks on this point are worth quoting at length:

> The Nazis had intended the destruction of the Jews to be total: they were to have been removed from history and memory. . . . But beginning with an ordinance in 1936 forbidding German stonemasons to carve gravestones for Jews, continuing through the Nazis' methodical destruction of documents in Vilna recording past persecutions, and ending with Hitler's plans for a museum in Prague to the extinct Jewish race, it grows clear that if the first step toward the destruction of a people lay in the blotting out of its memory, then the last step would

lie in its calculated resurrection. Through the Prague museum and other monuments to his victory over the Jews, Hitler never planned to "forget" the Jews, but rather to supplant their memory of events with his own. (1988, 189)

Young implies that the meaning of the Holocaust as a relentless project of forgetting is inseparable from the Nazis' elaborate efforts to erect a monumental state memory. A studied understanding and calculated use of historical memory was integral to their attempted genocide: "The Nazis," Young continues, "seemed to understand all too well this historically minded—which is to say analogically minded—nature of the Jews. By reinstituting the Renaissance ghetto, the medieval yellow star, and the seventeenth-century Jewish councils" (94), they preserved historical memory (in admittedly macabre and distorted fashion) precisely in seeking to eradicate it and its inheritors. By these methods, David Roskies remarks, the Third Reich "created a world that was both utterly terrifying and strangely familiar" (1984, 191). Viewed in this light, one might describe the Holocaust not simply as a war against memory but one in which forgetting depended upon (and, as such, weirdly preserved) the historical past.

The true source of evil involved in the Nazis' program of forgetting might not have been forgetting in and of itself but its use in the production of a violently manipulated regime of memory. By extension, memory in this specific circumstance assumes the character of evil as well. Elisabeth Domansky's words crystallize the counterintuitive lesson here: "The Jews were not to be annihilated and then forgotten," she writes, "but annihilated and then remembered forever" (1992, 60). The Nazis' synthesis of forgetting and remembrance indicates the categorical difference between such a gruesome leveling of the historical record and the ideal of public forgetting defended throughout this book. According to that ideal, public forgetting can assist in producing and productively altering symbolic forms of memory through which members of the *polis* enter into and sustain constructive relations with one another. Public forgetting can be commendable precisely because it produces these outcomes (which admittedly might involve gross revisions of the historical record) without recourse to violence, suspension of laws or rights, and other nonrhetorical, oppressive measures. Neither forgetting nor remembering transpired throughout the Third Reich as a result of healthy public deliberation and decision-making. Both were sources of evil because they constituted differing masks of the same naked state power.

Judicious instances of public forgetting may not yield perfect remedies to collective ills, but they reflect decisions arrived at nonetheless through a publicly articulated rhetoric of forgetting without the use of violence or other oppressive measures. Hence, public forgetting, as illustrated in the preceding case studies, necessarily involves both a stated rationale in support of its ends as well as an artfully, and thus transparently, constructed vernacular with which to symbolically enact it. In the broadest terms, public forgetting is desirable when it reflects open and voluntary procedures of judgment and detestable when it contributes to denying opportunities for communal judgment as such—indeed, as a substitute for deliberative judgment altogether.

## Archival Poverty or Abundance

The mere fact that public forgetting may be warranted in particular circumstances, however, does not secure the ideal ends envisioned for it throughout this book. Public forgetting stands a better chance of securing those ends when its advocates (however large or small in number they may be) base their advocacy on a sensitivity to *kairos,* or the loosely appropriate term in Greek classical literature for "timing." When, or under what circumstances, a public decides to forget elements of its shared past is a fundamental determining factor in allowing members of a community to begin again, to release one another from burdensome or corrosive dimensions of their common history and mutually enter into new and improved relations.

The question of how well the past in question has been remembered and documented is an especially critical matter of *kairos,* or timing. Forgetting can represent a constructive ground of public judgment when the significance of former people, places, and events has already been documented in abundant detail. John W. Draper's historical forgetting proved appealing to well-educated readers, including fellow experts, who could have cited plentiful evidence invalidating his version of events. Gypsies maintain their distinctive culture of forgetting, choosing not to formally document their history of recurrent persecutions, because the effects of that history are all too evident, amply remembered in their daily lives. And Abraham Lincoln uttered his rhetoric of moral and political forgetting at a time when unprecedented bloodshed and heinous acts of violence between North and South were obvious, copiously documented, and viscerally remembered facts of

American life. The abundance of remembrance and documentation in such circumstances accommodates willed forgetting: the community feels at liberty to symbolically forget elements of its past because it can do so without risking fundamental loss; yet organized gestures of relinquishing the past nevertheless reduce the symbolic weight those elements exert on the present. When accompanied by sufficient (if not abundant) remembrance and documentation, public forgetting stirs a community to remember its past anew, in politically transformative ways, as a result of choosing to forget the past in its former shape and significance.

Advocating public forgetting, however, when communities possess only impoverished resources for understanding the past will likely produce destructive rather than publicly enriching forms of forgetting. If forgetting holds situational value as a ground of public judgment, then particular judgments will reflect specious, easily manipulated deliberation and decision-making when communities arrive at them without a sober, transparent understanding of the past in question. The contrast between recent state apologies for historical atrocities and Lincoln's wartime rhetoric of forgetting supports this claim particularly well. Contemporary state apologies represent admirable exercises in public memory because they promote a frank and therefore responsible awareness of hitherto undocumented, inadequately remembered injustices. Lincoln's rhetoric of public forgetting, however, represents a symbolic device with which audiences steeped in their own wartime history may conscientiously reframe and reinterpret that history instead of literally abolishing it.

One should not assume, however, that the differences between poverty and abundance in historical documentation or communal recollection may be readily apparent. Consider, once again, the example of John Draper. Fellow scientists and historians might have known better (and probably did) than to uncritically accept his version of history; but lay readers accustomed to accept lively historical myth as an approximation of historical fact might have mistakenly believed themselves to possess sufficient resources for evaluating the veracity of his narrative and the particular brand of forgetting it advocated. Historical revisionism in totalitarian societies grandly exploits this sense of belief: members of the state assume they are well informed concerning its past because they have been indoctrinated in official, exceedingly selective and distorted versions of it *ad infinitum*. Notice, then, that impoverished public knowledge of the past threatens to produce more dangerous effects without opportunities for inclusive public judgment. The excesses of historical forgetting committed by Draper's less-informed readers seem more palatable (however naïve they were) compared to the historical revision-ism practiced by members of authoritarian societies who lack self-regulated forums for deliberation and decision-making independent of those pre-scribed by the state. In the former case, the poverty of public understanding can be amply corrected at once; in the latter, state authorities propagate a manipulated version of history or spectacles of memory precisely in order to prevent this correction. In whatever circumstance, however, public for-getting is most productive in communal affairs—indeed, is something of a luxury—when the public that endorses it already possesses abundant docu-mentation and memory of the past in question, and can forget precisely in order to reconsider its meaning and value as it has been preserved therein.

## Historical Distance or Proximity

A public's historical distance from, or proximity to, particular events is an equally critical *kairotic* factor in measuring the value and effectiveness of appeals to public forgetting. A sense of historical proximity, or immediacy, prevails throughout the preceding case studies. Draper's true rhetorical aim is not simply to persuade readers to forget a more accurate narrative of dis-tant scientific and religious history but to forget, as a result, any remaining allegiances to religious authority in the present. For the Gypsies, forgetting is a productive activity that defines their responses to, and degrees of agency within, their immediate past—the one within living memory. Lincoln did not beseech the wartime public to forget the nation's incipient dedication to the principle of equality, much less the sacrifices its soldiers made in defend-ing that principle, but the sectional rancor and idle fondness for empty com-memorative rituals with which the county was allegedly enthralled. Based on these observations, public forgetting holds commendable value as a form of civic deliberation and decision-making in direct response to ongoing affairs, and therefore as a productive, formative dynamic therein. Excising significant portions of relatively distant history or memory from public con-sciousness long after the historical record and commemorative rituals have been established more closely resembles an arbitrary relegation of the past to oblivion rather than principled reflection on the uses and disadvantages of history and memory.

Measuring historical distance or proximity in matters of communal memory, however, can be complicated. In the Israeli-Palestinian conflict, for example, distant biblical history apparently overwhelms contemporary efforts to achieve peace in the region. Those who propose that Israeli-Palestinian hostilities might be lessened if both parties forgot large portions of that history presume, in a sense, that chronologically distant events have never receded into historical memory, that they remain viscerally and tragically proximate elements of daily life in Israel, Gaza, the West Bank, and indeed throughout the surrounding Middle East. This observation suggests that the difference between historical distance and proximity may not be categorically apparent when questions of communal forgetting or remembering arise. Processes of collective judgment that culminate in public forgetting implicitly endorse a contingent understanding of the degree to which either the historically remote or immediate past remains a salient aspect of ongoing sociopolitical affairs.

## Morning Memory, Evening Forgetting

Kundera posits that the differences between the creative freedoms of young and old artists are as clear as those between morning and evening. "For a young person's freedom and an old person's freedom," he writes, "are separate continents" (2007, 141). The freedom of young artists is brash, conquering, always in danger of overreaching. Morning freedom wants to claim or seize, whereas evening freedom is content to do the opposite. Kundera describes an older and sager Picasso, "inspired by his vesperal freedom," who "transforms his style and abandons the image people had of him" (143). The young artist labors in the bright glare of his or her morning freedom to produce monuments that will be remembered and revered by all. The artist who discovers the profound impermanence of such monuments, and learns how to reinvent herself outside their glare, enjoys the "vesperal freedom" of artistic evening (143).

The imagery of morning and evening, of day and night, recurs as well in numerous commentaries on memory and forgetting. Such imagery recalls the signal differences between memory as Mnemosyne and forgetting as Lethe, and with them a rich train of allusive contrasts delineated at the outset of this book: between light and dark, presence and absence, wisdom and ignorance, care and neglect, fertility and decay, life and death. The imagery of morning and evening in this context also symbolizes the relative freedoms of memory and forgetting as explored in the preceding case studies: the freedom to retain and to relinquish, the freedom to begin and begin again.

The meaning of such freedoms in their respective morning and evening, like that of Mnemosyne and Lethe, is ambiguous. For some, memory is the dawn that banishes the darkness of night, the darkness in which our works and days recede into oblivion. But the evening of forgetting need not signify a terminal end to memory. Memory needs the freedom of its evening, the repose that tempers its heat and light. Those things that shimmer in the radiance of morning can endure among the shadows of evening, even in dramatically eclipsed form, waiting to be seen anew when morning breaks again.

# NOTES

## NOTES TO INTRODUCTION

1. See Hobsbawm and Ranger 1992; Lowenthal 1998; and Wallace 1996.

2. In the course of my research, I discovered that Andreas Huyssen had previously advanced the idea of "public forgetting" in print (2005). My use of the term, however, is distinct from his in two decisive respects. First, his illustrations of public forgetting are broad enough that they equate such forgetting with the necessarily selective, fragmented, or revisionist nature of public memory in its normal evolution. My conception of public forgetting, however, refers to unusually conspicuous, consciously undertaken and maintained practices of collective forgetting that stand apart from more commonplace processes of memorial selection, fragmentation, and revision. Second, Huyssen speaks of public forgetting as a self-evident phenomenon, not requiring further specification or qualification, whereas my conception of public forgetting is constituted by a cluster of secondary or supporting terms that define and identify its specific nature and effects.

3. See Margalit 2002; Volf 2006; and Wiesel 1962.

4. Luria (2006) documents a similar case.

5. See also Bartlett 1932 for a similar approach to memory based on the presumption that even individual memory consists of constructive processes dependent on social frameworks rather than isolated mental retrieval.

6. Although other memory scholars are not as specific about the rhetorical nature of public or collective memory as Bodnar is, they consistently stress either its interested character—as a ground of social, ethical, or political advocacy, or its discursive, textual, or symbolic nature—in ways compatible with basic rhetorical categories. In the former case, James Young writes that "memory is never shaped in a vacuum; the motives of memory are never pure" (1993, 2); in the latter, Edward Casey proposes that "the very basis" of collective commemoration "is found in the mediation of ritual and text" (2000, 221).

## NOTES TO CHAPTER I

1. Simonides' legendary feat of memory is recounted in the *Rhetorica ad herennium*, Cicero's *De oratore*, and Quintilian's *Institutione oratoria*. Augustine also notably describes memory as a vast storehouse of valuable goods (*Confessions* 10.8, 214–20).

2. See Kerenyi 1977.

3. On Lethe, see Ayto 1990, 322; Barnhart 1988, 590; and Partridge 1966, 339, 349. On *alethia*, see Peters 1967, 16–17.

4. See Avery 1972, 323. Charles Scott (1999) provides a rich and dexterous use of Mnemosyne as an essential figure of memory.

5. Socrates' comments in Plato's *Phaedo* (62c–69e) provide an excellent illustration of this concept. See also Peters 1967, 156–57. All direct quotations from Plato are from the *Collected Dialogues*, edited by Edith Hamilton and Huntington Cairns.

6. For background on Jewish memory, see Childs 1962 and Yerushalmi 2005.

7. All quotations from the *Confessions* are from Chadwick's translation (Augustine 1991).

8. All quotations from the *Divine Comedy* are from Ciardi's translation (Dante 1977).

9. See Weinrich 2004, especially 57–61.

10. Francis Bacon's influence permeates Locke's treatments of language, memory, and understanding; see Bacon 2000a, II, and 2000b, I.

11. See also Freud 1957, 237–58.

12. See Freud 1961a and 1966. Bergson's prior insights into memory and its psychological dynamics also gesture to a notion of pure, original memory. See Bergson 1990.

13. Adorno, in a different national context, expresses an even starker version of this same point when he likens archives to mausoleums: "The German word *museal* [museumlike]," he notes, "has unpleasant overtones. It describes objects to which the observer no longer has a vital relationship and which are in the process of dying" (1981, 175).

14. See Draaisma 2000 for a detailed survey of the ways in which metaphors taken from the language of science, technology, and computer engineering have infused modern conceptions of memory since long before the advent of contemporary digital technology.

15. Two nonetheless deeply informed and insightful works are especially relevant here. Edward Casey interprets the fact that computer or audiovisual storage systems today represent the dominate models of memory writ large as a symptom of our more general denigration of memory and the subsequent reduction of the past itself, in our perceptions thereof, to "a dead weight" (2000, 4). More recently, David Gross has interpreted modernist losses of confidence over the durability of memory and anxieties over the inevitability of forgetting as a putative affirmation of the latter in late modern culture; yet his interpretation is based on canonical literary or intellectual works, and he declines to consider how examples of the sort raised in this study might reveal that memory survives as an enthusiastically pursued ideal in altered popular forms (2000).

NOTES TO CHAPTER 2

1. For instructive commentary on antecedents of institutionalized forgetting in classical Greek drama and politics, see Booth 2006, 143–63.

2. Yet Cicero rejects the possibility that this insight somehow gives equal value to forgetting as a technique: "But this response of Themistocles," he says, "is no reason why we should neglect to expend our effort on our memory" (*De oratore* 2.300; Cicero 2001).

3. See, in particular, Augé 2004; Erdelyi 2008; Forty and Kuchler 1999; Gross 2000; Margalit 2002; Ricoeur 2004; Singer and Conway 2008; Todorov 1996; Weinrich 2004; and Wessel and Moulds 2008.

4. See Plato *Meno* 274c–278b and *Phaedo* 191c–195a. For expanded commentary on Plato's likening of memory to a wax tablet and its larger influences on cultural perceptions of memory, see Draaisma 2000, chap. 2, and Yates 2001, chap. 2. In addition to later Greek and Roman writers, who reproduced this metaphor as an axiom, Freud (1961b) amplifies its meaning most resoundingly in modernity, defining the unconscious as a realm where memories of traumatic events are imprinted, as a kind of writing, waiting to be translated from inscrutable traces back into lucid speech.

5. See Margalit 2002, chap. 6, for an extended discussion of Old Testament tropes of forgetting and forgiveness.

6. An especially notable classical precursor to such early modern forms of political amnesty, or forgetting, was the Athenian reconciliation (403–2 B.C.) following the reign of the Thirty, which granted amnesty to them by with a pledge "not to remember evil" (Aristotle "Athenian Constitution" sec. xxxix).

7. See Augé 2004; Connerton 2008; Erdelyi 2008; Forty and Kuchler 1999; Gross 2000; Huyssen 2005, 165–84; Margalit 2002; Ricoeur 2004; Singer and Conway 2008; Todorov 1996; Weinrich 2004; and Wessel and Moulds 2008.

8. Lowenthal's early remarks on forgetting also follow this pattern (1985, 205 – 6).

9. *Oxford English Dictionary* 1989, s.v. "forget."

## NOTES TO CHAPTER 3

1. An introductory list of sources pertaining to the artistic form or civic functions of epideictic includes Aristotle *On Rhetoric* 1.9; Beale 1978; Burgess 1987; Chase 1961; Condit 1985; Consigny 1992; DeNeef 1973; Duffy 1983; Hauser 1999; Loraux 1986; Ober and Strauss 1990; O'Malley 1979; Oravec 1976; J. Poulakos 1986; T. Poulakos 1987 and 1990; Rosenfield 1980 and 1989; Sullivan 1993; and J. Walker 1989.

2. See, especially, Casey 1993 and 1997; Jorgensen-Earp and Lanzilotti 1998; and Nora 1996.

3. See also "We Owe It" 2002, Hampson 2002; Matthews 2002; J. Scott 2002; and Stashenko 2002.

4. Thanks to David Depew for his interpretation of these addresses as politically neoliberal.

5. For additional commentary on neoliberal politics and economics, see Baldwin 1993; Campbell and Pedersen 2001; Comaroff and Comaroff 2001; and Rothenberg 1984.

6. Rhetorical scholarship on allegory includes Hariman 2002; Irvine 1987; Rowland 1989; Tejera 1975; and P. Walker 1956.

7. On the democratic or postmodern qualities of allegory, see Hariman 2002; Hirsch 1994; and Longxi 1994.

8. See also Adler and Gorman 1975, 121, 127, 132; and Dumbauld 1950, 58.

9. On Lincoln's expansion of the Declaration's original meaning, see Detweiler 1962; Jaffa 2002; Lucas 1989; Maier 1997; Peterson 1970, 92; and C. Warren 1945.

10. See Adler and Gorman 1975, 107; and Kromkowski 2002, 136.

11. Roosevelt 1999 [1941], 274.

12. Representative examples of this trend include Ambrose 1992, *Band of Brothers* 2002; Brokaw 1998; and *Saving Private Ryan* (1999). For commentary, see Biesecker 2002; Bostdorff 2003; and Goldstein 1999.

13. On the militarism and xenophobia of eulogies in the classical tradition, see Loraux 1986, 45, 80, 221–62.

14. See, for example, Bailey 1983; Lutz and Abu-Lughod 1990; Jorgensen-Earp and Lanzilotti 1998; Hariman and Lucaites 2001; and Maffesoli 1996.

15. Edelman's analysis (1988) is a classic study of political spectacles in this vein. See Procter 1990 for a rhetorical analysis of more recent ceremonial spectacles.

16. See Pocock 1971.

17. The origins of this tendency are suggestively explored in Bercovitch 1993. See also Bostdorff 2003.

## NOTES TO CHAPTER 4

1. For an analogous example in the history of science, see Lessl 1999.

2. The question of religion and science preoccupied thinkers in all domains of knowledge during the nineteenth century. See, for example, Buckle 1970; Fiske 1885; Frederic 2002; Gray 1876; and James 1929.

3. See Whewell 1837; and A. White 1896. Whewell is credited with identifying the atypical medieval figures who professed a faith in a flat earth, and whose writings would later serve as evidence for the flat earth narratives of many scientific historians (including

Draper's). Whewell's flat earth account, however, never approached the popularity or influence of Draper's, even though it remained a formative nineteenth-century text in the history of science. White, on the other hand, benefited from the popularity of Draper's texts, as his book enjoyed a wide public reception. White's use of anecdotes such as the flat earth narrative is nonetheless more accepting of religion than Draper's. While Draper used such narratives to demonstrate the villainy of religion (chiefly in the form of the pope or Roman Catholicism), White argued against dogmatism of any kind, thus admitting the possibility of a religion not ruled by repression or ignorance, and therefore harmonious with science.

4. On this subject, see Fuller 1997, 40–76.

5. On this subject, Bruce Gronbeck writes, "History is not to be confused with the past, for history is a collection of stories and arguments about some set of events from before" (1998, 48) Other relevant sources on rhetoric and history include Carpenter 1995; Clark and McKerrow 1998; Hexter 1971, 15–76; Jasinski 1998; Struever 1985, 249–71; H. White 1973 and 1987; and Zarefsky 1998.

6. See also R. Scott 1976.

7. The use of the word "awful" here may seem pejorative to modern readers but common usage in the nineteenth century meant being full of awe. *Oxford English Dictionary* 1989, s.v. "awful."

8. Draper was actually English-born, but he emigrated to the United States at the age of twenty-one.

9. A significant portion of *A History of the Intellectual Development of Europe* served as a precursor to *History of the Conflict*.

10. Draper is highly selective in his attacks on religion. He singles out some religious figures, such as Martin Luther, as brave guardians of knowledge working against a theologically enforced intellectual oppression. But he relentlessly attacks Roman Catholicism; popes from past and present receive the brunt of his invective.

11. Fleming (1950, 76) points out that Draper doesn't even use footnotes.

12. Higham (1965, 241) also writes that Draper "contributed to the end of showing what America was by investigating what it was not."

13. See Lactantius *Divine Institutes.*

14. See Cosmas *Christian Topography.*

15. Turner makes a similar point, arguing that "accuracy" in cases such as this "is only one minor and rather elusive consideration; the power of such stories and images as symbolic constructions of reality for their publics is precisely the stuff of the rhetorical historian" (1998, 5).

16. The power of this ethos does not obscure Draper's rhetorical strategy. As indicated throughout this essay, Draper's intent to gain a wide audience for his arguments about science and religion, and to petition the reading public into acting on behalf of science, were well documented. Consequently, the power of the prophetic ethos that Darsey describes is, far from being contradictory to an apprehension of Draper's intent, integral to his rhetorical strategies.

17. Curiously, the inverse was not true at the time: in debates over evolution, many theologians resorted not to the Bible but to scientific argument. Bishop Wilberforce, who clashed with T. H. Huxley on the subject of evolution in 1860, objected to Huxley on scientific grounds. See Cosslet 1984, 1.

NOTES TO CHAPTER 5

1. See Tong 1989 for a collection of Gypsy folktales that have nevertheless found their way into print.

2. Huttenbach provides the following statistical summary concerning the extent of Gypsy losses during World War II: "Given present research data, the total number of Gypsies killed by the Nazi genocidal policy can only be estimated, ranging from a conservative low of 250,000 to a possible high of 500,000, out of an estimated population of 885,000 European Gypsies in 1939. One source claims that 75 percent of Europe's Gypsies were killed by the Nazis, while others, using much higher prewar European Gypsy population estimates, have claimed that 1 million to 4 million died in the *Poŕajmos*. Simon Wiesenthal, among others, has stated that up to 80 percent of all Gypsies in Nazi-occupied Europe were exterminated; some scholars feel 70 percent is more accurate" (1992, 45).

3. See Hancock 1987, 61–87, and 1992, 11–30, and Tong 1989, 5, on the complex politics of memory in this context.

4. See also Vivian 2001 on the resonance between Kotre's work on memory and conventional ideals of public memory.

5. In its Greek root, cryptomnesia means "hidden memory." Kotre 1995, 36.

6. Brooks 1963, 326.


NOTES TO CHAPTER 6

1. Scholarly as well as popular literature on Lincoln is, of course, both prodigious and ever expanding. Instead of burdening readers with comprehensive treatments of such works, evidentiary resources for this chapter are confined mainly to works that reflect two particularly relevant facets of Lincoln's legacy: (1) his influence over U.S. historical memory and culture; and (2) analyses of Lincoln's rhetorical or literary skill pertaining to his Gettysburg Address and Second Inaugural. Scholarship concerning Lincoln's relevance to U.S historical memory and culture is represented in this chapter by Peterson 1994 and Schwartz 2000. See also Boritt 2001; Braden 1990; R. Browne 1996; Diggins 2000; Fehrenbacher 1988; and Holzer 2000. Scholarship focusing on the rhetorical or literary aspects of Lincoln's Gettysburg Address and Second Inaugural specifically will be acknowledged in relevant sections to follow. General sources on Lincoln's skill as a speaker or writer, however, include Angle 1981; Barzun 1972; Braden 1988; Berry 1943; Briggs 2005; Grossman 1985; Edwards and Haskins 1962; Einhorn 1992; R. White 2005; Wiley 1943; and Wilson 2006.

2. This reflection on forgetting in Lincoln's July 10, 1858, speech was inspired by Booth (see Booth 2006, 56, 152, 173, 175).

3. See Lincoln 1989a and 1989d.

4. Wills provides an excellent treatment of both stylistic distinctions between Everett's and Lincoln's addresses at Gettysburg as well as the more general stylistic significance of Lincoln's elegy (1992, 41–62). The striking contrast between Everett and Lincoln, however, is routinely invoked throughout scholarship on Lincoln's most famous address; see also, for instance, Briggs 2005, 304, 311–13. On the larger stylistic significance and popular reception of Lincoln's Gettysburg Address, see Peterson 1994, 109–10, 113–14, 138, 396; and Schwartz 2000, 133, 241.

5. At the time, for instance, Democratic newspapers such as the *Chicago Times* opined, "The cheek of every American must tingle with shame as he reads the silly, flat and dishwatery utterances of the man who has to be pointed out to intelligent foreigners as the President of the United States" (Harper 1951, 187). On controversy regarding whether Lincoln himself considered the speech a rhetorical failure, see Wilson 2006, 225–28.

6. All citations of Lincoln's Gettysburg Address will be taken from Lincoln 1989b, 536. My analysis of Lincoln's Gettysburg Address is especially indebted to Black 1994; Boritt 2006; Braden 1988, chap. 6; Briggs 2005, 303–15; Einhorn 1992; and Wills 1992. See also Brann

1972; Gramm 2001; Nevins 1964; Pease 1964; Petersen 1963; Stripp 1968; L. Warren 1964; Watson 2000; R. White 2005, chap. 9; and Wilson 2006, chap. 8.

7. Bryson 1994, 80.

8. All citations of Lincoln's Second Inaugural will be taken from Lincoln 1989f, 686–87. My analysis of Lincoln's Second Inaugural is especially indebted to Black 2000; Braden 1990, chap. 7; Briggs 2005, 315–27; Leff 2005, 564–69; Slagell 1991; and R. White 2002. See also Aune 1988; Carpenter 1988; Hansen 2004; Miller 1980; Solomon 1988; Watson 2000; R. White 2005, chap. 11; Wilson 2006, chap. 9; and Zarefsky 1988.

9. David Herbert Donald interprets Lincoln's theological imagery here as an expression of the doctrine of exact retribution familiar to religious communities of the time (1995, 567). Other scholars, however, perceive in Lincoln's diffuse theological language references to any number of similar religious doctrines. Allen C. Guelzo (1997), for instance, characterizes it as the doctrine of necessity.

# REFERENCES

Adler, Mortimer J., and William Gorman. 1975. *The American Testament.* New York: Praeger.

Adorno, Theodore W. 1981. "Valéry Proust Museum." In *Prisms,* trans. Samuel Weber and Shierry Weber. Cambridge: MIT Press.

————. 1982. "Commitment." In *The Essential Frankfurt School Reader,* ed. Andrew Arato and Eike Gebhardt, 300–318. New York: Continuum.

Ambrose, Stephen E. 1992. *Band of Brothers: E Company, 506th Regiment, 101st Airborne.* New York: Simon and Schuster.

Angle, Paul M. 1981. "Lincoln's Power with Words." *Journal of the Abraham Lincoln Association* 3, no. 1: 9–27.

Apple, Inc. 2008. http://www.apple.com/ilife (accessed September 17).

Archibold, Randal C. 2002. "Political Ad and 9/11 Speech May Be an Unwelcome Mix." *New York Times,* August 15, B4.

Ardant, Philippe, ed. 1990. *Les textes sur les Droits de l'Homme.* Paris: Presses Universitaires de France.

Arendt, Hannah. 1993. *Between Past and Future: Eight Exercises in Political Thought.* New York: Penguin.

————. 1998. *The Human Condition.* 2nd ed. Chicago: University of Chicago Press.

Aristotle. 1952. "The Athenian Constitution." In *The Athenian Constitution, The Eudemian Ethics, On Virtues and Vices,* 2–188. Loeb Classical Library. Cambridge: Harvard University Press.

————. 2006. *On Rhetoric: A Theory of Civic Discourse.* 2nd ed. Trans. George A. Kennedy. New York: Oxford University Press.

Auden, W. H. 1945. *For the Time Being.* In *The Collected Poetry of W. H. Auden.* New York: Random House.

Augé, Marc. 2004. *Oblivion.* Trans. Marjolijn de Jager. Minneapolis: University of Minnesota Press.

Augustine, Saint. 1991. *Confessions.* Trans. Henry Chadwick. Oxford: Oxford University Press.

Aune, James Arnt. 1988. "Lincoln and the American Sublime." *Communication Reports* 1:14–19.

Avery, Catherine B., ed. 1972. *The New Century Handbook of Greek Mythology and Legend.* New York: Appleton-Century-Crofts.

Ayto, John. 1990. *Dictionary of Word Origins.* New York: Arcade.

Bacon, Francis. 2000a. *The Advancement of Learning.* Ed. Michal Kiernan. Oxford: Oxford University Press.

————. 2000b. *The New Organon.* Ed. Lisa Jardine and Michael Silverthorne. Cambridge: Cambridge University Press.

Bailey, F. G. 1983. *The Tactical Uses of Passion: An Essay on Power, Reason, and Reality.* Ithaca: Cornell University Press.

References

Baldwin, David, ed. 1993. *Neorealism and Neoliberalism: The Contemporary Debate*. New York: Columbia University Press.

*Band of Brothers*. 2002. Various directors. New York: HBO Video.

Barnes, Harry Elmer. 1963. *A History of Historical Writing*. 2nd ed. New York: Dover Publications.

Barnhart, Robert K., ed. 1988. *The Barnhart Dictionary of Etymology*. New York: H. W. Wilson.

Barry, Dan. 2002. "Vigilance and Memory." *New York Times*, September 12, A1.

Barthes, Roland. 1977a. "Death of the Author." In *Image Music Text*, trans. Stephen Heath. New York: Hill and Wang.

————. 1977b. "From Work to Text." In *Image Music Text*, trans. Stephen Heath. New York: Hill and Wang.

Bartlett, F. C. 1932. *Remembering: A Study in Experimental and Social Psychology*. New York: Macmillan.

Bartov, Omer. 1993. "Intellectuals on Auschwitz: Memory, History, and Truth." *History and Memory* 5:87–129.

Barzun, Jacques. 1972. "Lincoln the Writer." In *Jacques Barzun on Writing, Editing, and Publishing*, 65–81. 2nd ed. Chicago: University of Chicago Press.

Baudrillard, Jean. 1995. *Simulacra and Simulation*. Trans. Sheila Glaser. Ann Arbor: University of Michigan Press.

Beale, Walter H. 1978. "Rhetorical Performative Discourse: A New Theory of Epideictic." *Philosophy and Rhetoric* 11:221–46.

Beckett, Samuel. 1970. *Krapp's Last Tape, and Other Dramatic Pieces*. New York: Grove Press.

Benjamin, Walter. 1968. "Theses on the Philosophy of History." In *Illuminations: Essays and Reflections*, ed. Hannah Arendt, 253–64. New York: Schocken Books.

Benson, Lee. 1972. *Toward the Scientific Study of History: Selected Essays*. Philadelphia: J. P. Lippincott.

Bercovici, Konrad. 1928. *The Story of the Gypsies*. New York: Cosmopolitan Book Corporation.

Bercovitch, Sacvan. 1993. *The Rites of Assent: Transformations in the Symbolic Construction of America*. New York: Routledge.

Bergson, Henri. 1990. *Matter and Memory*. Trans. N. M. Paul and W. S. Palmer. New York: Zone Books.

Berry, Mildred Freburg. 1943. "Abraham Lincoln: His Development in the Skills of the Platform." In *A History and Criticism of American Public Address*, vol. 2, ed. William Norwood Brigance, 828–57. New York: McGraw-Hill.

Biesecker, Barbara A. 2002. "Remembering World War II: The Rhetoric and Politics of National Commemoration at the Turn of the 21st Century." *Quarterly Journal of Speech* 88:393–409.

Black, Edwin. 1994. "Gettysburg and Silence." *Quarterly Journal of Speech* 80:21–36.

————. 2000. "The Ultimate Voice of Lincoln." *Rhetoric and Public Affairs* 3:49–57.

Bodnar, John. 1992. *Remaking America: Public Memory, Commemoration, and Patriotism in the Twentieth Century*. Princeton: Princeton University Press.

Bolzoni, Lina. 1995. *La stanza della memoria*. Turin: Einaudi.

Boorstin, Daniel J. 1991. *The Discoverers*. Vol. 1. New York: Harry N. Abrams.

Booth, W. James. 2006. *Communities of Memory: On Witness, Identity, and Justice.* Ithaca: Cornell University Press.

Borges, Jorge Luis. 1998. "Funes, His Memory." In *Collected Fictions,* trans. Andrew Hurley, 131–37. New York: Viking Penguin Books.

Boritt, Gabor. 2001. *The Lincoln Enigma: The Changing Faces of an American Icon.* New York: Oxford University Press.

———. 2006. *The Gettysburg Gospel: The Lincoln Speech That Nobody Knows.* New York: Simon and Schuster.

Bostdorff, Denise M. 2003. "George W. Bush's Post-September 11 Rhetoric of Covenant Renewal: Upholding the Faith of the Greatest Generation." *Quarterly Journal of Speech* 4:293–319.

Bostdorff, Denise M., and Steven L. Vibbert. 1994. "Values Advocacy: Enhancing Organizational Images, Deflecting Public Criticism, and Grounding Future Arguments." *Public Relations Review* 20:141–58.

Braden, Waldo Warder. 1988. *Abraham Lincoln: Public Speaker.* Baton Rouge: Louisiana State University Press.

———, ed. 1990. *Rebuilding the Myth: Selected Speeches Memorializing Abraham Lincoln.* Urbana: University of Illinois Press.

Brann, Eva. 1972. "A Reading of the Gettysburg Address." In *Abraham Lincoln, The Gettysburg Address, and American Constitutionalism,* ed. Leo Paul S. de Alvarez, 21–52. Dallas: University of Dallas Press.

Breisach, Ernst. 1983. *Historiography: Ancient, Medieval and Modern.* Chicago: University of Chicago Press.

Briggs, John Channing. 2005. *Lincoln's Speeches Reconsidered.* Baltimore: Johns Hopkins University Press.

Brokaw, Tom. 1998. *The Greatest Generation.* New York: Random House.

Brooke, John Hedley. 1991. *Science and Religion: Some Historical Perspectives.* Cambridge: Cambridge University Press.

Brooks, Cleanth. 1963. *William Faulkner: The Yoknapatawpha Country.* New Haven: Yale University Press.

Browne, Ray B., ed. 1996. *Lincoln-Lore: Lincoln in the Popular Mind.* 2nd ed. Bowling Green: Bowling Green State University Popular Press.

Browne, Stephen Howard. 1999. "Remembering Crispus Attucks: Race, Rhetoric, and the Politics of Commemoration." *Quarterly Journal of Speech* 85:169–87.

———. 2004. "Arendt, Eichmann, and the Politics of Remembrance." In *Framing Public Memory,* ed. Kendall R. Phillips, 45–64. Tuscaloosa: University of Alabama Press.

Browne, Thomas. 1963. *Religio Medici.* Cambridge: Cambridge University Press.

Bryson, Bill. 1994. *Made in America: An Informal History of the English Language in the United States.* New York: Perennial.

Buckle, H. T. 1970. *History of Civilization in England.* Chicago: University of Chicago Press.

Burgess, Theodore C. 1987. *Epideictic Literature.* New York: Garland.

Burke, Kenneth. 1969. *A Rhetoric of Motives.* Berkeley and Los Angeles: University of California Press.

Bush, Douglas. 1969. "Shakespeare's Sonnets: Introduction." In *William Shakespeare: The Complete Works,* ed. Alfred Harbage, 1449–52. New York: Penguin Books.

Bush, George W. 2003. "Presidential Address to the Nation from Ellis Island Marking the Observance of the September 11th Attacks." In *"We Will Prevail": President George W. Bush on War, Terrorism, and Freedom,* ed. Jay Nordlinger, 181–83. New York: Continuum.

Calvin, John. 1977. *Institutes of the Christian Religion.* Trans. Ford Lewis Battles. Philadelphia: Westminster.

Campbell, John L., and Ove K. Pedersen, eds. 2001. *The Rise of Neoliberalism and Institutional Analysis.* Princeton: Princeton University Press.

Carpenter, Ronald H. 1988. "In Not-So-Trivial Pursuit of Rhetorical Wedgies: An Historical Approach to Lincoln's Second Inaugural Address." *Communication Reports* 1:20–25.

———. 1995. *History as Rhetoric: Style, Narrative, and Persuasion.* Columbia: University of South Carolina Press.

Casey, Edward S. 1993. *Getting Back into Place: Toward a Renewed Understanding of the Place-World.* Bloomington: Indiana University Press.

———. 1997. *The Fate of Place: A Philosophical History.* Berkeley and Los Angeles: University of California Press.

———. 2000. *Remembering: A Phenomenological Study.* 2nd ed. Bloomington: Indiana University Press.

Cervantes, Miguel de. 2005. *Don Quixote.* Trans. Edith Grossman. New York: Harper Perennial.

Chase, Richard. 1961. "The Classical Conception of Epideictic." *Quarterly Journal of Speech* 47:293–300.

Childs, Brevard S. 1962. *Memory and Tradition in Israel.* London: SCM Press.

Cicero. 2001. *On the Ideal Orator (De Oratore).* Trans. James M. May and Jakob Wisse. New York: Oxford University Press.

Clark, E. Culpepper, and Raymie E. McKerrow. 1998. "The Rhetorical Construction of History." In *Doing Rhetorical History: Concepts and Cases,* ed. Kathleen J. Turner, 33–46. Tuscaloosa: University of Alabama Press.

Clive, John. 1989. *Not by Fact Alone: Essays on the Writing and Reading of History.* New York: Alfred A. Knopf.

Comaroff, Jean, and John L. Comaroff, eds. 2001. *Millennial Capitalism and the Culture of Neoliberalism.* Durham: Duke University Press.

Condit, Celeste M. 1985. "The Function of Epideictic: The Boston Massacre Orations as Exemplar." *Communication Quarterly* 33:284–98.

Connerton, Paul. 2008. "Seven Types of Forgetting." *Memory Studies* 1:59–71.

Consigny, Scott. 1992. "Gorgias's Use of the Epideictic." *Philosophy and Rhetoric* 25:281–97.

Cosmas Indicopleustes. 1967. *The Christian Topography of Cosmas, an Egyptian Monk.* Trans. J. W. McCrindle. New York: B. Franklin.

Cosslet, Tess, ed. 1984. *Science and Religion in the Nineteenth Century.* Cambridge: Cambridge University Press.

Crowe, David M. 1994. *A History of the Gypsies of Eastern Europe and Russia.* New York: St. Martin's Press.

Crowe, David M., and John Koltsi, eds. 1992. *The Gypsies of Eastern Europe.* Armonk, N.Y.: M. E. Sharpe.

Daniels, George H., ed. 1972. *Nineteenth-Century American Science: A Reappraisal.* Evanston: Northwestern University Press.

Dante Alighieri. 1977. *The Divine Comedy.* Trans. John Ciardi. New York: W. W. Norton.

Darsey, James. 1997. *The Prophetic Tradition and Radical Rhetoric in America.* New York: New York University Press.

de Certeau, Michel. 1988. *The Writing of History.* Trans. Tom Conley. New York: Columbia University Press.

Deleuze, Gilles. 1994. *Difference and Repetition.* Trans. Paul Patton. New York: Columbia University Press.

Demosthenes. 2000. "The Funeral Speech." In *Demosthenes VII,* trans. Norman W. DeWitt and Norman J. DeWitt, 7–37. Loeb Classical Library. Cambridge: Harvard University Press.

DeNeef, A. Leigh. 1973. "Epideictic Rhetoric and the Renaissance Lyric." *Journal of Medieval Studies* 3:203–31.

Derrida, Jacques. 1998. *Archive Fever: A Freudian Impression.* Trans. Eric Prenowitz. Chicago: University of Chicago Press.

Descartes, René, 2006. *A Discourse on the Method.* Trans. Ian Maclean. Oxford: Oxford University Press.

Detweiler, Phillip P. 1962. "The Changing Reputation of the Declaration of Independence: The First Fifty Years." *William and Mary Quarterly* 19:557–74.

Diggins, John P. 2000. *On Hallowed Ground: Abraham Lincoln and the Foundations of American History.* New Haven: Yale University Press.

Donald, David Herbert. 1995. *Lincoln.* New York: Simon and Schuster.

Dow, Bonnie J. 1989. "The Function of Epideictic and Deliberative Strategies in Presidential Crisis Rhetoric." *Western Journal of Speech Communication* 53:294–310.

Draaisma, Douwie. 2000. *Metaphors of Memory.* Trans. Paul Vincent. Cambridge: Cambridge University Press.

Draper, John William. 1897. *History of the Conflict Between Religion and Science.* New York: D. Appleton.

Duffy, Bernard K. 1983. "The Platonic Function of Epideictic Rhetoric." *Philosophy and Rhetoric* 16:79–93.

Dumbauld, Edward. 1950. *The Declaration of Independence and What It Means Today.* Norman: University of Oklahoma Press.

Edelman, Murray. 1988. *Constructing the Political Spectacle.* Chicago: University of Chicago Press.

Edwards, Herbert Joseph, and John Erskine Haskins. 1962. *Lincoln the Writer: The Development of His Literary Style.* Orono: University of Maine.

Einhorn, Lois J. 1992. *Abraham Lincoln the Orator: Penetrating the Lincoln Legend.* Westport, Conn.: Greenwood Press.

Erdelyi, Matthew Hugh. 2008. "Forgetting and Remembering in Psychology: Commentary on Paul Connerton's 'Seven Types of Forgetting' (2008)." *Memory Studies* 1:273–78.

Everett, Edward. 1870. "Oration at Gettysburg." In *Orations and Speeches on Various Occasions,* 4:622–59. Boston: Little, Brown.

Fehrenbacher, Don E. 1988. *Lincoln in Text and Context: Collected Essays.* Stanford: Stanford University Press.

Fenster, Julie M. 2003. *Mavericks, Miracles, and Medicine: The Pioneers Who Risked Their Lives to Bring Medicine into the Modern Age.* New York: Carroll and Graf.

"Finding a Way to Remember." 2002. *U.S. News and World Report,* August 26, 10.

Fisch, Jörg. 1979. *Krieg und Frieden im Friedensvertrag: Eine universalgeschichtliche Studie über Grundlagen und Formelemente des Friedensschlusses.* Stuttgart: Klett-Cotta.

Fiske, John. 1885. *The Idea of God as Affected by Modern Knowledge.* Boston: Houghton Mifflin.

Fleming, Donald H. 1950. *John William Draper and the Religion of Science.* Philadelphia: University of Pennsylvania Press.

Fonseca, Isabel. 1995. *Bury Me Standing.* New York: Knopf.

Forty, Adrian. 1999. Introduction to *The Art of Forgetting,* ed. Adrian Forty and Susanne Kuchler, 1–18. Oxford: Berg.

Forty, Adrian, and Susanne Kuchler, eds. 1999. *The Art of Forgetting.* Oxford: Berg.

Foucault, Michel. 1977a. "Nietzsche, Genealogy, History." In *Language, Counter-Memory, Practice,* ed. Donald F. Bouchard, trans. Donald F. Bouchard and Sherry Simon, 139–64. Ithaca: Cornell University Press,

———. 1977b. "What Is an Author?" In *Language, Counter-Memory, Practice,* ed. Donald F. Bouchard, 113–38. Ithaca: Cornell University Press.

———. 1979. *Discipline and Punish: The Birth of the Prison.* Trans. Alan Sheridan. New York: Vintage.

———. 1990. *The History of Sexuality: An Introduction.* Trans. Robert Hurley. New York: Vintage.

———. 1994. "On the Genealogy of Ethics." In *Ethics, Subjectivity, Truth: Essential Works of Foucault, 1954–1984,* vol. 1, ed. Paul Rabinow, 253–80. New York: New Press.

Fraser, Angus. 1992. *The Gypsies.* Oxford: Blackwell.

Frederic, Harold. 2002. *The Damnation of Theron Ware, or, Illumination.* New York: Modern Library.

Freud, Sigmund. 1957. "Mourning and Melancholia." In *The Complete Psychological Works of Sigmund Freud,* trans. James Strachey, 14:237–58. London: Hogarth Press.

———. 1958. "Remembering, Repeating and Working-Through." In *The Complete Psychological Works of Sigmund Freud,* trans. James Strachey, 12:147–56. London: Hogarth Press.

———. 1961a. *Civilization and Its Discontents.* Trans. James Strachey. New York: W. W. Norton.

———. 1961b. "A Note upon the 'Mystic Writing-Pad.'" In *The Complete Psychological Works of Sigmund Freud,* trans. James Strachey, 19:225–32. London: Hogarth Press.

———. 1966. *The Psychopathology of Everyday Life.* Trans. Alan Tyson. New York: Norton.

Frow, John. 1997. "Toute la mémoire du monde: Repetition and Forgetting." In *Time and Commodity Culture: Essays in Cultural Theory and Postmodernity,* 218–46. New York: Oxford University Press.

Fuller, Steve. 1997. *Science.* Minneapolis: University of Minnesota Press.

Gay, Peter. 1969. *The Enlightenment: An Interpretation.* Vol. 2, *The Science of Freedom.* New York: W. W. Norton.

Gillis, John R., ed. 1994. *Commemorations: The Politics of National Identity.* Princeton: Princeton University Press.

Goethe, Johann Wolfgang von. 1965. *Faust.* Trans. Charles E. Passage. Indianapolis: Bobbs-Merrill.

Goldstein, Richard. 1999. "World War II Chic." *Village Voice,* January 19, 47.

Golinski, Jan. 1998. *Making Knowledge Natural: Constructivism and the History of Science.* Cambridge: Cambridge University Press.

Gooch, G. P. 1952. *History and Historians in the Nineteenth Century.* 2nd ed. London: Longmans.

Gould, Stephen Jay. 1995. "The Late Birth of a Flat Earth." In *Dinosaur in a Haystack: Reflections in Natural History,* 44–48. New York: Harmony Books.

Gramm, Kent. 2001. *November: Lincoln's Elegy at Gettysburg.* Bloomington: Indiana University Press.

Grant, Edward. 1986. "Science and Theology in the Middle Ages." In *God and Nature: Historical Essays on the Encounter Between Religion and Science,* ed. David C. Lindberg and Ronald L. Numbers, 49–75. Berkeley and Los Angeles: University of California Press.

Gray, Asa. 1876. *Darwiniana: Essays and Reviews Pertaining to Darwinism.* New York: D. Appleton.

Gronbeck, Bruce E. 1998. "The Rhetorics of the Past: History, Argument, and Collective Memory." In *Doing Rhetorical History: Concepts and Cases,* ed. Kathleen J. Turner, 47–60. Tuscaloosa: University of Alabama Press.

Gross, David. 2000. *Lost Time: On Remembering and Forgetting in Late Modern Culture.* Amherst: University of Massachusetts Press.

Grossman, Allen. 1985. "The Poetics of Union in Lincoln and Whitman: An Inquiry Toward the Relationship of Art and Policy." In *The American Renaissance Reconsidered,* ed. Walter Ben Michaels and Donald E. Pease, 183–208. Baltimore: Johns Hopkins University Press.

Guelzo, Allen C. 1997. "Abraham Lincoln and the Doctrine of Necessity." *Journal of the Abraham Lincoln Association* 18:57–81.

Haberman, Clyde. 2002. "Speechless in the Face of History." *New York Times,* August 30, p. B1.

Halbwachs, Maurice. 1992. *On Collective Memory.* Trans. Lewis A. Coser. Chicago: University of Chicago Press.

Hampson, Rick. 2002. "NYC Unveils Plans for Sept. 11 Events." *USA Today,* August 7, p. 3A.

Hancock, Ian. 1987. *The Pariah Syndrome.* Ann Arbor: Karoma.

———. 1992. "Gypsy History in Germany and Neighboring Lands: A Chronology Leading to the Holocaust and Beyond." In *The Gypsies of Eastern Europe,* ed. David Crowe and John Kolsti, 11–30. Armonk, N.Y.: M. E. Sharpe.

Hansen, Andrew C. 2004. "Dimensions of Agency in Lincoln's Second Inaugural." *Philosophy and Rhetoric* 37:223–54.

Hariman, Robert. 2002. "Allegory and Democratic Public Culture in the Postmodern Era." *Philosophy and Rhetoric* 35:267–96.

Hariman, Robert, and John Louis Lucaites. 2001. "Dissent and Emotional Management in a Liberal-Democratic Society: The Kent State Iconic Photograph." *Rhetoric Society Quarterly* 31:4–31.

## References

Harper, Robert S. 1951. *Lincoln and the Press.* New York: McGraw-Hill.

Harvey, David. 1990. *The Condition of Postmodernity: An Enquiry into the Origins of Cultural Change.* Cambridge: Blackwell.

Hauser, Gerard. 1999. "Aristotle on Epideictic: The Formation of Public Morality." *Rhetoric Society Quarterly* 29:5–23.

Heidegger, Martin. 1996. *Being and Time.* Trans. Joan Stambaugh. Albany: State University of New York Press.

Herodotus. 2003. *The Histories.* Ed. John M. Marincola. New York: Penguin Press.

Hexter, J. H. 1971. "The Rhetoric of History." In *Doing History,* 15–76. Bloomington: Indiana University Press.

Higham, John. 1965. *History.* Englewood Cliffs, N.J.: Prentice-Hall.

Hirsch, E. D., Jr. 1994. "Transhistorical Intentions and the Persistence of Allegory." *New Literary History* 25:549–67.

Hobsbawm, Eric, and Terence Ranger, eds. 1992. *The Invention of Tradition.* Cambridge: Cambridge University Press.

Holzer, Harold. 2000. *Lincoln Seen and Heard.* Lawrence: University Press of Kansas.

Huttenbach, Henry R. 1992. "The Romani Pořajmos: The Nazi Genocide of Gypsies in Germany and Eastern Europe." In *The Gypsies of Eastern Europe,* ed. David Crowe and John Kolsti, 31–49. Armonk, N.Y.: M. E. Sharpe.

Huyssen, Andreas. 2003. *Present Pasts: Urban Palimpsests and the Politics of Memory.* Stanford: Stanford University Press.

———. 2005. "Resistance to Memory: The Uses and Abuses of Public Forgetting." In *Globalizing Critical Theory,* ed. Max Pensky, 165–84. Lanham, Md.: Rowman and Littlefield.

Irvine, Martin. 1987. "Interpretation and the Semiotics of Allegory in Clement of Alexandria, Origen, and Augustine." *Semiotica* 63:33–71.

Jaffa, Henry V. 2002. "Abraham Lincoln and the Universal Meaning of the Declaration of Independence." In *The Declaration of Independence: Origins and Impact,* ed. Scott Douglas Gerber, 29–44. Washington, D.C.: CQ Press.

James, William. 1929. *The Varieties of Religious Experience: A Study in Human Nature.* New York: Modern Library.

Jasinski, James. 1997. "Instrumentalism, Contextualism, and Interpretation in Rhetorical Criticism." In *Rhetorical Hermeneutics: Invention and Interpretation in the Age of Science,* ed. Alan G. Gross and William M. Keith, 195–224. Albany: State University of New York Press.

———. 1998. "A Constitutive Framework for Rhetorical Historiography: Toward an Understanding of the Discursive (Re)constitution of 'Constitution' in the Federalist Papers." In *Doing Rhetorical History: Concepts and Cases,* ed. Kathleen J. Turner, 72–94. Tuscaloosa: University of Alabama Press.

Jefferson, Thomas. 1994. "The Declaration of Independence." In *The Essential Thomas Jefferson,* ed. John Gabriel Hunt. New York: Random House.

Joinet, Louis. 1989. "L'amnistie: Le droit à la mémoire entre pardon et oubli." *Communications* 48:213–24.

Jorgensen-Earp, Cheryl R., and Lori A. Lanzilotti. 1998. "Public Memory and Private Grief: The Construction of Shrines at the Sites of Public Tragedy." *Quarterly Journal of Speech* 84:150–70

Keats, John. 1907. *The Complete Poetical Works of John Keats.* Edited by H. Buxton Forman. Oxford: Oxford University Press.

Kellner, Hans. 1989. *Language and Historical Representation: Getting the Story Crooked.* Madison: University of Wisconsin Press.

Kerenyi, Karl. 1977. "Mnemosyne-Lesmosyne: On the Springs of 'Memory' and 'Forgetting.'" *Spring,* 120–30.

Kierkegaard, Søren. 1964. *Works of Love: Some Christian Reflections in the Form of Discourses.* Trans. Howard V. Hong and Edna H. Hong. New York: Harper and Row.

———. 1991. *Practice in Christianity.* Trans. Howard V. Hong and Edna H. Hong. Princeton: Princeton University Press.

Knight, David. 1986. *The Age of Science: The Scientific World-View in the Nineteenth Century.* New York: Basil Blackwell.

Kotre, John. 1995. *White Gloves: How We Create Ourselves Through Memory.* New York: Free Press.

Kromkowski, Charles A. 2002. "The Declaration of Independence, Congress, and Presidents of the United States." In *The Declaration of Independence: Origins and Impact,* ed. Scott Douglas Gerber, 118–41. Washington, D.C.: CQ Press.

Kundera, Milan. 2007. *The Curtain.* Trans. Linda Asher. New York: HarperCollins.

LaCapra, Dominick. 1983. *Rethinking Intellectual History: Texts, Contexts, Language.* Ithaca: Cornell University Press.

Lactantius. 1964. *The Divine Institutes, Books I–VII.* Trans. Sister Mary Francis McDonald. Washington, D.C.: Catholic University of America Press.

Leff, Michael. 2005. "Dimensions of Temporality in Lincoln's Second Inaugural." In *Readings in Rhetorical Criticism,* 3rd ed., ed. Carl R. Burgchardt, 564–69. State College, Pa.: Strata.

Le Goff, Jacques. 1996. *History and Memory.* Trans. Steven Rendall and Elizabeth Claman. New York: Columbia University Press.

Lessl, Thomas. 1999. "The Galileo Legend as Scientific Folklore." *Quarterly Journal of Speech* 85:146–68.

Liegeois, Jean-Pierre. 1986. *Gypsies.* Trans. Tony Berrett. London: Al Saqi Books.

Lincoln, Abraham. 1989a. "Address at Cooper Institute, New York City, February 27, 1860." In *Speeches and Writings, 1859–1865,* 111–30. New York: Library of America.

———. 1989b. "Address at Gettysburg, Pennsylvania, November 19, 1863." In *Speeches and Writings, 1859–1865,* 536. New York: Library of America.

———. 1989c. "Annual Message to Congress, December 1, 1862." In *Speeches and Writings, 1859–1865,* 393–415. New York: Library of America.

———. 1989d. "'House Divided' Speech at Springfield, Illinois, June 16, 1858." In *Speeches and Writings, 1832–1858,* 426–34. New York: Library of America.

———. 1989e. "First Inaugural Address, March 4, 1861." In *Speeches and Writings, 1859–1865,* 215–24. New York: Library of America.

———. 1989f. "Second Inaugural Address, March 4, 1865." In *Speeches and Writings, 1859–1865,* 686–87. New York: Library of America.

———. 1989g. "Speech at Chicago, Illinois, July 10, 1858." In *Speeches and Writings, 1832–1858,* 439–58. New York: Library of America.

————. 1989h. "Speech on the Dred Scott Decision at Springfield, Illinois, June 26, 1857." In *Speeches and Writings, 1832–1858,* 390–403. New York: Library of America.

Lindberg, David C. 1986. "Science and the Early Church." In *God and Nature: Historical Essays on the Encounter Between Religion and Science,* ed. David C. Lindberg and Ronald L. Numbers, 19–48. Berkeley and Los Angeles: University of California Press.

Locke, John. 1959. *An Essay Concerning Human Understanding.* New York: Routledge.

Longxi, Zhang. 1994. "Historicizing the Postmodern Allegory." *Texas Studies in Language and Literature* 36:212–31.

Loraux, Nicole. 1986. *The Invention of Athens: The Funeral Oration in the Classical City.* Trans. Alan Sheridan. Cambridge: Harvard University Press.

Lowenthal, David. 1985. *The Past Is a Foreign Country.* Cambridge: Cambridge University Press.

————. 1998. *The Heritage Crusade and the Spoils of History.* Cambridge: Cambridge University Press.

————. 1999. Preface to *The Art of Forgetting,* ed. Adrian Forty and Susanne Kuchler, xi–xiii. Oxford: Berg.

Lucas, Stephen E. 1989. "Justifying America: The Declaration of Independence as a Rhetorical Document." In *American Rhetoric: Context and Criticism,* ed. Thomas W. Benson, 67–130. Carbondale: Southern Illinois University Press.

Luria, Aleksandr R. 2006. *The Mind of a Mnemonist: A Little Book About a Vast Memory.* Trans. Lynn Solotaroff. Cambridge: Harvard University Press.

Lutz, Catherine A., and Lila Abu-Lughod, eds. 1990. *Language and the Politics of Emotion.* New York: Cambridge University Press.

Lyon, Janet. 1999. *Manifestoes: Provocations of the Modern.* Ithaca: Cornell University Press.

Maffesoli, Michel. 1996. *The Contemplation of the World: Figures of Community Style.* Trans. Susan Emanuel. Minneapolis: University of Minnesota Press.

Maier, Pauline. 1997. *American Scripture: Making the Declaration of Independence.* New York: Alfred A. Knopf.

Margalit, Avishai. 2002. *The Ethics of Memory.* Cambridge: Harvard University Press.

Matsuda, Matt K. 1996. *The Memory of the Modern.* New York: Oxford University Press.

Matthews, Karen. 2002. "Former Mayor Giuliani to Read Victims' Names at WTC Ceremony." Associated Press State and Local Wire, August 6.

McCarthy, Joseph. 2000. "Speech at Wheeling, West Virginia, February 9, 1950." In *In Our Own Words: Extraordinary Speeches of the American Century,* ed. Andrew Carroll, Robert Torricelli, and Doris Kearns Goodwin, 173–76. New York: Washington Square Press.

McChesney, Robert W. 1999. *Rich Media, Poor Democracy: Communication Politics in Dubious Times.* Urbana: University of Illinois Press.

McGee, Michael Calvin. 1990. "Text, Context, and the Fragmentation of Contemporary Culture." *Western Journal of Communication* 54:274–89.

McPherson, James M. 1992. "How Lincoln Won the War with Metaphors." In *Abraham Lincoln and the Second American Revolution,* 93–112. New York: Oxford University Press.

Megill, Allan, and Donald N. McCloskey. 1987. *The Rhetoric of the Human Sciences: Language and Argument in Scholarship and Public Affairs.* Ed. John S. Nelson, Allan Megill, and Donald N. McCloskey, 221–38. Madison: University of Wisconsin Press.

Microsoft Research. 2008. http://www.microsoft.research.com/barc/mediapresence/MyLifeBits.aspx (accessed September 17).

Miller, William Lee. 1980. "Lincoln's Second Inaugural: The Zenith of Statecraft." *Center Magazine* 13, no. 4 (July/August): 53–64.

Milton, John. 2007. *Paradise Lost.* Annotated edition, ed. Alistair Fowler. New York: Longman.

Montaigne, Michel de. 1957. *The Complete Works of Montaigne.* Trans. Donald M. Frame. Stanford: Stanford University Press.

Murphy, John M. 1990. "'A Time of Shame and Sorrow': Robert F. Kennedy and the American Jeremiad." *Quarterly Journal of Speech* 76:401–14.

———. 2003. "'Our Mission and Our Moment': George W. Bush and September 11th." *Rhetoric and Public Affairs* 4:607–32.

Musil, Robert. 2006. "Monuments." In *Posthumous Papers of a Living Author,* trans. Peter Wortsman, 64–68. Brooklyn, N.Y.: Archipelago Books.

Nevins, Allan. 1964. *Lincoln and the Gettysburg Address: Commemorative Papers.* Urbana: University of Illinois Press.

*The New Oxford Annotated Bible.* 2001. 3rd ed. Ed. Michael Coogan. Oxford: Oxford University Press.

Nietzsche, Friedrich. 1990. *Beyond Good and Evil.* Trans. R. J. Hollingdale. New York: Penguin Books.

———. 1997. "On the Uses and Disadvantages of History for Life." In *Untimely Meditations,* ed. Daniel Breazeale, 57–123. Cambridge: Cambridge University Press.

Nora, Pierre. 1989. "Between Memory and History: Les Lieux de Mémoire." *Representations* 26:7–25.

———. 1996. *Realms of Memory: Rethinking the French Past.* Vol. 1. New York: Columbia University Press.

Ober, Josiah, and Barry Strauss. 1990. "Drama, Political Rhetoric, and the Discourse of Athenian Democracy." In *Nothing to Do with Dionysos: Athenian Drama in Its Social Context,* ed. John J. Winkler and Froma I. Zeitlin, 237–70. Princeton: Princeton University Press, 1990.

O'Malley, John W. 1979. *Praise and Blame in Renaissance Rome: Rhetoric, Doctrine, and Reform in the Sacred Orators of the Papal Court, c. 1450–1521.* Durham: Duke University Press.

Ovarec, Christine. 1976. "'Observation' in Aristotle's Theory of Epideictic." *Philosophy and Rhetoric* 9:162–74.

*Oxford English Dictionary.* 1989. 2nd ed. Oxford: Clarendon Press.

Partridge, Eric. 1966. *Origins: A Short Etymological Dictionary of Modern English.* New York: Macmillan.

Pease, Noval F. 1964. "The Forgotten Gettysburg Address." *Central States Speech Journal* 15:107–11.

Perelman, Chaïm, and Lucie Olbrechts-Tyteca. 1971. *The New Rhetoric: A Treatise on Argumentation.* Trans. John Wilkinson and Purcell Weaver. Notre Dame: University of Notre Dame Press.

Peters, F. E. 1967. *Greek Philosophical Terms: A Historical Lexicon*. New York: New York University Press.

Petersen, Svend. 1963. *The Gettysburg Addresses: The Story of Two Orations*. New York: F. Ungar.

Peterson, Merrill D. 1970. *Jefferson and the New Nation: A Biography*. New York: Oxford University Press.

————. 1994. *Lincoln in American Memory*. New York: Oxford University Press.

Piaget, Jean. 1962. *Play, Dreams and Imitation in Childhood*. Trans. C. Gattegno and F. M. Hodgson. New York: W. W. Norton.

Plath, Sylvia. 1966. *Ariel*. New York: Harper and Row.

Plato. 1989. *The Collected Dialogues of Plato*. Ed. Edith Hamilton and Huntington Cairns. Princeton: Princeton University Press. All quotations from Plato are from the translations in this edition.

Pocock, J. G. A. 1971. *Politics, Language and Time: Essays on Political Thought and History*. New York: Atheneum.

————. 2003. *The Machiavellian Moment: Florentine Thought and the Atlantic Republican Tradition*. Rev. ed. Princeton: Princeton University Press.

Poulakos, John. 1986. "Gorgias' and Isocrates' Use of the Encomium." *Southern Speech Communication Journal* 51:300–307.

Poulakos, Takis. 1987. "Isocrates's Use of Narrative in the *Evagoras:* Epideictic, Rhetoric and Moral Action." *Quarterly Journal of Speech* 73:317–28.

————. 1990. "Historiographies of the Tradition of Rhetoric: A Brief History of Classical Funeral Orations." *Western Journal of Speech Communication* 54:172–88.

Procter, David. 1990. "The Dynamic Spectacle: Transforming Experience into Social Forms of Community." *Quarterly Journal of Speech* 2:117–33.

Proust, Marcel. 1934. *Remembrance of Things Past*. Trans. C. K. Scott Moncrieff and Frederick A. Blossom. New York: Random House.

Purnick, Joyce. 2002. "A Modern Rite of Mourning: Must-See TV." *New York Times,* September 12, A22.

Quintilian. 1996–98. *Institutio oratoria*. Trans. H. E. Butler. 4 vols. Loeb Classical Library. Cambridge: Harvard University Press.

Ranke, Leopold von. 1956. "Fragment from the 1860's." In *The Varieties of History: From Voltaire to the Present,* ed. Fritz Stern, 60–62. Cleveland: Meridian Books.

Reagan, Ronald. 2005. "Speech to the National Association of Evangelicals (The 'Evil Empire' Speech)." In *American Rhetorical Discourse,* 3rd ed., ed. Ronald F. Reid and James F. Klumpp, 796–803. Long Grove, Ill.: Waveland Press.

Reingold, Nathan. 1964. *Science in Nineteenth-Century America: A Documentary History*. New York: Hill and Wang.

*Rhetorica ad herennium*. 1954. Trans. Harry Caplan. Cambridge: Harvard University Press.

Ricoeur, Paul. 2004. *Memory, History, Forgetting*. Trans. Kathleen Blamey and David Pellauer. Chicago: University of Chicago Press.

Ritter, Harry. 1986. *Dictionary of Concepts in History*. Westport, Conn.: Greenwood Press.

Rittner, Carol. 1990. "An Interview with Elie Wiesel." In *Elie Wiesel: Between Memory and Hope,* ed. Carol Rittner, 30–41. New York: New York University Press.

Roosevelt, Franklin D. 1946. "Annual Message to Congress—the Economic 'Bill of Rights.'" In *Nothing to Fear: The Selected Addresses of Franklin Delano Roosevelt, 1932–1945,* ed. B. D. Zevin, 387–97. Boston: Houghton Mifflin.

———. 1999 [1941]. "President Franklin D. Roosevelt Tries to Convince a Skeptical Nation Why It Must Defend the World Against Nazism." In *In Our Own Words: Extraordinary Speeches of the American Century,* ed. Senator Robert Torricelli and Andrew Carroll, 120–23. New York: Washington Square Press.

———. 2005 [1932]. "Progressive Government." In *American Rhetorical Discourse,* 3rd ed., ed. Ronald F. Reid and James F. Klumpp, 734–46. Long Grove, Ill.: Waveland Press.

Rosenfield, Lawrence W. 1980. "The Practical Celebration of Epideictic." In *Rhetoric in Transition,* ed. Eugene E. White, 131–56. University Park: Pennsylvania State University Press.

———. 1989. "Central Park and the Celebration of Virtue." In *American Rhetoric: Context and Criticism,* ed. Thomas W. Benson, 221–66. Carbondale: Southern Illinois University Press.

Roskies, David. 1984. *Against the Apocalypse: Responses to Catastrophe in Modern Jewish Culture.* Cambridge: Harvard University Press.

Rothenberg, Randall. 1984. *The Neo-Liberals: Creating the New American Politics.* New York: Simon and Schuster.

Rowland, Robert C. 1989. "On Limiting the Narrative Paradigm: Three Case Studies." *Communication Monographs* 56:39–54.

Rowse, A. L. 1963. *The Use of History.* New York: Collier Books.

Russell, Jeffery Burton. 1991. *Inventing the Flat Earth: Columbus and Modern Historians.* New York: Praeger.

Santayana, George. 1906. *The Life of Reason.* Vol. 1. New York: Charles Scribner's Sons.

Sartre, Jean-Paul. 1955. "On *The Sound and the Fury:* Time in the Work of Faulkner." In *Literary and Philosophical Essays,* trans. Annette Michelson, 79–87. London: Rider.

*Saving Private Ryan.* 1999. VHS. Directed by Stephen Spielberg. Redwood City, Calif.: Dreamworks Home Entertainment.

Schacter, Daniel L. 2001. *The Seven Sins of Memory: How the Mind Forgets and Remembers.* New York: Houghton Mifflin.

Schlesinger, Jr., Arthur M. 1966. *The Bitter Heritage: Vietnam and American Democracy.* Boston: Houghton Mifflin.

Schwartz, Barry. 2000. *Abraham Lincoln and the Forge of National Memory.* Chicago: University of Chicago Press.

Schwartz, Barry, and Horst-Alfred Heinrich. 2004. "Shadings of Regret: America and Germany." In *Framing Public Memory,* ed. Kendall R. Phillips, 113–44. Tuscaloosa: University of Alabama Press.

Scott, Charles E. 1999. *The Time of Memory.* Albany: State University of New York Press.

Scott, Janny. 2002. "Sept. 11 Leaves Speakers at a Loss for Their Own Words." *New York Times,* August 11, A29.

Scott, Robert L. 1967. "On Viewing Rhetoric as Epistemic." *Central States Speech Journal* 18:9–17.

————. 1976. "On Viewing Rhetoric as Epistemic: Ten Years Later." *Central States Speech Journal* 27:258–66.

Shakespeare, William. 1969. *William Shakespeare: The Complete Works*. Ed. Alfred Harbage. New York: Penguin Books.

Singer, Jefferson A., and Martin A. Conway. 2008. "Should We Forget Forgetting?" *Memory Studies* 1:279–85.

Slagell, Amy R. 1991. "Anatomy of a Masterpiece: A Close Textual Analysis of Abraham Lincoln's Second Inaugural Address." *Communication Reports* 42:155–71.

Solomon, Martha. 1988. "'With Firmness in the Right': The Creation of Moral Hegemony in Lincoln's Second Inaugural Address." *Communication Reports* 1:32–37.

Sontag, Susan. 2002. "Real Battles and Empty Metaphors." *New York Times,* September 10, A25.

Spenser, Edmund. 1962. *The Shepherd's Calendar and Other Poems*. New York: Dutton.

Stashenko, Joel. 2002. "Pataki Will Read Cherished Speech on Sept. 11." Associated Press State and Local Wire, September 8.

Steinhauer, Jennifer. 2002. "New York to Observe Sept. 11 with Dawn-to-Dusk Tributes." *New York Times,* August 7, A1.

Stevens, Thaddeus. 2005. "Congressional Speech in Favor of Radical Republican Reconstruction Policy (Abridged)." In *American Rhetorical Discourse,* 3rd ed., ed. Ronald F. Reid and James F. Klumpp, 466–73. Long Grove, Ill.: Waveland Press.

Stewart, Michael. 1997. *The Time of the Gypsies*. Boulder, Colo.: Westview Press.

Stripp, Fred. 1968. "The Other Gettysburg Address." *Western Speech* 32:19–26.

Struever, Nancy S. 1985. "Historical Discourse." In *Handbook of Discourse Analysis,* vol. 1, *Disciplines of Discourse,* ed. Teun A. van Dijk, 249–71. London: Academic Press.

Sullivan, Dale L. 1993. "The Ethos of Epideictic Encounter." *Philosophy and Rhetoric* 26:113–33.

Tejera, V. 1975. "Irony and Allegory in the *Phaedrus*." *Philosophy and Rhetoric* 8:71–87.

Thucydides. 1973. "The Funeral Speech of Pericles." Trans. Richard Crawley. In *The Speeches of Thucydides,* ed. H. F. Harding, 52–62. Lawrence, Kans.: Coronado Press.

Todorov, Tzvetan. 1996. "The Abuses of Memory." *Common Knowledge* 5:6–26.

Tong, Diane. 1989. *Gypsy Folktales*. San Diego: Harcourt Brace Jovanovich.

Truman, Harry. 1995. "The Truman Doctrine." In *American Rhetorical Discourse,* 2nd ed., ed. Ronald F. Reid, 747–53. Long Grove, Ill.: Waveland Press.

Turner, Kathleen J. 1998. "Rhetorical History as Social Construction." In *Doing Rhetorical History: Concepts and Cases,* ed. Kathleen J. Turner, 1–18. Tuscaloosa: University of Alabama Press.

Vickery, Olga W. 1964. *The Novels of William Faulkner: A Critical Interpretation*. Baton Rouge: Louisiana State University Press.

Vivian, Bradford. 2001. "'Always a Third Party Who Says Me': Rhetoric and Alterity." *Philosophy and Rhetoric* 34:343–54

Volf, Miroslav. 2006. *The End of Memory: Remembering Rightly in a Violent World*. Grand Rapids, Mich.: William B. Eerdmans.

Walker, Jeffrey. 1989. "Aristotle's Lyric: Re-imagining the Rhetoric of Epideictic Song." *College English* 51:5–28.

Walker, Phillip. 1956. "Arthur Miller's *The Crucible:* Tragedy or Allegory?" *Western Speech* 20 (Fall): 222–24.

Wallace, Mike. 1996. *Mickey Mouse History and Other Essays on American Memory.* Philadelphia: Temple University Press.

Warren, Charles. 1945. "Fourth of July Myths." *William and Mary Quarterly* 2:237–45.

Warren, Louis Austin. 1964. *Lincoln's Gettysburg Declaration: "A New Birth of Freedom."* Fort Wayne: Lincoln National Life Foundation.

Watson, Martha. 2000. "Ordeal by Fire: The Transformative Rhetoric of Abraham Lincoln." *Rhetoric and Public Affairs* 3:33–48.

"'We Owe It to Those That We Lost to Expand Our Quest': Perspectives." 2002. *New York Times,* September 11, A15.

Weinrich, Harald. 2004. *Lethe: The Art and Critique of Forgetting.* Trans. Steven Rendall. Ithaca: Cornell University Press.

Wessel, Inke, and Michelle L. Moulds. 2008. "How Many Types of Forgetting? Comments on Connerton (2008)." *Memory Studies* 1:287–94.

Westbury, Chris, and Daniel C. Dennett. 2000. "Mining the Past to Construct the Future: Memory and Belief as Forms of Knowledge." In *Memory, Brain, and Belief,* ed. Daniel L. Schacter and Elaine Scarry, 11–32. Cambridge: Harvard University Press, 2000.

Whewell, William. 1837. *History of the Inductive Sciences: From the Earliest to the Present Times.* London: J. W. Parker.

White, Andrew Dickson. 1896. *A History of the Warfare of Science with Theology in Christendom.* New York: Appleton.

White, Hayden. 1973. *Metahistory: The Historical Imagination in Nineteenth-Century Europe.* Baltimore: Johns Hopkins University Press.

———. 1987. *The Content of the Form: Narrative Discourse and Historical Representation.* Baltimore: Johns Hopkins University Press.

White, Ronald C., Jr. 2002. *Lincoln's Greatest Speech: The Second Inaugural.* New York: Simon and Schuster.

———. 2005. *The Eloquent President: A Portrait of Lincoln Through His Words.* New York: Random House.

Wiesel, Elie. 1962. *The Accident.* Trans. Anne Borchardt. New York: Hill and Wang.

———. 2006. *Night.* Trans. Marion Wiesel. New York: Hill and Wang.

Wiley, Earl W. 1943. "Abraham Lincoln: His Emergence as the Voice of the People." In *A History and Criticism of American Public Address,* vol. 2, ed. William Norwood Brigance, 859–77. New York: McGraw-Hill.

Wilkins, Roger. 1995. "The Case for Affirmative Action: Racism Has Its Privileges." *Nation,* March 27, 409–16.

Willems, Wim. 1997. *In Search of the True Gypsy.* Trans. Don Bloch. London: Frank Cass.

Wills, Garry. 1992. *Lincoln at Gettysburg: The Words That Remade America.* New York: Simon and Schuster.

Wilson, Douglas L. 2006. *Lincoln's Sword: The Presidency and the Power of Words.* New York: Alfred A. Knopf.

Yates, Frances A. 2001. *The Art of Memory.* Reprint. Chicago: University of Chicago Press.

Yerushalmi, Yosef Hayim. 2005. *Zakhor: Jewish History and Jewish Memory.* Seattle: University of Washington Press.

Young, James E. 1988. *Writing and Rewriting the Holocaust: Narrative and the Consequences of Interpretation.* Bloomington: Indiana University Press.

———. 1993. *The Texture of Memory: Holocaust Memorials and Meaning.* New Haven: Yale University Press.

———. 2000. *At Memory's Edge: After-Images of the Holocaust in Contemporary Art and Architecture.* New Haven: Yale University Press.

Zarefsky, David. 1988. "Approaching Lincoln's Second Inaugural Address." *Communication Reports* 1:9–13.

———. 1998. "Four Senses of Rhetorical History." In *Doing Rhetorical History: Concepts and Cases,* ed. Kathleen J. Turner, 19–32. Tuscaloosa: University of Alabama Press.

Zelizer, Barbie. 1998. *Remembering to Forget: Holocaust Memory Through the Camera's Eye.* Chicago: University of Chicago Press.

# INDEX

# Index

# Index

oblivion, 13, 35, 39, 53–54. *See also* amnesia; *ars oblivionis* (art of oblivion); forgetting
Draper's rhetoric and, 92–93, 108
forgetting as, 7, 19, 20, 37, 168–69
Gypsy folklore and, 115
Lincoln and, 133, 149
as a literary term, 2–3, 21–22, 24, 168
*Oblivion* (Augé), 44–45
"Ode on Melancholy" (Keats), 25
"Ode to a Nightingale" (Keats), 25
Olbrechts-Tyteca, Lucie, 65
Old Testament, 22–23, 31, 161
*On the Ideal Orator* (Cicero), 19–20, 40
"On the Uses and Disadvantages of History for Life" (Nietzsche), 51–52
oppression, 4–5, 71, 83, 176–77. *See also* totalitarianism
oration, 19–20. *See also* epideictic speech; eulogies
*Oratore, De* (Cicero), 19–20, 40
Oresme, Nicole, 105
"Ozymandias" (Shelley), 1–2, 6

Palestine, 10, 179–80
"Papusza," 118
*Paradise Lost* (Milton), 24
Pataki, George, 66, 68
peace treaties, 43–44
pedagogy, 21–22, 25–28
Perelman, Chaïm, 65
Pericles, 64–65, 68, 69
Peterson, Merrill, 134, 136, 146
*Phaedrus* (Plato), 22
philosophy, 21–22, 26–27, 30–31, 39. *See also* specific philosopher
Piaget, Jean, 125
Picasso, 180
Plath, Sylvia, 25
Plato, 21–22, 23, 37, 39, 40, 184 n. 4
Pocock, J. G. A., 82, 86
poetry, 2–3, 21, 37–38
postwar era, 4, 31–38
power, productiveness of, 89–90, 91, 102
preservationist ethic, 3–5, 6, 15, 128, 171–72. *See also* archival documentation; monuments; museums
promises, faculty to make and keep, 58–59, 88, 167
prophecy, 22, 83–85
Draper, 97–98, 100–101, 102, 106–7, 109, 186 n. 16
Lincoln, 75–76, 157–62, 166

Proust, Marcel, 30, 31, 38
psychoanalysis, 28–30, 38, 184 n. 4
psychology
brain research, 11, 126, 127
cognitive psychology, 11–12, 27, 45–46, 48–50, 126
Freud's psychoanalytic theory, 28–29, 38, 184 n. 4
imagery of forgetting, 41–42
Kotre's autobiographical memory, 124–27
Lockes' analysis of memory, 27–28
Ptolemy, 106
public forgetting, 6–16, 169–73, 176–79. *See also* amnesia; amnesty; historical forgetting; oblivion; state forgetting
defined, 14, 59, 60, 183 n. 2 (intro)
inadvertent encouragement of, 63–64
productive aspects of, 89–90, 91, 102
reciprocity of with public memory, 129–30, 131–32
as source of well-being, 47–48
*telos* of, 50–51, 84, 108, 153
public goods, 54–55, 56, 59, 67, 78, 122
public history. *See* historical memory
public memory, 11, 13–16, 50. *See also* recollection
defined, 13
individual *vs.*, 10–13, 48–49, 115, 124–27, 183 n. 5 (intro)
nomadic nature of, 115–16, 121, 124, 125–32
public time, 59, 60, 171
Arendt's "odd in-between period" of, 170
Draper's sense of, 109, 166
eternal return and, 51–52, 54
Lincoln's sense of, 166
*Purgatory* (Dante), 24

Ranke, Leopold von, 95
*Rape of Lucrece* (Shakespeare), 2
Reagan, Ronald, 83
recollection, 21–22, 29–30, 45, 113–14, 115–16, 124–27. See also *ars memoriae* (art of memory)
reconciliation, 10, 133, 136–37, 150, 165, 167
religion, 10, 24, 37, 84. *See also* flat earth narrative; theology
covenant to remember, 22–23, 31–32
forgiveness, 42–44, 56, 136–37, 148–49, 155–62, 159–61, 163–66
freedom of, 77, 146
Gypsy folktales and, 117–18

Made in the USA
Lexington, KY
01 April 2013